CW00469915

Retu
time
and

6 797 057 000

THE INTERCITY STORY

1964 – 2012

THE INTERCITY STORY
1964 – 2012

CHRIS GREEN & MIKE VINCENT

First published 2013

ISBN 978 0 86093 652 7

© Chris Green and Mike Vincent 2013

Published by Oxford Publishing Co

An imprint of Ian Allan Publishing Ltd, Hersham, Surrey KT12 4RG.

Printed in England

Visit the Ian Allan Publishing website at **www.ianallanpublishing.com**

FRONT COVER InterCity of the future? A model of the InterCity 250 – note the similarity to the Eurostar powercar.

BACK COVER TOP LEFT A beautiful train in a beautiful setting: No 43010 heads west towards Teignmouth on 15 September 1990. *Gavin Morrison*

BACK COVER TOP RIGHT For many years the Class 86 electrics were the mainstay of the West Coast route. This example, painted in corporate Rail Blue, leaves Crewe in 1985. *Gavin Morrison*

PAGE 2 With Battersea Power Station in the background, No 73028 leaves London Victoria for Gatwick. The date is 17 October 1993. *Gavin Morrison*

PAGE 4–5 Evidence that cross-franchise motive-power support occurs even in a fragmented railway: East Coast HST power car No 43310 heads CrossCountry's 0608 Edinburgh–Plymouth service at Dawlish on 23 March 2011. *Antony Christie*

ABOVE Eurostar trains at St Pancras International hint at the excitement to come for those taking HS1 to Europe. *Eurostar International Limited*

CONTENTS

INTRODUCTION

In 1994 during the last months of British Rail, we wrote *The InterCity Story* to highlight a public industry delivering a quality service. As an opportunity to take stock of two very different worlds, we are now re-issuing the book exactly twenty years since the announcement to privatise the rail industry. This updated second edition shows the way the InterCity legacy has changed and prospered over the last decade, as well as highlighting the stories of those people who have helped to make that change happen.

Our story starts by examining how a vertically integrated InterCity railway was fragmented into a number of businesses that were put up for sale or franchise. It then traces the ongoing progress of the original InterCity routes as they became seven fully independent train companies. The final chapters address the key question of whether these intercity passenger businesses deliver a better or worse set of products some twenty years later and explore where those diverse businesses are likely to be heading in the next twenty years.

We have sought to base our judgments on evidence rather than sentiment, and we have received tremendous help from every quarter of the rail industry in researching the post-privatisation era. Indeed, we were extremely fortunate in being able to interview over sixty of the senior managers who have been running the ex-InterCity railway since 1993 and the result is a unique inside record of events and achievements as seen through their eyes. Supporting tables and Factfiles have been collated from well-recognised, national sources and will hopefully provide a useful archive for future historians.

The new InterCity story is one of remarkable evolution. The InterCity vision of fast, civilised travel between the main cities was previously and crucially restrained by a lack of funds whilst the post-1994 story has seen the intercity sector expand with long-distance rail passenger travel doubling since the book's first edition. The future looks even more promising provided that the high hopes of tight cost control and a strengthened franchising process can become hard reality over the next few years. The only sadness is that the country that gave the InterCity name to the world has now become the only country determined not to use it! InterCity is an iconic name which is internationally recognised and understood. One wonders whether one day it will return home.

LEFT A Virgin West Coast Pendolino emerges purposefully into the daylight at Birmingham New St on 23 May 2008. *Paul Bigland*

Chapter 1
INTERCITY'S ROOTS:
THE 1950s AND 1960s

ABOVE Racing down Hildenborough Bank with full exhaust flying, 'Battle of Britain' No 34071 *601 Squadron* heads towards Dover on its journey from London Victoria. *Brian Morrison*

The term 'Inter-City,' or 'InterCity' as it became from the early 1980s, conjures up a picture of a high profile, high quality, customer-focused passenger railway. This chapter sets out to explore the formative years of InterCity in the 1950s and 1960s when so many of the seeds sown were reaped with such success in the following decades. It looks back to the radical nationalisation of 1948 and through to the commercialism of the Beeching era which finally launched the InterCity we know today.

InterCity began in earnest in 1966 when it became the product name of the new electric expresses between London, Liverpool and Manchester. An historic perspective of the intervening years offers a fascinating pattern of evolution culminating in a profitable £1 billion turnover business in the 1990s.

The 1950s and 1960s provided the seed-bed for InterCity in a slow and disjointed period of gestation. The 1970s accelerated the growth in every sense of the word with the development of the world famous High Speed Train (or HST) which provided InterCity with both an identity and a means to beat the competition. The 1980s saw InterCity establishing itself as a profitable marketing sector and brand alongside its sisters, Network SouthEast and Regional Railways. Finally, the 1990s saw InterCity reaching its fulfilment as a self-contained business within British Rail with its own balance sheet, assets, staff and marketing.

It would have been a small step to complete the logical process with the privatisation of the total InterCity business. It was certainly considered, but the 1993 Railways Act determined that InterCity should instead be broken back into the individual routes which had formed it. History is often circular and there may well be lessons for future pioneers as we begin our exploration of the seeds of the InterCity business in the postwar decades of the 1950s and 1960s.

The pre-Beeching 1948-1961 period

InterCity as we know it began in earnest in the Beeching era of the 1960s. It is, however, important to set those years in their historic perspective with a quick look at express train operations before and after the second world war.

It is also important to note that the British railway system did not develop as a planned and unified network. It grew instead from an unplanned explosion of small, competing private ventures. The InterCity network of 1994 represented the extreme change to a single, national product of consistent, high speed services across the country. How did this dramatic change come about?

By the outbreak of the first world war in 1914, a clearly identifiable pattern of train services had grown up with key main lines serving the principal centres of population. Express trains plied those main lines whilst stopping services served all stations. A number of semi-fast services fitted uneasily between the other two categories, often running to no clear pattern. Nonetheless, it seems fair to say that by 1923 when over 100 railway companies amalgamated into the 'Big Four' – the Great Western Railway (GWR), the London, Midland & Scottish Railway (LMSR), the London & North Eastern Railway (LNER) and the Southern Railway (SR) – Britain had achieved faster and more frequent inter-city services than its continental counterparts.

Exhausted and starved of investment after the enormous strains and demands placed upon them by the second world war, the railways were nationalised on 1st January 1948. Not only were the main line railways nationalised within the transport portfolio, but so were certain elements of road freight, bus operation, canals and London Transport (both buses and underground railways). The British Transport Commission was formed to administer the whole enterprise, with a Railway Executive established to manage the railways. Day to day rail operations were in the hands of six Regional Boards – organised geographically – whilst the whole complex series of organisations traded as British Railways.

At last, the opportunity seemed to have arrived in the 1950s to have a long, hard look at the railway system and to see how best it might be brought together into a coherent whole. This could have included the birth of a national express intercity network of services but the opportunity was missed for a decade. Perhaps, because the railways paid their way until 1952, the unique chance to take a close look at the opportunities for national networks and marketing were not truly grasped. However, a small profit swiftly turned into an ever-growing loss which eventually led, some ten years later, to the publication of the Beeching Report and to the creation of the early InterCity services as a means of returning to profit.

To bring about economies in scale, it was planned that all equipment would be purchased in large quantities and could be used, as appropriate, anywhere in the country. It was intended that the standard designs of locomotives and coaches would draw together the best operational practices of the 'Big Four' railways and in April 1948 a series of comparative trials of pre-nationalisation locomotives was held in order to obtain the optimum designs for BR's range of standard classes.

At the same time a standard coach was commissioned which was to become the ubiquitous Mark I vehicle. Designed to be able to travel over most lines throughout the country, the standard body shell could accommodate all types of interiors from First and Third (later renamed Second) Class, to catering facilities, sleeping cars and parcel vans. With the introduction of these coaches, the 'buckeye' automatic coupling gave greater rigidity throughout the train when running and helped to prevent serious damage in the event of an accident. The first standard locomotives and coaches appeared in 1951.

The 1955 Modernisation Plan

By the mid 1950s, major investment in the railways was essential if an express passenger network was to have any hope of surviving into the future. In January 1955 the Chairman of the Railway Executive, Sir Brian Robertson, finally published a £1,200m Modernisation Plan which would take 15 years to complete and which, he believed, would totally revolutionise the whole railway system laying the foundation stones for InterCity in the 1960s. The key features of this Plan were the abolition of the steam locomotive in favour of diesel and electric traction; electrification where density of traffic could justify the heavy initial investment required; improvements to track to permit higher speeds together with the extension of colour-light signalling, track circuiting and automatic warning systems (AWS) controlled from new power-operated signal boxes. There was to be a total modernisation of the rolling stock fleets and considerable expenditure on stations and parcels' depots.

Until the mid-1950s electrification schemes had been based on medium voltage, direct current systems, but post-war developments in France established 25kV alternating current as a more efficient system which was becoming adopted as standard for new projects in mainland Europe. One of the best long-term decisions for InterCity was the 1955 agreement to adopt the new 25kV ac system for all future main line electrification. The Modernisation Plan still called for an extension of the existing systems around London, but new electrification in the Glasgow suburbs and on the whole of the West Coast main line of the London Midland Region from London to Manchester and Liverpool via Stoke on Trent and Crewe, was to be on the 25kV ac system. With considerable foresight, electrification of the Eastern Region main line from London to Leeds via Doncaster was also recommended but this work was deferred and did not actually start until the mid 1980s.

West Coast electrification

Work began immediately on the London Midland route and, being new technology, its design and construction took some time. However, in 1960, the first section of the 'New Railway' from Crewe to Manchester began operation. The other northern section, from Crewe to Liverpool, was commissioned in 1962 and work gradually extended southwards towards London. In the meantime, the other main plank of the Modernisation Plan was taking shape in the delivery of main line diesel locomotives for the rest of the UK network.

The Blue Pullmans

In 1960 the so-called 'Blue Pullmans' were introduced in their attractive and special blue and grey livery. Five complete trains were built with a 1,000hp diesel electric power car at either end of a rake of passenger coaches. The self-contained trains formed the first step along the path to the production of one of the most successful passenger trains in the world, the InterCity 125. The 'Blue Pullmans' ran on fast, limited-stop schedules and offered air-conditioning, individually-adjusted Venetian blinds at each window and meals served at every seat. A supplementary fare was payable in order to gain that exclusivity.

Both the London Midland and Western Regions operated 'Blue Pullmans', the former having First Class accommodation only. They provided an early morning service from Manchester to London via Derby and, in order to make full use of the trains with their quick turnround capability, were employed on midday journeys to Nottingham. The Western Region's trains had both First and Second Class seating and provided business services from Bristol, Wolverhampton and Birmingham to Paddington. In addition, the WR sets provided a daytime 'fill-in' service to Oxford.

Whilst the business concept behind the trains was very successful, the trains themselves were not. They were 'one-offs' in a world of growing standardisation and they were expensive to operate and maintain. The bogies began to give a very rough ride after a period of service and the 'Blue Pullmans' were withdrawn in 1973. Nonetheless, they had demonstrated a demand for superior customer service from specific sectors of the travelling public and had provided the inspiration for InterCity's diesel train of the future, the High Speed Train – or InterCity 125 – as it later became.

'Deltics' for the East Coast

As work progressed on West Coast electrification, BR decided to buy high-powered diesel locomotives

ABOVE Its Pullman cars tucked away to the rear of the train, the London King's Cross-Newcastle 'Tees-Tyne Pullman' stretches down Holloway Bank behind No 9003 *Meld* on 12 September 1972. *Brian Morrison*

for the East Coast route's passenger services between London King's Cross, Leeds, Newcastle and Scotland. Faced with growing competition from the private car and the expanding network of domestic air services, the forward-thinking East Coast management felt that they could wait no longer for electrification in this competitive environment. Fortunately, some real foresight had been shown by the English Electric Company who had designed and built a new high-powered diesel prototype locomotive known as the 'Deltic' at their own financial risk. Way ahead of its time and its competitors, this remarkable machine was capable of cruising at 100mph on the long journeys between London and Scotland. The East Coast managers saw this as the ideal candidate to bridge

the gap until the East Coast main line was eventually electrified.

Twenty-two production models were built in total and the first of these 100mph locomotives began to appear on East Coast services during 1961. With the start of the 1962 timetables, dramatic cuts were made to the times of all East Coast services. Over an hour was cut between King's Cross and Edinburgh to create new six hour schedules between London and Scotland. Although six hour timings had been achieved by the pre-war steam-hauled 'Coronation' train, that particular service had run just once a day, on Mondays to Fridays only with a special supplement payable. In 1962, the average timing of all the route's daytime trains was down to a little over six hours and none required a supplement.

Diesel power was shrinking journey times quite considerably. To raise train speeds between London Paddington, Bristol, South Wales and the West of England, a fleet of diesel hydraulic locomotives had made it possible for the Western Region to phase out steam locomotives and upgrade its services. As dieselisation spread, train services on other trunk routes such as London St Pancras to Nottingham, Derby and Sheffield and Liverpool Street to Norwich were accelerated and upgraded. As yet though, standards of service and image varied significantly over BR's main routes. Something was needed to bring these different services together in a consistent, coherent and marketable kind of way. A major opportunity presented itself with the introduction of the new electric services from Euston to Liverpool and Manchester in 1966. Inter-City as a corporate brand name was about to be born.

In 1960, the Conservative Government had become increasingly concerned at the rising annual deficit of British Railways, and appointed the Stedeford Committee as a special advisory group to the Minister of Transport, Ernest Marples, to inquire into and report on the steadily worsening financial position of the railways. One member of that Committee was a certain Dr Richard Beeching, Technical Director of Imperial Chemical Industries Limited. Mr Marples believed Dr Beeching had just the right qualities to become the Chairman of British Railways. The incumbent Chairman, Sir Brian Robertson, was due to retire in May 1961, and Dr Beeching duly replaced him as Chairman of the new British Railways Board. His purpose was singularly clear. He was required to carry out a deep and searching investigation into every aspect of the railways' operations and finances.

The Beeching Era: 1961-1969

The InterCity story accelerated during the Beeching era when a radical Board was seeking radical means to beat the new competition from motorways, cars and domestic airlines. The Beeching Report was published in March 1963 and revealed that over half the mileage carried only 4% of the passenger miles. Very large sections therefore did not even cover their day-to-day operating costs, such as wages, fuel, etc let alone track, signalling and other maintenance costs. The other half of the system, on the other hand, had earnings which covered route costs by more than six times.

It was at last clear that the railway was at its best when concentrating on specific traffics such as fast passenger services, rather than trying to play the nineteenth century role of common carrier. Even with reduced operating costs which the rapidly spreading

diesel traction was bringing – in some areas diesel railcar operation of local lines was cutting costs by up to 50% – there was no way in which many local and rural lines could ever be made viable. On the positive side, Beeching recommended that far more attention should be paid to the speed, reliability and comfort of the inter-city services which he believed should be provided by the fast and semi-fast trains at the expense of the local stopping services. Overall the Report suggested the closure of some 5000 route miles of track and 2000 stations. Many of the stopping services ran over lines used by express passenger trains and their removal would release track capacity to allow the higher speeds demanded for the inter-city services. Not all the proposed passenger closures were delivered but most were and at a pace that many considered to be indecent.

The Beeching era was an important period in the InterCity story. It was during that time that the importance of inter-city traffic for a forward-looking and potentially profitable railway was first clearly spelt out, even though the evidence for this state of affairs had long been available. It was in the Beeching era that the need for much finer, more precise costing procedures, which would enable the viability of much smaller parts of the total operation to be assessed, was brought much more sharply into focus. Although fast inter-urban traffic had had a long and honourable place on the railway scene, it was really during the Beeching years that the foundations were put in place for the subsequent and successful InterCity business.

The Inter-City name

The Beeching Report of 1963 was the first occasion when the term 'inter-city' was used to loosely describe the whole long-distance, express network. The specific words had first been used in a railway context on 25th September 1950 when the Western Region continued the GWR's tradition of giving names to its most prestigious trains by calling the 0900 from London Paddington to Wolverhampton and its return, 'The Inter-City'. Following a revision of services over the route from Paddington to Birmingham and the North West, 'The Inter-City's' destination was extended to Chester in 1962. The name was then dropped in 1965 in anticipation of its adoption for the whole of the Euston to Liverpool and Manchester electric services the following year.

Another pioneering use of the word also came from BR's 1957 staff magazine when it stated that: The first of the new series of inter-city express diesel trains to enter service in Great Britain started work on the

ABOVE A member of the Class 40 fleet – for many years the mainstay of London Midland, Eastern and Scottish Region's long-distance services - powers an Anglo-Scottish express over the Settle & Carlisle. *Gavin Morrison*

Glasgow to Edinburgh route on 7th January'. A series of diesel multiple units, built at Swindon in 1963 for services between Cardiff and Derby and Cardiff and Bristol were also described as 'inter-city' units. Indeed, the 1957 Annual Report of the British Transport Commission stated that it had been decided to provide three categories of express train called; Pullman deluxe, special inter-city and ordinary express.

BRB's Corporate Identity Programme 1965

One especially significant aspect for the InterCity story was Sir Brian Robertson's initiative in 1956 in forming a British Transport Commission Design Panel charged with advising on 'the best means of obtaining a high standard of appearance and amenity in the design of equipment'. The Design Panel influenced virtually every major development from then on.

A new corporate design initiative in 1965 launched a new BR image and the now world-famous and much emulated double arrow logo. Longer distance trains were picked out in a distinctive blue and grey livery, whilst stopping trains were plain blue. This early recognition that long distance trains were different to other trains was the start of the idea which culminated in the sophisticated InterCity livery of the 1990s.

In 1963, the British Railways' workshops at Swindon had introduced a revised passenger coach bogie design.

Designated B4 and capable of 100mph, it had superior riding qualities to the ageing 90mph Mark I coaches. At the same time, Swindon was also perfecting the associated Mark II coach body designs in which the whole body was built as a rigid box with no separate underframe. This radical design saved weight, gave extra rigidity and offered a safer environment compared to the Mark I type of 1951. The first of the new Mark II coaches came into extensive use on the 'New Railway' between Euston and the North West on its electrification in 1966 and completed the image of the rebirth of a modern, high speed railway complete with smart blue and grey livery.

In 1962 the British Railways Board authorised a further build of eight prototype coaches which were introduced in 1964 as the XP64 project.

InterCity dateline -1966

One of the most significant dates in the InterCity story was that of 18 April 1966 which was the inaugural day of the long-awaited electric services between London Euston, Liverpool and Manchester. The new timetable was based on a consistent regular-interval concept and included journeys timed at an average of over 80mph with sustained running at 100mph for the first time ever in Britain. Stations were rebuilt including those at Manchester, Lichfield, Tamworth, Stafford and Euston.

ABOVE The first 'Inter-City' – hauled by a 'King'-class locomotive in 1959. *Authors*

The new service was an immediate success and demonstrated the phenomenon which came to be known as the 'sparks effect' – instant and sustained increases in passenger travel on newly electrified railways. The new service was such a success that additional trains had to be arranged to cope with the business. After just three months of the new service, traffic between Manchester, Liverpool and London was up by a remarkable 66% on the previous year. When electrification was extended to Birmingham and Wolverhampton in March 1967 the results were equally dramatic and positive.

Instead of giving names to individual expresses as had been the practice previously, an historic decision was taken to brand the whole of the new service 'Inter-City' for promotional purposes. Promotion of the route also marked a major change in the practice of marketing and advertising in the railways. Instead of station posters preaching to the converted, television commercials, newspaper and magazine advertising and mailshots now delivered the message to the homes and offices of those who had seldom used railways. Specialist marketing teams were set up with many members recruited from outside the railway and external advertising agencies were increasingly used to

improve professionalism. Since that time the skills of the marketeer have been central to the success of the InterCity operation.

The InterCity route electrification was extended via Birmingham in 1967 where it coincided with the total reconstruction of Birmingham New Street station. Here a new office was opened dealing with ticket sales, information, advance bookings and reservations, for both business and leisure travel. This was one of the first of a new type of Travel Centre, now taken-for-granted, yet so important to InterCity's future sales drive.

Political initiatives to put British Rail and its fledgling InterCity on a sounder business footing occurred in 1968 following the return of a Labour Government in 1964. Under the Transport Act of 1968, the Minister of Transport, Barbara Castle, announced an '11,000 mile basic railway network, which the Government and the British Railways Board have decided should be retained and developed'. The accumulated deficit, of some £153 million, was written off. The 'social railway' was separated from the 'commercial railway', the government being prepared to support the 'social railway' only for as long as it felt it was necessary. The intention was that 'commercial' businesses would move towards profitability and open competition but it was to take InterCity another 20 years to achieve that profitability against severe deregulated competition from coach and air.

Work began in 1966 on the first major national InterCity promotional campaign with the slogan 'Inter-City: Heart to Heart'. This required 40 separate television commercials to highlight facilities in each area. This was the start of marketing all the principal long-distance routes which were at last starting to form themselves into a much more integrated network with its own identity. The new promotions increasingly used market research to establish customers' opinions and reactions. In 1968, a survey found a significant shift in public perception had taken place following the new InterCity network of services compared to those pre-1966. The spread of the new services was also an important factor in the public's new approval.

A key decision for InterCity's future competitiveness was made in 1969 when the Board announced that all new coaches to be built for InterCity would be air-conditioned regardless of class of travel. The transition to a fully air-conditioned fleet would take twenty years to implement but it was to put the UK ahead of other world rail operators and gave it a vital edge in comfort and luxury which came to be recognised as part of rail's unique advantage for relaxed travel. Other railways

were beginning to offer air-conditioning but usually in First Class coaches only and with supplements payable. InterCity was uniquely farsighted in making air-conditioning standard in both First and Second Class and without supplements. It was to prove a highly successful decision in the competitive era of the 1980s.

In the same year a decision was made to market all Britain's sleeper services as a single InterCity Sleeper product. This followed a similar decision to create a national Motorail product for accompanied cars in 1966. In both cases the significance was the end of local regional promotions in return for the added-value of national product management. InterCity grew into its full strength from these early acts of national product management and branding.

The seeds of InterCity were undoubtedly sown in the 1950s and 1960s when the evolution began from the steam railway to gradual, but sustained, advances in speed and business planning. Railways throughout Europe had started to encounter unprecedented levels of competition from other modes of transport. In order to fight back, the railways started to focus on exploiting the potential of their long distance, high speed services between major centres. From 1966 onwards, the InterCity concept had caught the public's imagination in Britain and had started along a path that would place it amongst the world's leaders in the provision of quality rail transport in the next decades.

ABOVE One of the West Coast electrics passes an almost empty M1 motorway in the 1960s. *Authors*

Chapter 2
TECHNOLOGY FOR THE PEOPLE 1970-1982

ABOVE Prototype High Speed Diesel Train No 252001 rests at London Paddington's platform 4 on 5 May 1975. *Colin J. Marsden*

In May 1970, InterCity's future as Europe's only profitable railway turned on one decision made at a meeting of the British Railways Board's Investment Committee. At that meeting, the Committee authorised £70,000 for the development of a prototype high speed diesel-electric train. Today we call that train the InterCity 125. Its service history is distinguished by spectacular journey time reductions and a series of record runs which have all made it the fastest diesel train in the world. But, for the InterCity business, it was the train's earning power which was so decisive. With its unique blend of performance and comfort, combined with steadily improving standards of on-board service, 1C125 became a moneyspinner wherever it entered service.

However, unlike the much-publicised bullet trains in Japan, the TGV in France and the ICE trains in Germany, 1C125 has achieved its success the hard way, running on existing rail routes laid down by the great Victorian engineers. InterCity 125 was the uniquely British way to high speed and its development is the story of InterCity in the years of the 1970s.

High speed policy

By the end of the 1960s, there was agreement within BR that average journey times had to be reduced if the developing InterCity was to survive in a market where Government investment and technical development was favouring the car, the coach and the aeroplane. But the way forward to higher average speeds divided engineers and managers alike.

In December 1968, British Rail Research had finally received funding to develop its vision of an Advanced Passenger Train (APT) capable of running at up to 150mph on existing track. The Government would provide half of the £4.8 million needed to produce a prototype train for trial running: BR would fund the other half.

The APT programme was set up independently of BR's established traction and rolling stock engineers who had launched the InterCity revolution back in the 1960s. It was, however, the latter group of engineers who had been intimately involved in the 'sparks effect' of the London-North West electrification which had boosted ridership so dramatically by 66%. In partnership with the civil engineers, and with each new summer timetable, they were now reducing journey times on the East Coast route from London King's Cross to Edinburgh by using the high powered, high speed Class 55 Deltic diesel locomotives.

Nonetheless, however significant these developments were held to be by BR's engineers, their professional

colleagues in the Research Division chose to see them as the work of yesterday's technology compared with their 150mph gas-turbine powered, tilting train. Their view was that while conventional technology chipped gently away at the minutes, APT would slash up to an hour from the longer runs.

A new technical vision

Then, in 1968, BR appointed a new Chief Engineer, Traction & Rolling Stock. His name was Terry Miller and he had the ideal pedigree to take conventional high speed trains into the 1970s. As a young man he had trained under the great railway engineer Sir Nigel Gresley who, with the development of the 'Silver Jubilee' on the LNER in the 1930s, had created the concept of the high speed, fixed-formation train. In the more recent past, Miller had been Chief Engineer of the Eastern Region of British Railways responsible for the mould-breaking Deltic diesels. Clearly, Terry Miller was the right person at the right time. He had the vision to see that conventional technology could build on the successes already experienced on the East and West Coast routes and he had the leadership ability to make major change happen again, and quickly.

It was also fortunate for Miller that much of the technology was already in place. His engineers had already begun to develop new coaching stock which was designed to replace the InterCity Mark II vehicles then in production. Significantly, and with considerable foresight, Miller had decided that this new stock should have the previously undreamed of design speed of 125mph – about twice the legal road limit.

To be commercially viable, a new high speed train would have to be able to operate with the minimum number of changes to the existing track, structures, etc. One critical area that needed consideration was that of possible track damage incurred by trains travelling at higher speeds. The civil engineers specified that any new locomotive or power car would have to produce the same forces on the track at 125mph as an existing 99 tonne Class 55 Deltic produced travelling at 100mph. Fortunately, the far-sighted diesel engine builders, Paxman Engineering, had a new engine under development which would put 2,250 hp into a 68 tonne power car. This light weight would meet the civil engineers' track force requirements whilst, for the railway operators, two of these power cars would still take seven of the new Mark III coaches up to 125mph.

Having dealt with the issues of running softly, safely and at high speed, it was also clearly important to consider the signal engineers' famous dictum of 'your right to speed is your power to stop'. As resignalling

ABOVE No 55018 *Ballymoss* leaves London King's Cross on the 16.00 to Edinburgh on 10 July 1976. *Gavin Morrison*

at that time was both impracticable and unaffordable, raising line speeds to 125mph on existing track meant stopping within existing braking distances. Once again, in a fortuitous case of 'here's one we designed earlier', the right technology was available in the form of a British-designed disc brake allied with new anti-slide brake controls.

A key decision

Meanwhile, the technical challenges of the APT programme were beginning to worry BR's commercial managers. So, when Terry Miller offered them a 125mph train with a prototype up and running in just 22 months, the proposal to make this happen soon appeared before the British Railways Board. The then Chairman, Sir Henry Johnson, quickly became convinced that BR could not wait for APT to prove itself. At the same time, road and air competition continued to grow stronger. It was Johnson who

expressed what was to become InterCity's traction and rolling stock philosophy for the next 20 years when he said: 'We cannot stand still, we must go on improving track and trains on orthodox lines.'

Once that decision was taken development of the new train accelerated. In August 1970 the development authorisation was changed to the construction of a prototype High Speed Diesel Train (HSDT) with six coaches and two power cars. In June 1972, the train which would take InterCity into the 21st century rolled out at Derby Works as promised, just 22 months after authorisation and only a month after the experimental Advanced Passenger Train (APT-E) had appeared. Coincidentally, at the same time on the other side of the English Channel, French Railways unveiled the prototype Train à Grande Vitesse, the TGV. Interestingly, the British train would not only enter commercial service first but it would be the first to be sold abroad.

Tragically, a year of vital development was lost when both HSDT and APT were immediately boycotted by the trades' unions for having a single central seat in the cab with all the implications that the cab would be single-manned. But in many ways, the race between the two trains was already over. While the HSDT was a true prototype, fully equipped to run in revenue service, the APT-E was no more than a test train with only one part of one coach fitted out as a VIP saloon.

At this point, the stories of the two trains began to diverge. HSDT became a commercial success, thanks to heroic efforts on the part of the maintenance engineers and the manufacturers to overcome design weaknesses which had not been exposed by the truncated development testing process. On the other hand, APT ended up as a national disappointment; a bold strategic concept, starved of technical resources which should have developed into another winner alongside the HSDT but did not. InterCity was still paying the price on the West Coast in the 1990s.

HSDT on test

Once HSDT began running, its performance exceeded all expectations. For example, its disc brakes stopped it in 1,930 yards at 125mph compared with the 2,200 yards allowed for a train travelling at 100mph. In addition, its acceleration was better than hoped for and later on in its development it would be discovered that the train's aerodynamics were so good that another coach could be added to the original seven-car formation without having to increase the output of the two power cars.

The prototype went to the East Coast main line for high speed trials. On 12 June 1973, it set a new diesel-powered world rail speed record of 143mph whilst running on the fast, straight racetrack between York and Darlington. On the same line it also demonstrated an invaluable ability to get the train home on a single engine when failures occurred. On level track, the train can run at 110mph on one power car thus maintaining a reasonable service.

When the Duke of Edinburgh opened the new National Railway Museum in September 1975, what better form of transport from London to York than the HSDT? Suddenly, however, in mid-journey the senior engineer on the train was called away from the official party. In one of the power cars a French-built circuit breaker had blown up. Would the same component do the same thing at the other end of the train? Fortune favoured InterCity and the journey was completed uneventfully – at least as far as the royal party was concerned.

Higher customer standards

For InterCity's customers this new technology has meant much more than shorter journey times. The Mark III coach, the cheapest and lightest steel-built air-conditioned coach in Europe, gives a quality of ride, even on poor track, that later designs have struggled to emulate. Whilst the internal ambience was not significantly better than that of the later models of the air-conditioned Mark IIe and IIf coaches, the positive overall impression for those 1970s customers, reinforced by the new buffet cars and the higher standards of on-board service, made the train a winner right from the start.

With electrification on the West Coast main line being extended to Preston, Carlisle and Glasgow and with the East Coast's route engineers still pulling further cuts in journey times from their fleet of untiring 'Deltics', the Western Region's main lines to Bristol and South Wales were chosen to receive the first fleet of what were now to be simply called High Speed Trains or HSTs.

Built for speed

As part of a major upgrade for 125mph operation, the Western Region's civil engineers, led by Chief Civil Engineer Phil Rees, turned Isambard Kingdom Brunel's great way west into a veritable billiard table and exploited its high speed potential to the maximum. Indeed, in some places so great were the changes to be made that only complete renewal of the track bed could meet the new standards required. Between Wootton Bassett (to the west of Swindon) and Bristol Parkway station, the track bed had to be blanketed with sand and polythene sheeting to restore effective drainage. Faced with the prospect of three years' disruption while this work was carried out under a series of weekend possessions, the decision was taken to shut the line down completely and do the work in five months. This entailed shift working around the clock during the summer of 1975 to get the work finished.

Brunel, of course, had been an early apostle of high speed and high levels of ride comfort and had, therefore, endowed the Great Western Railway's alignment with gentle gradients and sweeping curves. Building on this magnificent foundation and attending to some of the areas where Brunel's 19th century vision had actually faltered, Rees and his 20th century engineers improved upon the master's work, slewing the track to ease curves and raising line speeds wherever possible to the full 125mph. Take the 112 miles between Paddington and Bristol Parkway as an example. After the upgrading work had taken place only 14 miles would be run at less than 125mph and all but two of those miles were at speeds over 100mph.

With the prototype HSDT up and running, the 27 production trains for the Great Western main line on order and the infrastructure engineers hard at work, it was now time for the timetablers and marketeers to work out how InterCity was going to exploit fully its new assets. Pathing the 125mph HST into the existing passenger and freight services was a major challenge but one which would get easier as successive fleets were introduced. The sheer performance of the HST reduced the impact of station stops and gave the operators something in hand. On one test run from Reading to Taunton, an HST gained eight minutes purely on its acceleration away from stops and speed restrictions.

The people's train

Hard though it may seem for us to believe today, one of the major concerns for the railway marketeers of 1975 was to persuade the everyday travelling public that a train like the HST was a train for them. High speed trains on other railways had almost invariably been sold as a premium product with business travellers prepared to pay a supplement for superior service and performance. In contrast, HST was InterCity's new standard product providing hourly, high speed services throughout the day. The concern was that ordinary members of the public would not perceive that such a train was for them.

Selling HST as the people's train meant playing down some of its features. Speed for speed's sake was out as were images of luxury travel. Instead the emphasis was on shorter journey times, greater comfort and improved onboard service. For business travellers, of course, there was no such resistance to a high quality service – in fact, it was long overdue. In the case of the Western Region services from London to Bristol and South Wales, the parallel M4 motorway had been abstracting traffic steadily. Now InterCity was striking back at the company car with a highly effective weapon. In 1975, as the production trains began to leave the works at Crewe and Derby, the HST had gained a new name. On the side of the power cars, the legend 'Inter-City 125' had appeared in large letters and figures. The marketing revolution had started.

The 'nose cone' effect

On Monday, 4th October 1976, InterCity's high speed revolution began with a service of sixteen 1C125s a day each way on the London-Bristol-Swansea routes. A decade earlier 70mph had been considered the desirable commercial speed for InterCity trains. Now the fastest 1C125 averaged just under 92mph between Paddington and Bristol Parkway and much faster timings were to come. Nevertheless, in 1976, a 23 minute reduction on the best London-Cardiff time and a 15 minutes reduction off the London-Bristol trains were impressive enough to be getting on with and ridership began to climb. At a time of recession, the public responded with enthusiasm.

In the first six months of that service, ridership rose by 15% and in two years it was up by 33%. In the first two years of HST squadron service on the Western Region ten million passengers had been carried and business was up by a third on a highly competitive corridor. The economists had to coin a new phrase to describe the extraordinarily strong pulling power of the new train. InterCity 125 had been launched with the slogan 'It's the changing shape of rail'. Now its commercial impact was being dubbed the 'nose cone' effect.

With the introduction of the May 1977 timetables, and with 82 services a day running at 125mph, the twenty seven strong HST fleet was in full service. There was nothing to match this combination of speed and intensity anywhere in the world other than the Japanese Shinkansen. Meanwhile, as permanent way improvements were being completed, journey times continued to fall. Bristol Parkway was now only 70 minutes from Paddington on the fastest train, a start to stop average speed of 96mph. On the South Wales route, the London to Cardiff time came down to 105 minutes.

Record runs

In 1977, Her Majesty Queen Elizabeth II celebrated the silver jubilee of her reign. For InterCity it was too good a chance to miss and so the Western Region decided to show that when it came to special runs the 1C 125 was in a class of its own. On 7 May 1977, a standard seven-car train in the charge of Drivers W. Francis and R. Sandercock pulled out of Bristol Temple Meads Station bound for London. The aim of this run of the 'Jubilee Special' was to average 100.1mph. The train took just 68 minutes 19 seconds to arrive at Paddington – a start to stop average of 103.3 miles per hour without exceeding the 125mph line limit.

On the return journey the train did even better. By Twyford, 31 miles out from Paddington, the average speed was 100mph: by Bristol Parkway the average had gone up to 110 whilst, even after the slow run around the curves into Bristol, the start to stop average was 104.4 miles an hour. Not surprisingly, this was a world record for diesel traction.

ABOVE Intercity steam in decline (1): 60025 *Falcon* leaves Leeds Central with the last steam working to London King's Cross from the Leeds' area. In happier times, King's Cross shed would have cleaned the locomotive especially for the occasion. Equally unkempt D9016 is on the down 'Queen of Scots Pullman'. *Gavin Morrison*

BELOW Intercity steam in decline (2): Trafford Park-allocated 70032 *Tennyson* seen here in terrible external condition readies itself to leave Leeds City on the up 'Thames-Clyde Express' on 7 August 1960. *Gavin Morrison*

In later years there would be even faster high speed runs culminating in the inauguration on 27 September 1985 of the new 'Tyne Tees Pullman' from Newcastle to London. As they would do with the launch of the electrified InterCity 225 some seven years later, the East Coast main line engineers and operators pulled out all the stops for what would be the ultimate demonstration of InterCity 125 performance. Considerable care went into the selection of the train for the run, even down to ensuring that the wheelsets were new to maximise the gearing. With the civil engineers having given special permission for the line speed to be raised to 140mph in some key locations, the 268.6 miles to King's Cross was scheduled to be covered in 139 minutes. In fact, King's Cross was reached some 9.5 minutes early at a start to stop average of 115.4mph. Newcastle was potentially only 2 hours 9 minutes from London by rail!

In spite of the success of the 1C125s, however, there was more disappointing news on the horizon when it came to the size of the HST fleet itself. Originally, InterCity had planned a production programme which would see a 161 strong fleet of 1C

125s operating on all the non-electrified main lines. These sets would cover services on the East Coast main line, on the West of England services from Paddington, on the Cross Country services from the North of England and Scotland to the South West as well as a number of secondary InterCity routes such as Edinburgh-Glasgow and the Trans-Pennine route. But it was not to be. By the time that the Western Region's services had started, Britain was falling into recession and British Rail was having to fight to justify investment in every new train.

East Coast expectations

When the East Coast inaugurated its new high speed services in May 1978 there were not enough InterCity 125s for the full timetable due to delays in their delivery. Instead a hybrid service with additional locomotive-hauled trains was provided. Once again the 'nose cone effect' was demonstrated. Passengers were willing to stand to get the speed and comfort advantages of the InterCity 125 while there were seats to spare in the slower locomotive-hauled trains.

ABOVE No 55010 *The King's Own Scottish Borderer* passes Doncaster diesel depot and approaches Bridge Junction on the 12.05 London King's Cross-Hull on 26 March 1981. *Gavin Morrison*

ABOVE The 13.00 London King's Cross-Edinburgh threads its way along the cliff tops near Burnmouth heading for Edinburgh on 2 June 1978. *Gavin Morrison*

BELOW A young passenger talks to the driver of a High Speed Train at King's Cross. *Authors*

ABOVE In strong profile, a trio of HSTs rest at the buffer stops inside London Paddington station on 22 July 1978. *Gavin Morrison*

BELOW Three generations of East Coast motive power line up at York in March 1978. They are Gresley's 'A4' Pacific, a Class 55 'Deltic' and an Inter-City 125. *Gavin Morrison*

Then, just as the East Coast main line was preparing for the full launch of its Anglo-Scottish InterCity 125 services in May 1979, tragedy struck as a tunnel collapsed at Penmanshiel in Scotland killing two workers. It was, therefore, not until August 1979 that the full InterCity 125 services were introduced.

Improvements on track

On the East Coast too, the role of the civil engineers was vital in making sustained, high speed cruising possible. They had been driven since the 1960s by the commercial need to reduce journey times on a route with severe air and motorway competition and they had worked relentlessly to save precious minutes. They developed an incremental programme of improvements which simplified the authorisation of funding compared to a total route upgrading scheme. Improvements were worked up which saved two minutes here and three minutes there. For example, in 1967 line speed improvements gave a benefit of some 15 minutes between London and Newcastle for a total expenditure of just £750,000.

Even better, the cumulative effect of journey time savings made each scheme more affordable than the last. As an example, in 1969, it became feasible to realign curves at Offord in Cambridgeshire to raise the speed limit from 70mph to 100mph even though this work meant encroaching upon and diverting the course of the River Ouse.

As a result of all of these small but vital improvements, at the start of the 1970 timetable a line speed of 95/100mph was available for some 160 out of the 268 miles between London and Newcastle. The figure just three years earlier had been a mere 77 miles.

These steady steps to success paved the way for even more ambitious schemes which saw the remodelling of Peterborough station where line speed through the station itself was raised from 20 to 105mph. In addition, other major improvements were also carried out at Hatfield, Grantham, Selby and between Darlington and Newcastle.

The first trains to exploit this engineering work were the famous 'Deltic plus eight' formations. These trains, limited to eight coaches with a 3,300 hp diesel-electric at the head end, brought journey times down dramatically in advance of the introduction of InterCity 125s. When the Deltics were launched in 1962 they introduced a 6-hour London to Edinburgh timing. By the time that they handed over to 1C125s, this had been cut to 5 hours 27 minutes.

Transport economists have calculated that it is journey time and not distance that is the critical factor in the competition between rail and air, there being a changeover point from one mode to the other around the three hours' mark. On the East Coast, 1C125 made London to Newcastle a three-hour journey, nearly one hour being slashed off the best Deltic timing. This was achieved through the East Coast's relentless strategy of route improvements with no less than 260 of the 393 miles on the London to Edinburgh journey being run at 100mph and above by the end of the 1970s.

Winning in the West of England

Meanwhile, the Government had authorised a further 14 sets for the Western Region for operation of its West of England services to Somerset, Devon and Cornwall. That the investment case could be made for a line with hardly any track cleared for more than 110mph west of Reading demonstrated yet another of the strengths of 1C125: even when the sets were unable to run at their full design speed, the superior acceleration and braking characteristics could bring valuable time savings whilst the improved ambience would also attract passengers. A partial West Country service was introduced in October 1979, with the full 1C125 timetable starting in May 1980.

The HST's ability to save time without needing to exploit its 125mph potential was one of the key reasons for the InterCity 125 being so attractive to the State Rail Authority of New South Wales in Australia. Re-geared for 100mph, acceleration was even better and InterCity XPT was able to transform journeys which had previously required an overnight stop into straightforward day returns.

Cross Country goes HST

Back in the UK, however, and despite InterCity 125's commercial success, investment was getting increasingly difficult to obtain. InterCity sought authority in 1978 to add a further 36 trains to its North East/South West services better known today as the CrossCountry business.

Implementation was planned in two stages. An initial batch of 18 trains would provide services from Edinburgh, Newcastle and Leeds to Cardiff, Bristol, Plymouth and Penzance. A second tranche would extend 1C125 to services between the North West and South West and South Coast destinations. However, with nationalised industry investment under severe pressure and InterCity ridership also suffering from the recession, approval for the first batch was finally obtained in 1978 with the planned second stage being abandoned.

East Coast overcrowding

Meanwhile, the success of 1C125 on the East Coast was causing severe overcrowding, highlighting the shortsighted decision to cut back the original submission for 42 trains sets. In response, InterCity put forward a submission for a further seven 1C125s. These would be used to give Sheffield a peak hour service to and from King's Cross and would add Middlesbrough and Hull to the high speed network as well as beefing-up midday Anglo-Scottish services.

When the Department of Transport said that it could justify only two sets, a public storm erupted over what became known as the 'two for seven' affair. With BR's frustrated aspirations made public for once, the Department was forced to reconsider and four trains were eventually authorised in January 1980. These sets brought the total number ordered to 95 and marked the end of production. From then on there were never to be enough of these superb trains and the shortage became particularly clear when the re-organisation of BR into business sectors in 1982 resulted in a widescale reallocation of the fleet onto the most profitable routes.

An unfulfilled promise

In contrast, the Advanced Passenger Train never overcame the year-long boycotting by the unions which meant that it was always in the shadow of the increasingly commercially successful 1C125. Yet, when APT-E began running it soon demonstrated the potential of tilting trains. Sadly, in the late 1980s, this capability was to be exploited commercially elsewhere by ABB of Sweden and by FIAT of Italy until the appearance of the Pendolino in 2002. Nevertheless, in trial running APT-E demonstrated the speed potential for a tilting train to clip journey times on curving routes before it was eventually consigned to the National Railway Museum at York. In August 1975 the high speed test programme was completed in spectacular style with a number of runs on the Western Region between Swindon and Reading. On the final run the four-car train maintained 152mph for a distance of six miles.

More significant in many ways was the run between London and Leicester in October the same year when the twisting 99 miles were covered in 58 minutes at an average speed of 102.4mph. The line speed was raised from 110mph to 125mph for this run with a burst of 135mph allowed between Luton and Bedford. The notorious Market Harborough curve, then a 50mph restriction, was taken at 75mph. It is interesting to contrast this future potential with the 1993 schedule for the 1C125 Pullman running non-stop south from

Leicester which took 71 minutes with the line speed still limited to 110mph.

According to the original programme, APT-E was to have been followed by four pre-series trains designated APT-P. With InterCity 125 already being ordered for the non-electrified routes and the gas-turbine power plants of APT-E having failed to meet expectations, the pre-series trains were destined for the Euston to Glasgow route which was due to be fully electrified in 1974.

But the APT programme was already slipping. The original 1968 prospectus had planned to have the pre-series trains in service in 1974. Instead, they were not even ordered until that year and the quantity was cut back from four to three. It was now the intention to get them into service in 1977 with a London to Glasgow timing of four hours offering an average of just over 100mph.

To achieve this, each train had two 4000 hp power cars marshalled between two rakes of six articulated trailer cars. This formation was put forward because only one pantograph could be used at any one time to avoid creating a bounce in the contact wire. BR was not allowed to run a high voltage cable along the train to provide a power car at each end despite the use of this solution on the French TGV fleet. This meant duplicating catering and other facilities in the rakes of coaches on either side of the power cars as passengers were not allowed to pass through these. Not surprisingly, such a formation could not have been used economically in commercial service.

APT-P spawned a number of innovations, possibly the most significant of which was the use of long, extruded aluminium sections welded together to produce the coach bodies. British Rail pioneered this 'plank' production method with the Swiss firm Alusuisse on the APT-P. It was subsequently to transform the use of aluminium in rail vehicle construction world-wide and was employed in Britain in multiple unit trains such as Regional Railways Class 158 and the family of Networker trains.

Technical innovations

Another innovation was the hydrokinetic brake. With a maximum speed of 155mph, it was considered that APT-P needed to go beyond the friction disc brake used in InterCity 125. Instead of discs, the passenger vehicles had tubular axles inside which were small water turbines. To apply the brakes, fluid was allowed into the axle and the churning action of the turbine blades slowed the train.

Although tilting had been proved to work on APT-E, a new design of tilt mechanism was developed and this was providing a greatly improved response. So

ABOVE The pre-production APT negotiates the curvaceous West Coast route. *Authors*

good a response, in fact, that it was easy to be fooled into believing that the train was still upright. However, in spite of these many clear technological benefits APT-P struggled, partly because of a mid-project re-organisation when APT was transferred from the Research Division to the Mechanical & Electrical Engineering Department and partly because the project continually lived in the shadow of the 1C 125 which continued to go from strength to strength.

The first APT power car did not roll out until mid 1977. One year later, the first three trailer cars were ceremonially unveiled but it was not until 1979 that the first test train started running with two power cars and six trailers. Nonetheless, progress was encouraging once testing started. So much so that it culminated in a new United Kingdom speed record of 160mph between Quintinshill and Beattock on the West Coast main line on 20 December 1979. As a result, there was well-grounded confidence that APT, running at 125mph, would start revenue earning service between London and Glasgow with the introduction of the May 1980 timetable.

It was not to be. On 18 April 1980, during a high-speed proving run, the bolts holding one of the hollow axles together failed and the train derailed at 125mph with the British Rail Vice-Chairman on board. Happily, no-one was hurt but the project never seemed to recover from this blow. Despite the APT being central to the future of the West Coast route, the project never received the resourcing needed to make it an early success.

Following APT-P, Inter-City planned to acquire a fleet of 60 trains for the West Coast, with the first being delivered in 1983 and with timetabled services starting in 1984. However, the service entry date slipped continuously.

In the end APT-P made its first run in revenue earning service between Glasgow and London on 7 December 1981. Leaving Glasgow Central at 0700, it arrived one minute early at Euston at 1115. It had averaged 102mph between Preston and London and had reached a top speed of 137mph. This run was hailed as the beginning of success but two subsequent runs were dogged with problems, from freezing brake pipes to a chafing wire and to tilt failure. Service running was abandoned after just one week.

West Coast options

In 1982, sectorisation had been introduced and InterCity became a business in its own right. The APT programme was then put under very close scrutiny. The conclusion was that APT was no longer what the business needed and high speed, locomotive-hauled options began to be considered for the West Coast route.

During 1982, trial running restarted with APT-P carrying railway staff and their families to test on board systems. At the same time, however, the London Midland Region team was actively investigating the possibility of converting HSTs to electric traction for that route. This too was to be a lost opportunity and, in one last throw, John Mitchell, one of the original members of the Research Division's team which created the APT concept, was appointed APT Project Manager and more engineers were drafted into the development team.

The APT was made to work reliably in just a few months but already the future of the project was looking less than promising. In 1983, the train was withdrawn once more as the bolts in the hollow axles again proved troublesome. Meanwhile, the design of the APT had evolved through an alphabet of variants until APT-U was proposed with tilting coaches marshalled with a non-tilting power car with driving cab. Gone was articulation, to be replaced by conventional bogies. Gone was the hydrokinetic brake, now to be replaced with discs. This concept then evolved into IC225, of which more later, which was adopted as a common design for both the West Coast and for the East Coast main line electrifications.

By the time IC225 went out to tender for the East Coast electrification, the power car had become the Class 91 locomotive, an entirely new design by GEC Alsthom. Similarly, the lightweight aluminium vehicles had become the steel-bodied Mark IV coach. The only hint of the original dream were the tapered sides of the Mark IV body, which would allow it to tilt – that is if fitting tilting equipment could ever be justified.

And that was the end of APT which, nonetheless, saved its best for last. On 12 December 1984, there was a tantalising reminder of what might have been with a run from Euston to Glasgow in 3 hours 52 minutes 45 sec. It was not enough to save the project, unfortunately, and one train was preserved in 1986 with the remainder of the vehicles sold for scrap. By then the Class 91 had been ordered. Significantly, key posts on

that project were held by former APT engineers who had left BR as they saw the original vision fail. This time, they were determined to get it right and from the moment it rolled out on schedule on St Valentine's Day 1988, the Class 91 has proved to be the real success that APT could have been.

Weaver to Glasgow electrification

On the darker side, the failure of the APT was to handicap the West Coast main line for the rest of the century. In 1970, the Government had authorised the extension of the 1966 London to Liverpool/ Manchester electrification northwards from Weaver Junction, via Preston, Lancaster and Carlisle to Glasgow. That further electrification, authorised at a time when the railway's finances were under severe pressure, was, in large part due to the success of the original sixties' scheme.

Those new services to and from Manchester and Liverpool were inaugurated in 1966 and by 1970 this intensive electric service had doubled ridership on the route, had given InterCity a 40% share of the market and had forced competing airline operators to cut back their schedules, thus presaging the opening of the TGV between Paris and Lyons some two decades later. Completed in the spring of 1974, the Crewe to Glasgow electrification repeated the earlier success story as the 'sparks effect' again caught the travelling public's imagination. Overnight, the northern fells were tamed. Where trains had required double heading with diesel locomotives to achieve acceptable times over the difficult climbs of Shap and Beattock, the new 5,000 hp Class 87 electric locomotives stormed up these gradients at line speed. At the same time, the route received its first locomotive-hauled Mark III coaches and, from the customer's viewpoint, the West Coast main line had achieved its total route modernisation. One result was a five-hour timing for the London to Glasgow 'Royal Scot', half an hour faster than the then best time of the 'Deltics' on the East Coast. Day trips between Euston and Glasgow were offered to popularise the memorable new service.

'Sparks effect' again

By the autumn of 1974, passenger traffic on the West Coast line, the former London & North Western Railway's 'Premier Route', was already up by over 50% on the previous year. In 1978 there were 165 runs in the West Coast timetable averaging 80mph or more but, by that time, the rival East Coast was preparing to launch its Anglo-Scottish IC 125 service with a 4 hour 37 minutes timing. Had the APT programme proceeded

ABOVE A Class 45 hauling Mark I coaches leaves London St Pancras for Nottingham in 1978. *Gavin Morrison*

to plan, the West Coast route would have seen its next step as a four-hour London-Glasgow timing at the end of the 1980s to challenge the air market. Instead, the route remained trapped in the mid-1970s timetable whilst south of Crewe, infrastructure laid in the 1960s began to deteriorate from years of hammering under the intensive locomotive-hauled services.

Hard times ahead
We have seen how the introduction of HSTs on the Great Western and East Coast main lines had revolutionised travel. On other routes, however, there was a very different picture. Elderly Mark II coaches and even more elderly Mark I stock dating from the early 1960s continued to be hauled by ageing diesel locomotives on such major arteries as the Midland main line from St Pancras to Nottingham and Sheffield, on the Great Eastern between Liverpool Street and Norwich and on the crosscountry link

between the North East and South West England. In all, services with traction and trains not designed to give the most positive image for InterCity.

Nor were prospects for improvement good. The 1970s were coming to a close during the country's regularly-occurring economic recessions and the Labour Government announced in a 1977 White Paper on Transport Policy that InterCity services 'must aim to make their full contribution to the cost of providing the infrastructure, if they are to justify continuing investment in this development'.

Politicians demand profits
It was no surprise that the new Conservative Government continued this commercial policy for InterCity. On 17 March 1980 the Conservatives announced new interim targets for the InterCity business which had been agreed with the Board and which were clearly intended to concentrate InterCity minds.

Chapter 3
PUSHING FOR PROFIT: 1982-1993

ABOVE No 90016 rounds the curve at Beckfoot just south of the Lune Gorge heading a Glasgow-London Euston express on 13 May 1989. *Gavin Morrison*

The 1982 to 1993 era was one of dramatic change and growth within InterCity. It saw the business come of age and become an independent, profitable sector competing successfully with deregulated coach and air services and with its strongest competitor – the private motor car.

InterCity's progress in the 1980s and 1990s makes an interesting business case study. The change in InterCity's strategic direction linked with a focused attack on basic costs helped to provide the foundation stones for success. The main theme running through the 1980s was the push for profit. It began as a desire to differentiate InterCity as the commercial arm of British Rail. It culminated in a major financial turnround which delivered a profit for six consecutive years. The means of this achievement were to be found in business sectorisation and in the emphasis on productivity, marketing initiatives, redefinitions of the InterCity portfolio and strategic investment. This chapter will place these ingredients in their historical context up to its achievement of full business brand status in 1993.

Organising for InterCity

1982 saw the transformation of InterCity into a business sector under a new, much more accountable set of management arrangements. This provided the catalyst for change throughout the rest of the decade. On 4 January 1982 BR was split into five independent but inter-related sectors, each with bottom-line responsibility for control over costs and revenue, even if that resulted at times in difficult and complicated working relationships. It had to become a business with a clear and closely identifiable commercial role.

One of the 'five fingers of the late Sir Robert Reid's controlling hand' under the new sectorisation arrangements and the person appointed to meet InterCity 's difficult and somewhat ambitious target of breaking even by 1985, was Cyril Bleasdale, the former managing director of Freightliners Limited. The InterCity network was clearly defined in 1982 and was intended to include all the profitable main lines including:

- The East Coast between Kings Cross and Edinburgh with trains penetrating through as far as Aberdeen.
- The West Coast between Euston and Glasgow with sleeper trains penetrating into the Highlands.
- The Great Western between Paddington, Bristol, South Wales and the West Country route to Plymouth with penetrating services through to Penzance.

- The Midland between St Pancras, Derby, Nottingham and Sheffield
- The Cross Country services between North West and North East England and South Wales, the South West of England and the South Coast.

Productivity InterCity style

To operate InterCity's 2000 mile network the business used 3400 passenger vehicles and 362 locomotives. Under sectorisation, one team could take an overall view of the needs and resources of the InterCity network for the first time and could re-allocate assets and stock to meet the changing needs of customers. Within ten years InterCity would be operating roughly the same services with 33% less rolling stock.

HSTs had first been introduced with a generous allocation of new stock on the Western Region. By May 1980 all principal trains on the Region, including services on the West of England line were HSTs. Completion of the M4 motorway paralleling the Great Western main lines to Bristol and South Wales soon attracted low-cost coach competition and this led to a significant fall in rail traffic in the early 1980s. One of the advantages of sectorisation in its early days was the development of a national business strategy which overcame the old regional parochialism. The re-allocation of seven HSTs from the Western to the Midland main line in October 1982 was a classic example of a national InterCity decision which improved net profit for the business.

Up until this time, the Midland main line between London St Pancras, Sheffield, Derby and Nottingham had been treated as something of a poor relation when it came to allocating modern rolling stock to the route. Trains were powered by elderly Class 45 diesel locomotives, limited to 90mph, and formed of Mark II coaches offering journey times that fell far below standards on other InterCity main lines.

The image of the Midland was transformed when five HST units were cascaded from the Western Region at the beginning of the October 1982 timetable, to be joined by a further two units from the East Coast and three originally intended for Cross Country services. From May 1983, these sets provided the Midland with a complete HST service, save for one peak-hour train each way which continued to be locomotive-hauled. Not only had this new service been introduced by more efficient use of existing stock rather than through the provision of expensive new trains, but it had also reduced maintenance costs by ensuring that the trains formed part of a common pool of units used on both the Midland and East Coast. The cascade of HSTs to the Midland and the transformation

ABOVE No 89001 arrives at Leeds on 21 January 1989 with a special from London King's Cross to Carlisle via the Settle & Carlisle line. Diesel traction took the train forward from here. *Gavin Morrison*

of its services can be seen as one of the first benefits of InterCity sector thinking.

Marketing InterCity

On 3 October 1983 InterCity demonstrated its growing confidence by having a marketing re-launch. The most obvious sign of this to the travelling public was the decision to adopt a new and easily identifiable livery based on that formerly used on the APT. This livery was light and dark grey, separated by striking red and white bands. Internally, the re-liveried coaches – two complete sets on the Western Region and the Manchester Pullman set – received attention as InterCity experimented with new seat designs and decor to enhance the travellers' ambience. Payphones were also installed in the re-liveried units from 1984. They represented an early example of product marketing as payphones lost money but were seen as part of a larger business package. This enhanced package was aimed at attracting the First Class business traveller and included free car parking at the station, at-seat service of drinks, seat reservations on outward journey and vouchers for train meals.

A marketing setback occurred in 1983 when the Department of Transport allowed InterCity to construct no more than a third of the 180 new Mark IIIb coaches which it so badly needed to meet motorway competition. The first 32 Second Class coaches were intended to strengthen the Western Region's HST sets from a formation of two power cars plus seven coaches (2+7) to a 2+8 formation. The remaining twenty eight coaches were authorised to improve quality on the West Coast main line which had received little recent investment and where standards of both quality and speed were beginning to compare unfavourably with the rest of InterCity. From May 1984 however, maximum line speed on the West Coast was raised from 100mph to 110mph to exploit the new coaches and to help strengthen the investment case for the remainder.

Redefining InterCity's portfolio

A number of important UK routes nearly became part of the InterCity network in 1984. Following the Department of Transport's ruling that the InterCity business should receive no subsidy, it was invited by the Board to identify any other potentially profitable services which could fit into the InterCity portfolio. These routes included the TransPennine expresses, Edinburgh-Glasgow and Waterloo-Bournemouth. Only two routes offered the opportunity to help InterCity improve its net profitability and London Liverpool Street-Norwich and London Victoria-Gatwick Airport were duly transferred to InterCity in 1985.

It is relevant to later privatisation proposals to remember that a conflict of customer priorities had developed at Gatwick before 1984 between the needs of Southern Region commuters travelling between London and the South Coast and the demands of luggage-laden airport travellers. It was to address these differing customer needs that a dedicated 15 minute interval service called the 'Gatwick Express' was introduced at the beginning of the May 1984 timetable for those wishing to travel directly between the airport and central London.

This was a classic case of market segmentation by InterCity. Mark IId coaches were allocated to the route and refurbished, some seats being removed to provide additional luggage space. The trains were worked on a push-pull basis, power being provided by Class 73 electro-diesel locomotives. The newly transferred coaches and one locomotive (No 73123 'Gatwick Express') were repainted in the experimental InterCity livery. Ultimately, thirteen locomotives were designated Class 73/2 and wore the same livery to emphasise their new, exclusive InterCity use.

A strategic challenge: the Serpell Report

Just as InterCity was starting to develop as a new business sector, the Serpell Report was published by the Government in January 1983. Ironically, it saw no prospect of InterCity achieving its financial target of commercial viability as set out in the 1982 Rail Plan. The Committee had been asked in May 1982 by the then Secretary of State for Transport, David Howell, to: 'examine within six months the finances of the railway and its associated operations, in the light of all relevant considerations, and to report on options for alternative policies and their related objectives, designed to secure improved financial results in an efficiently run railway in Great Britain over the next twenty years'.

The options for change produced by the Committee could not have been more designed to destroy morale on the railways, with an Option A that identified a commercially viable system of only 1630 route miles. This option showed no railway south west of Bristol or north of Edinburgh or Glasgow. There was not even a line of railway between Newcastle and Edinburgh and the Midland main line had completely disappeared. After a bitter and protracted debate, public opinion won the day, the report was shelved, the railway network was retained and new investment was released for the start of InterCity's modernisation of the East Coast route.

East Coast Electrification

InterCity confidence in the future was materially enhanced by the announcement by the Secretary of State for Transport (the late Nicholas Ridley) on 27 July 1984 that the Government had approved a £306m scheme for the electrification of the East Coast main line northwards from Hitchin, in Hertfordshire, through to Leeds and Edinburgh on the basis that the scheme could be funded internally through increased productivity. Of the £306m investment, just over half was attributed to infrastructure with £62m, to motive power and £74m for rolling stock. The scheme was justified primarily on savings in maintenance costs of 60% whilst reduction in journey times of around ten minutes between London and Edinburgh were also assured.

Planning for profit

A Board strategy document was published in December 1984. It was called 'InterCity – Into Profit' and it sought to convert an InterCity loss of £107m in 1983 into a £5m surplus by 1989. The prime agents for financial success came to be the transfer of the Anglia and Gatwick services which, once they had transferred, increased InterCity income by some £25m. An additional boost occurred in the following year when the loss-making Gloucester-Chepstow-Newport service was moved out of InterCity's remit into that of Provincial Services.

A second major contribution to profit was the identification of cost savings totalling £47m which included a seven per cent reduction in train mileage over the following five years through better tailoring of services to demand. The business also planned a 1% income growth from marketing measures such as the re-introduction of Pullman services. The re-launch of the 'Tees-Tyne Pullman' was carried out in style on 27 September 1985 when an HST made a special run from Newcastle to London in 2 hours 9 minutes at an average speed of 115mph.

It is difficult to imagine now just how daunting was the task that InterCity faced in the mid 1980s in its quest to achieve profitability. Nevertheless, there was some good news. The Western Region had been worst hit by the drop in passenger traffic as a result of motorway competition but the loss was arrested in 1984 and was followed by a very welcome surge in demand. Loadings in 1985 averaged about ten per cent above those of the previous winter, helped by bad weather, bad road conditions and a coach strike in South Wales. At least five per cent of this traffic was believed to have been new business.

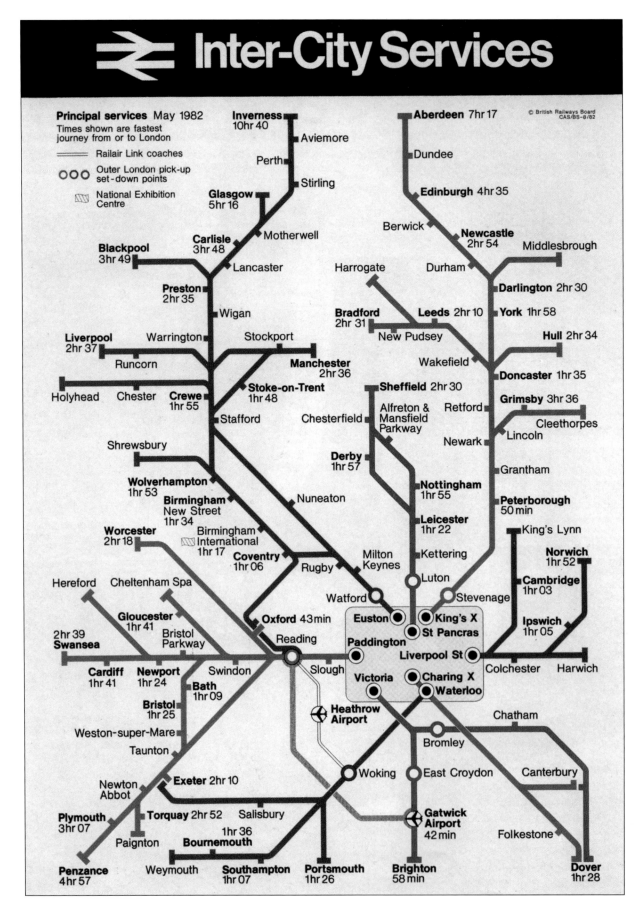

ABOVE InterCity route map 1982

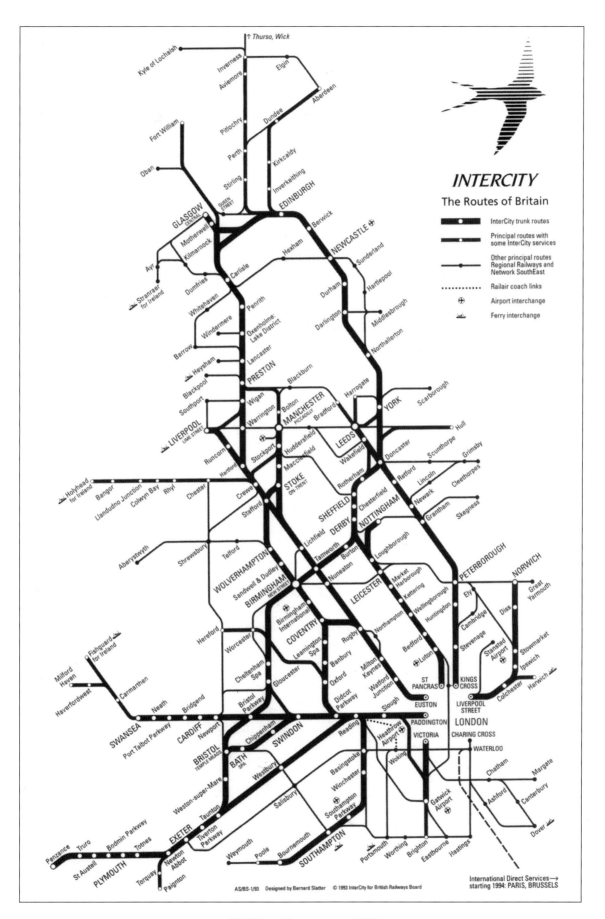

ABOVE InterCity route map 1993

Marketing in the boom

The non-stop Gatwick Express service was an immediate success. It took only 30 minutes, but a long layover at the end of each journey was built into the timetable so that a train was always available for boarding. A trolley service was provided from the outset and the format proved highly successful. This provided the model and inspiration for the 'InterCity Shuttle' services introduced on other routes in the 1990s. Passenger numbers on Gatwick Express increased by 38% in the first year of operation and revenue shot up by some 52%. By the 1990s rail had a quarter of all passenger travel to and from Gatwick Airport.

The mid-1980s also saw the beginning of long-distance commuting on a grand scale as people began to realise that they could travel daily to London by HST from Didcot, Swindon or even Bath and Bristol in far less time than was required for many shorter journeys on Network SouthEast's third-rail electric system from Surrey, Sussex and Kent. Indeed, journey numbers between Bristol and Paddington increased by no less than 20% in the 1986 boom. Season ticket price increases well in excess of the rate of inflation were being applied by the end of the 1980s but a fifteen minute interval service was still required between Swindon and Paddington to meet peak demands.

Commuters now accounted for some ten per cent of InterCity Great Western's income and that income helped to make it the first InterCity route to move into profit. The electrification of the East Coast at the end of the decade enabled additional HSTs to be returned to Great Western in order to meet this growing commuter demand and enabled all GW HSTs to be reformed into 2+8 sets to provide additional seats.

Financial performance 1987-88

John Prideaux took over as Managing Director at InterCity in February 1986. He focused on the need for major cost reductions. The Government target remained a 2.7% return on net assets and the Annual Report for 1987/88 recorded an encouraging 19% reduction in InterCity's operating loss together with a 5% increase in passenger volume. This impressive performance had been helped by a series of highly focused business activities. Refurbishment of the InterCity fleet brought a dramatic change in perception amongst customers. At the same time a more sophisticated approach to marketing was taken which involved streamlining products and restructuring the ticket range in order to optimise revenue per seat. The expansion of the Pullman network in 1987 helped to enhance product quality and to expand the First Class business market. New Pullman

services were introduced including 'The Master Cutler', 'The Golden Hind' and the 'Birmingham Pullman'. All of these had helped to contribute towards a 15% increase in First Class ticket sales.

Improved quality was introduced between Liverpool and London Euston with the introduction of Silver Standard service. This provided specially identified accommodation with free seat reservations and with an at-seat service of complimentary light refreshments to passengers holding full fare Standard tickets. One of the best achievements of InterCity in the late 1980s was maintaining its timetable of frequent, regular-interval services thoughout the recession.

Profit at last: 1988-89

The BRB's Annual Report for 1988/89 proudly announced that 'in its first year as a fully commercial business, InterCity turned an operating loss of £86m into a profit of £57m. Income rose by 10% and traffic volume rose by 4% to record levels.

The transfer of routes, the economic boom and a maintenance 'holiday' had all helped to deliver a profit. Electrification had reached Norwich by May 1987 and the results had been good. Both fleet and infrastructure made considerable contributions to the 1987/88 financial achievement. Substantial reductions in rolling stock unit costs were achieved by rationalising heavy maintenance work at key strategic depots, whilst an intense review of maintenance schedules led to cost savings of £15m. A review of infrastructure working practices in the late 1980s looked specifically at weekend engineering work and helped to lower the cost of track maintenance. The infrastructure cost initiative reaped major savings for the business but could never be a substitute for the economies that would flow from investment in major route modernisation.

West Coast interim strategy

In contrast with other InterCity routes, the West Coast main line had made little progress for a number of years. The failure of the APT experiment in the mid 1980s had left this important main line struggling with equipment which the tilting train had been designed to replace. By 1987 InterCity had recognised that its strength lay in competing for journeys of up to three hours in duration and had shifted its emphasis from the historically important Euston to Glasgow line to the more profitable routes from London to the West Midlands, Liverpool and Manchester, where the last deliveries of Mark III coaching stock had been introduced in 1987 to create an all air-conditioned service.

ABOVE No 43032 heads a Plymouth-London Paddington afternoon express as it passes Cockwood Harbour at full line speed on 16 September 1990. *Gavin Morrison*

In the following year, the West Coast received some welcome new equipment intended to enhance efficiency and productivity. Driving Van Trailers (DVTs), designed to save locomotives by creating self-contained train sets, began to be delivered to the route. Fifty two were ordered to work with new Class 90 locomotives, whilst existing Class 86 and 87 locomotives were converted to enable push-pull working to be introduced. The first 110mph Class 90 was delivered towards the end of 1987. There was some disappointment that 125mph locomotives had not been specified but, nonetheless, the new arrivals did mean that some increasingly troublesome older locomotives from the 1960s could be withdrawn. The new Class 90s and their DVTs improved reliability and efficiency on the West Coast even though there were some initial teething problems with the DVTs themselves. These rolling stock improvements bought time for the West Coast before the infrastructure fell due for renewal in the 1990s.

East Coast electrification commissioned

In the meantime, full electrification and other modernisation of the East Coast route took place between 1984 and 1991. In the same timescale the InterCity 225 train was developed, brought into production and introduced into full service. The IC225 consisted of the powerful new Class 91 electric locomotive and its stylish Mark IV coaches. The first Class 91 locomotive was rolled out at Crewe on 14 February 1988 and commenced its intensive running-in period.

Electric haulage of some services between Kings Cross and Leeds began in August of that year, using the experimental Brush Traction locomotive No. 89001 and Mark III coaches. The Leeds electrification was not only finished ahead of schedule but worked out at approximately half the cost of the pioneering West Coast project twenty years earlier after allowance for inflation.

Class 91s began revenue earning service on 3rd March 1989, and from the beginning of that summer's timetable five train diagrams were scheduled for haulage by these new locomotives. Their speed as well as their power was ably demonstrated later in the year when new Mark IV coaches and No 91001 'Swallow' were involved in high speed tests between Grantham and Peterborough, during which a top speed of 162.2mph was reached.

The thirty one new East Coast trains were known as InterCity 225s to reflect their top design speed of 225km/h (140mph). In practice, the line speed remained limited to 200km/h (125mph). The first complete IC225 train-Class 91 and Mark IV coaches – to enter passenger service did so on 2 October 1989 on the Leeds-London 'Yorkshire Pullman'. As deliveries proceeded apace further InterCity 225 formations were introduced regularly. On 14 May 1990, with the summer timetable, the full IC225 service to Leeds was introduced.

Wiring of the short stretch of railway from Carstairs to Edinburgh was planned as part of the Weaver Junction to Glasgow electrification back in the 1970s. It was finally sponsored by Cross Country – to eliminate diesel-haulage of trains between Edinburgh and West Coast destinations – but it also enabled East Coast IC225s to be extended to Glasgow allowing a much more attractive through service between that city and the North East of England and Yorkshire.

With electrification in place and completion of the Newcastle resignalling, IC225 services to Scotland began in mid-1991 and the then largest, single modernisation scheme ever to be undertaken on Britain's railways was completed. The whole package brought the best ever service between London, Yorkshire, North East England and Central Scotland and was based on hard, commercial planning.

InterCity becomes a business

In 1990 InterCity was still a small commercial organisation with a relatively small staff of its own – some 3,000 together with a further 2,400 in On Board Services. InterCity was required to provide passenger services over the main lines linking Britain's principal cities without any contribution from Government grant. The business was dependent on six geographical Regions with very different histories and business cultures for the actual delivery of the product it marketed. They provided lines, stations and rolling stock.

A successful new organisation, 'Organising for Quality', was implemented in shadow form in 1991. This united the General Managers of the former Regions as Directors of the five new InterCity routes. An InterCity Directors' Group was established and this was given the task of fully integrating the five InterCity routes into one, forward-looking profitable business.

In April 1991 the East Coast route, the Great Western and the Anglia/Gatwick operations were fully absorbed into the new organisation and in April 1992

ABOVE A Sheffield-London St Pancras HST headed by No 43075 passes Kibworth north of Market Harborough on a bitterly cold 12 December 1991. *Gavin Morrison*

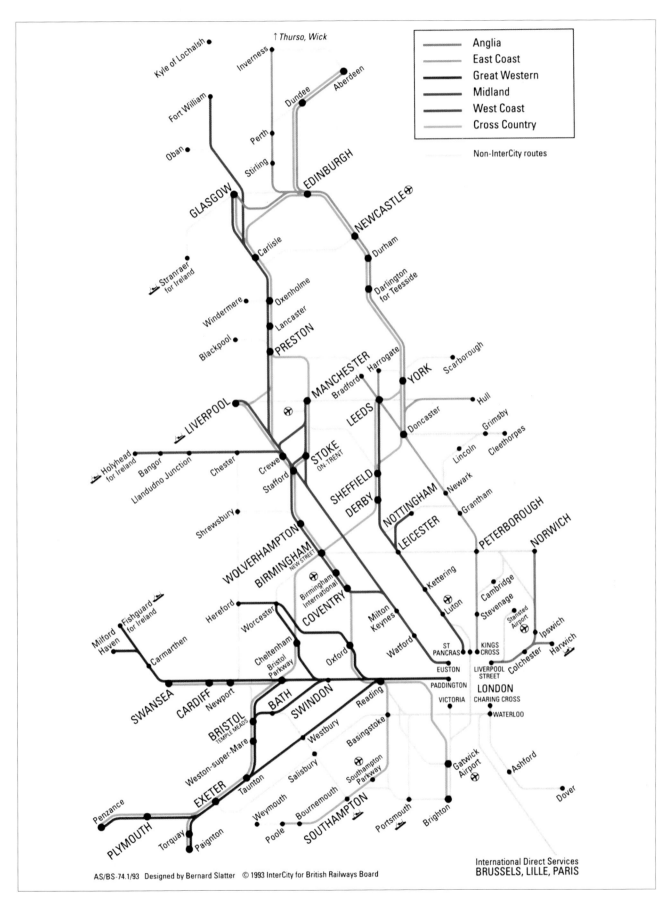

ABOVE InterCity route by route with associated feeder services.

ABOVE No 73211 approaches Gatwick Station with a down express on 21 September 1991. *Gavin Morrison*

BELOW Probably one of the most famous locations on the railway network is Horse Cove between Dawlish and Teignmouth. No 43010 heads west at this beautiful setting on 15 September 1990. *Gavin Morrison*

the dissolution of the London Midland Region allowed the final InterCity to emerge. It brought the providers of the services into one organisation and equipped them with all the assets needed to work and market those services. A real railway company was created; a company which owned its assets and employed its own staff. In addition, it managed its own £1 billion balance sheet under the control of a new Finance Director from Trust House Forte, Geoff Ashton. For the first time since 1948 a genuine railway business had been put together in a form the outside world could recognise.

Chris Green was appointed Managing Director in January 1992 with the remit to commission the new organisation from April and to maintain profitability despite the deepening economic recession. Radical changes would be needed in both the cost structures and the marketing of InterCity to deliver these targets and it was quickly recognised that a major shift would be needed in the company's culture. Such changes could not happen without much careful planning and great goodwill.

The new organisation set up specific levels of responsibility between the InterCity business headquarters and the five route headquarters. InterCity headquarters dealt with strategic planning, marketing and finance including the development of a strong national brand. In addition, considerable time and effort were devoted to training and development to create a proactive business culture. Inter-City's Infrastructure Director, John Elliott, ensured that a significant proportion of the savings the civil engineers contributed to the improvement of InterCity finances was re-invested. Revolutionary track renewal equipment was purchased to help them in their quest for higher productivity with minimal impact on the service to the customer.

What was put in place between 1990 and 1992 was, without doubt, the best organisation that British Rail ever had: the tragedy was that Organising for Quality came too late. For InterCity, it brought a very sharp focus to the railway, uniting a family of 30,000 staff in the common purpose of achieving the InterCity vision.

Cross Country strategy

InterCity was convinced of the positive merits of its HSTs and it put considerable energy into examining the case for forming half-HSTs to work on Cross Country services. However, not only would the cost of this solution have been too high, but there would have been an unbridgeable time-gap in which units were out of service. A study was made of the costs and benefits of running HSTs 'under the wires' to Aberdeen and other places off electrified routes. A similar study led to the introduction of HSTs on Euston-Holyhead services in 1991 which ran 'under the wires' from London to Crewe.

If there could be no half-HSTs, what was to be done for Cross Country? The answer was the short-train solution, with Class 47-hauled formations of Mark IIf vehicles able to run close to HST timings, which were limited on these routes. There was a problem with the elderly Class 47 locomotives which had been designed for a maximum speed of 95mph, but which had become used to working at significantly lower speeds. Approaching the end of their lives, they were being required to run at their maximum speed for long distances. A number of them were subsequently equipped with larger fuel tanks and bigger brake blocks and were concentrated on the former Bristol Bath Road depot for maintenance. The modifications and allocation to one depot all helped to deliver the product. What did not help was the conclusion that the clasp brakes of the Mark IIf vehicles were not predictable enough in their performance to allow lightweight five coach trains to be worked at 95mph so that eventually an increase of the formation to seven vehicles was required.

Maximising the InterCity fleet

Completion of the East Coast project allowed a huge shake-out of stock to take place, leaving a fleet properly reflecting the quality railway that the InterCity vision sought. Essentially, nothing earlier than Mark IIf remained and what was left was refurbished to a consistently high standard. The East Coast and the Great Western became 125mph railways and the Midland and the West Coast became 110mph railways with the latter being rationalised to three train types. Anglia operated at 100mph with Mark IIf vehicles, and Cross Country became a Class 47 short-train railway operating at 95/100mph. No less than two thirds of the core fleet was made up of Mark III vehicles built between 1974 and 1984. Such a chain of events demonstrated the strength of a national InterCity organisation able to survey its entire operation and deploy its fleet to the best advantage of the whole business and to the benefit of the greatest number of customers.

During the early 1990s InterCity also learnt to prioritise its markets. Rather than offering a token train service to a wide number of destinations it contracted its resources to ensure excellence on its core routes. This resulted in the scrapping of much second-rate rolling stock and the strengthening of primary services. InterCity's withdrawal from Shrewsbury and Blackpool in 1992 and Cleethorpes in 1993 enabled it to make significant savings and also allowed Great Western to withdraw all its locomotive-hauled passenger trains and provide a 100% HST operation for the first time in 1993.

The customer service revolution

The 1990s will be remembered as the era when InterCity made a major and very public commitment to the radical improvement of customer service. This was as a result of extensive research into customer needs which highlighted rising consumer expectations. It made good business sense to invest in customer service at a time of intense competition.

InterCity's customer service improvements came at a time when there was a growing awareness throughout the country of consumer rights and entitlements. There was pressure to raise standards and InterCity, along with the other passenger businesses, produced the 'Passenger's Charter' in March 1992. This set targets for customer service and promised to compensate customers if the railway failed to deliver its timetable promise. In October 1993, InterCity Anglia received a prestigious customer service award when it gained the coveted 'Charter Mark' for continuous customer service improvement. This achievement helps to demonstrate how far InterCity had come from the late 1970s.

The main theme from the customer research was that over half InterCity's customers made only one or two trips a year and found rail travel stressful and unfriendly. InterCity took this finding to heart in a big way and from 1992 Customer Welcome teams appeared in their bright claret uniforms on the concourses of all the larger InterCity stations. In 1993 porters were re-introduced at London King's Cross and Euston to the delight of the media and consumers alike. New Telesales services offered a freephone number for the immediate purchase of tickets using credit or debit cards. Stations were given improved directional signing, signposting, car parks were extended and new waiting rooms provided.

InterCity Shuttle

The introduction of InterCity Shuttle in May 1993 represented a culmination in the range of customer service initiatives. It brought together all these in a tangible way and presented them confidently in TV advertising. Four medium distance routes were designated Shuttle in 1993:

Route	Number of trains daily
Euston-West Midlands	56
St Pancras-East Midlands	57
Liverpool St-Norwich	32
Paddington-Bristol/South Wales	69

The total cost of Shuttle was small but the goodwill it generated was enormous and repeat business started to flow. This was particularly fortuitous since InterCity's top investment priority, the £750m West Coast modernisation, was not going well.

InterCity 250 for West Coast

The InterCity 250 project for a new West Coast train was fully approved by InterCity but was quickly stalled for funding at Board and Ministry level. This was a Total Route Modernisation project, and involved the extensive modernisation of the infrastructure, realignments for higher speed, re-electrification and the acquisition of a fleet of new trains. In 1992 InterCity wanted to buy complete trains rather than separate locomotives and coaches. This was something that had previously happened only with the HSTs – and it wanted to lay the foundations for a coherent fleet.

The aim was to get a Class 250 into service as the replacement for the obsolete Mark IIf stock and to test this thoroughly in service over a four or five year period before commissioning a high quality fleet. The new train was to be an evolution of the East Coast's InterCity 225 and could have been in service by 1995. In the summer of 1992 it finally hit the buffers for lack of funding in the depths of the recession and the tenders for the train lapsed.

Privatisation proposals precluded any further development and 1993 represented another watershed in InterCity's history. The 1980s and 1990s had been periods of great change and achievement for InterCity. The business had survived the worst post-war recession to hit the UK and had remained in profit throughout.

Profit in the recession

Despite the deepening recession, InterCity remained strongly in the black with results in 1992/93 revealing a £65m profit. This could not have been achieved without a grinding attention to attacking costs, committing the business to customer service and developing an aggressive marketing approach. The InterCity Directors' Group determined in 1993 that productivity savings of 6% should be made in such a way that customers would not see any deterioration in the service offered. There was to be no change to the InterCity vision even in a financial crisis. Extensive analysis revealed what could be done. It was finally agreed to risk delegating the task down the line and to trust the staff closest to the job to deliver the savings. This was done and the results exceeded the original target.

Clearly, the strength of the new InterCity did not come from a highly-centralised organisation. With day-

to-day working delegated to the lowest sensible level there was no central control point at headquarters, no central operating structure, no longer even a Director of Operations. The central management team at the business unit was there to develop policy, to think strategically and to ensure a strong voice for the routes in arguing the case for investment with Board and Government. It represented the whole InterCity business in the market place through, for example, multi-million pound television advertising initiatives which won several coveted awards and in major new ticketing initiatives such as Apex which offered road coach prices for rail speeds on selected trains.

The use of revenue management to maximise the available ticket revenue played a vital part in marketing initiatives in the 1990s. Over long distance routes, even more competitively-priced fares such as SuperApex were introduced which effectively fought-off coach competition and helped to increase InterCity's market share. Other national marketing promotions included the reinforcement of the First Class market at a time when customers were choosing to trade down in increasing numbers from First to Standard. In addition, there were further joint leisure promotions with household names such as Boots and Shell.

The InterCity team maintained its momentum on customer service, marketing and overall productivity. The reward was a £100m profit for 1993/94; a truly exciting achievement given the economic and political conditions under which the business was working. However, the greatest frustration remained the continuing shortage of investment funding. To run a steady-state railway which renewed its assets at the right time, InterCity needed to spend £225m a year on its infrastructure and trains but in 1993-94 it only had £90m, which was barely enough to keep the railway safe and secure. No clearer example could be given of the implications that short term funding decisions can have on long term profitability than the loss of the West Coast modernisation during this period. A disappointing end to what had been an otherwise powerful and positive period for the InterCity business.

Chapter 4
BUILDING A
WINNING BRAND

ABOVE InterCity branding at its best. *Authors*

The story of the famous InterCity brand was a long and fascinating one which deserves a chapter to itself. InterCity as a name evokes the ideas of relaxation, comfort and fast trains speeding through the British countryside. InterCity as a business was the first profitable, national passenger railway in Europe. But InterCity was, above all, a brand with which people enjoyed associating and which they choose to use again and again.

In fact, InterCity was one of the best established brand names in the United Kingdom with over ninety per cent of the population recognising the name. Its use began back in the 1960s when British Rail led branding in the travel market. Since that time the InterCity business had taken the concept forward in major strides. Today it has passed into the language as a general term for fast, long-distance trains – so much so that it has been widely copied by railways around the world – and imitation is the sincerest form of flattery.

Successful brands

Effective brands guarantee hard functional benefits to the customer. InterCity offered fast, frequent, comfortable trains. Really successful brands have an emotional appeal as well and a major element of InterCity's success was achieved by building on the British public's emotional attachment to trains, a feeling best described as 'train magic'. This became an emotion particularly associated with HSTs and the InterCity business.

The use of the name Inter-City was originally given to a London Paddington-Wolverhampton train that ran in the early 1950s. As a brand however, its origins lay in the Corporate Design Panel of 1965. The new name, British Rail, and the new logo that went with that new name, were a conscious decision to break with the past. Looking back after nearly five decades when company logos and corporate identities are the norm, it is difficult to remember just how innovative those changes were.

Breaking the mould

When electric trains began running between Euston, Manchester and Liverpool in April 1966 the improvement was so dramatic that it became known as the 'New Railway'. All the new trains on the service were called 'Inter-City' and all set new standards for speed, frequency and comfort. New television and press advertising supported the launch. Again, all emphasised the InterCity name; this was the launch of InterCity as a brand. It was also a turning point in that long-distance rail began to fight back against

competition from the car, growing use of which had led to a continuous decline in train travel during the 1950s and early 1960s.

InterCity was an immediate success with customers and further television advertising, such as the Inter-City 'Heart to Heart' campaign which was launched in 1967, built on this success. The use of the name was extended to other routes as coaches were upgraded or as new services were introduced. For example, the London to Birmingham electrification was completed in December 1967 and the new service on this line was promoted as 'Inter-City' too.

The marketeers always tried to ensure that the InterCity guarantee of quality meant something and that it was not just a promotional campaign or a label. In September 1969, in order to enhance this guarantee, it was announced that all new InterCity coaches including Second Class were to have air-conditioning. In 1971 the first such coaches entered service. Previously, only the 'Blue Pullman' and the 'Manchester Pullman' had enjoyed air conditioning. At the same time, the network was expanded away from routes based on London with the announcement that the North East/South West route from Newcastle to Bristol and Plymouth would have InterCity status.

Initiatives and innovations

Other quality improvements for the InterCity passenger included the development of Travel Centres focused on selling InterCity tickets. The partnership between the car for local journeys and the InterCity train for long distance travel was enhanced with Rail Drive car hire in 1969 and the first custom-built Parkway station at Bristol in 1972. There was a mix of success with some initiatives being less successful than others. The 'Travelling' quarterly magazine for rail passengers, for example, was relatively short-lived. On the other hand, the Executive Travel concept introduced on the East Coast between Newcastle, Bradford, Leeds and King's Cross, went on to give InterCity a long-term competitive edge.

By the mid 1970s, InterCity was well established with a modern image and a record for innovation in both product and advertising. The slogan 'Inter-City makes the going easy – and the coming back' emphasised the convenience and the famous 'Monica' posters were designed to stimulate leisure travel. Further afield, overseas railways such as those in West Germany began to adopt the InterCity name in 1971. The next major step forward in the development of the InterCity came with the launch of InterCity 125 trains in 1976. These trains gave the InterCity brand whole

ABOVE Building 'brand image' through product – as exemplified by this 1988 publicity shot. *Authors*

new dimensions of speed and comfort. They also gave a much clearer visual identity to the brand with the distinctive nose cone which quickly came to signify InterCity and all that was best in rail travel. InterCity 125 was an instant success both on the Great Western and the East Coast. New advertising with the slogan 'Have a good trip' stressed the benefits of speed, with the HST being known as 'The Journey Shrinker'.

However, the success of InterCity 125 led to BR overreaching itself with the InterCity brand application – possibly losing some of the quality guarantee that came with it. The brand name was extended through a range of 'secondary Inter-City services' such as London to Brighton which were fairly fast but which had few of the associations with comfortable long-distance travel that had been linked with InterCity. For many this loss of direction was typified by the 'This is the Age of the Train' advertising campaign intended to re-launch train travel generally. This 1980 campaign used InterCity simply as one of the many names BR presented to the market. The distinctive InterCity identity was in danger of being lost.

This loss of InterCity's focus as a brand continued as BR faced the recession of 1980/81. The bad economic news was combined in 1980 with increased competition from deregulated coaches and with the intensely difficult year of 1982 when strikes closed the railway for seventeen days. After these events, the natural reaction on the part of the railway authorities was to cut fares in order to get volume back. The Liverpool to London 'Saver' offer at £9 return did this very successfully, but the volume of traffic generated could only be carried by running extra trains. These cost money to run and, more importantly, were not generally of InterCity quality. This resulted in the whole offer merely breaking even and risked further loss of quality for the InterCity brand.

Policy and people

A marketing strategy was developed that recognised that 'Inter-City' had a major asset in the brand name, but stressed that it was vital that the name should only be used on those trains which met the quality standards associated with the brand. By definition, this killed any idea that there could be 'secondary Inter-City services'. Furthermore, the business should position itself as a quality and value-for-money operator in the travel market and should not try to compete with coach on price. InterCity should target its marketing activity more explicitly at specific segments of the market, for example, on business travellers and on leisure travellers, but should do so with the overall brand name. It was agreed that InterCity should not compete just on journey time but should be concerned with the customer's overall journey experience. Amongst other things, this would mean improving accessibility to the network as well as further developing the range and quality of customer services provided on the train.

Inter-City becomes InterCity

This strategy was put into practice over the four years 1982/86. One of the first changes to be implemented was to drop the hyphen; Inter-City became InterCity. Although this may sound a trivial step to take it began the process of creating a new and distinctive image for InterCity, now an independent business as well as a brand name. Up until this point different parts of BR had used different typefaces and had used the name InterCity in different ways. Now there was to be one clear and consistent usage and approach.

Much more significant in relation to its immediate and direct impact on the customer was the development of new services for the business traveller, culminating in the re-launch of Pullman in 1985. The business recognised that InterCity was losing out in terms of status to air as a way of travelling on business. Pullman's traditional high standards and InterCity's image of modernity redressed this balance. The leisure customer was not forgotten and the positive lessons from Savers on the Liverpool to London route were taken on board with a new range of Saver fares which was progressively extended across the country, culminating in 1985 in the introduction of a new national fares structure.

During this period further developments took place with InterCity publications. The InterCity Executive Guide (a high quality pocket timetable) was developed for the business traveller and was mailed to over 100,000 customers. It is better known today as the InterCity Guide, for all customers needing a network timetable. In 1985, the InterCity Magazine was launched for the First Class business traveller and it went on to become one of the most widely read publications of its type at the time.

Research carried out into InterCity's image in the mid-1980s suggested that some of the momentum that had been generated behind the InterCity brand had not, as yet, changed public perceptions. InterCity was still seen as a name for British Rail's long distance trains but it had lost some of its distinct identity as a specific brand. This led to a review of the advertising

campaign and to a demand for new commercials from new agencies. In 1984 distinctive campaigns were introduced for InterCity business travel. The still-remembered 'Plane to Train' and 'Train Jam' with their single, obvious, yet brilliantly presented messages were the most famous. They were produced by a small advertising agency which was soon taken over by Saatchi and Saatchi. This was the beginning of InterCity's long and successful relationship with Saatchis. Meanwhile, InterCity had begun to build up its own strong identity in other areas, for instance, through sponsorship of sporting activities such as that of the InterCity squash championships.

Alongside these particular InterCity campaigns, BR ran its own corporate advertising, which focused on customer service initiatives and on the number of trains operated. It was perhaps a tribute to the inbuilt strength of the InterCity brand that many rail customers saw these too as being InterCity commercials. These commercials also featured the last in the long line of BR slogans; 'We're getting there.'

In 1986, when John Prideaux took over as Managing Director of InterCity, he and Rob Mason, who continued as Marketing Director, identified the opportunity to build much more on the inherent strength of the InterCity brand. The key requirements were, firstly, to ensure that the brand was only applied in ways which were associated with high quality and, secondly, to distinguish the InterCity business much more sharply from British Rail which increasingly had negative associations for the public.

The InterCity vision

By 1990 InterCity had identified a new vision statement which was 'to be the best, most civilised way to travel at speed from centre to centre.' Meticulous attention to quality standards was to be paid in every way and to every aspect of InterCity trains and services. This in turn, led to a number of new initiatives. For instance, it was recognised that business customers in Second Class were not satisfied with the quality being offered. The very name Second Class was off-putting and a decision was taken to retitle this to 'Standard'.

The InterCity image

Following InterCity's lead, each of the BR businesses developed their own identity, image, and most importantly, their own marketing initiatives. In June 1986, Network SouthEast, for example, launched a massive re-branding of the London area services involving half of the BR fleet. The InterCity identity, albeit de-hyphenated, was still felt to be too closely

ABOVE "See a friend this weekend".

ABOVE "Inter-City makes the going easy" theme – 1985

associated with that of BR's. For example, it still used BR typeface and logo, and was ill-served in this connection in the public mind. It became obvious that there was a need to present a separate identity for InterCity. A design consultancy, Newell & Sorrell, was commissioned for this purpose and they produced the new INTERCITY logotype and the Swallow emblem. The emblem was specifically designed to emphasise speed and civilised movement. The new identity was launched in 1987 in time for the 21st anniversary of the InterCity brand.

'Train Magic'

By the late 1980s consumer expectations of all brands had developed significantly compared with those prevalent in the early days of InterCity. Successful brands still needed to have hard, functional benefits and InterCity clearly had these. But increasingly there was an emotional content with much more subjective

associations and links. To be a successful brand in the late 1980s InterCity needed to be much stronger in this emotional area, so that customers would see the sense in choosing InterCity in an increasingly competitive market place.

InterCity identified this missing link in the idea of 'train magic'. On an InterCity train people were cocooned in an environment away from the cares of the world and could relax. This led to the famous 'Relax' advertising launched in 1988. Totally different from anything which had gone before, it made customers think of InterCity in a new way. InterCity now had a very clearly defined identity which was all its own. It was a distinctive brand building its own special relationships with its customers.

One problem with this new strategy, however, was that it could be viewed as highly elitist. There was a risk that InterCity would be seen to be a service purely for the expense account business traveller, even though two-

thirds of InterCity's customers were, in reality, leisure travellers. A Marketing Manager for leisure travel was brought in to redress this imbalance facing a situation where InterCity was viewed by leisure travellers as expensive, poor value for money and having a complex fare structure as well.

Immediate actions were taken to review the price structure and to improve the ways in which prices were communicated. People were not interested in the structure. They were only interested in the price they had to pay. As a result, attractive, low-priced Apex fares were extended to a range of long-distance journeys around the country. For the longer term, a revenue management initiative was developed which enabled a much wider range of attractive leisure fares to be had without their being a risk of over-crowding. The new approach extended beyond pricing in that InterCity's advertising and promotion was consciously pushed towards the needs of the leisure market.

By 1990, InterCity had become clearly established as one of the top 150 businesses in the United Kingdom. Marketing success had been a key element in its move into profitability. The brand was now performing two roles; firstly, it was a corporate name and, secondly, it was a consumer brand in the market place. In addition, it became possible to develop subbrands within the total InterCity business, such as Pullman and First Class.

Although clearly a national brand, InterCity was also important to local communities and local markets that were proud of their link with the national network. These local differences were reflected in the organisation of InterCity marketing, where there were teams for national activities as well as for each geographical route. For example, the InterCity Apex fare from Glasgow to London was initiated on the West Coast route and became a £30m national product. InterCity in Scotland was re-launched because it was

ABOVE In this striking poster, InterCity promoted itself as one network for Britain. *David Ward*

felt important for InterCity to have a strong presence in the very competitive Anglo-Scottish travel market.

As so often before, the development of InterCity's image was linked inexorably to the introduction of new trains. The InterCity 225 was inaugurated on the Leeds-London route in 1989. However, it was consciously decided to hold back the main promotion until the service was extended to Newcastle and Edinburgh in 1991. Indeed, by 1991 InterCity was sufficiently closely associated in the public mind with the 'Relax' image that it was felt that its advertising could go back to InterCity's roots and promote speed and modernity. In addition, the British people could be reminded that InterCity was something to be proud of. Research demonstrated that InterCity ran more trains at over 100mph than any other railway in Europe and this fact went on to become the basis of new advertising.

Based on this strategy, the so-called 'Black Silk' commercial was used to launch the InterCity 225, the epitome of InterCity's strength of speed, frequency, comfort and modernity. It proved to be an effective campaign and research demonstrated a significant and positive impact on customer attitudes.

Deep recession: great ideas

By now the British economy was yet again deep in recession and InterCity, like virtually every other business, was badly affected. Thus the joint Boots' promotion was launched at the same time as the InterCity 225 was fully introduced. This promotion enabled three million people to travel at half price over two years. It also generated over £6m extra income for the InterCity business and created much goodwill in the leisure market.

Other initiatives unfortunately had to be curtailed. For example, the 'Frequent Traveller' programme for business travellers failed to meet its initial targets and could not be maintained in the harsh economic climate. Looking back, there must be considerable regret that such a potentially powerful customer loyalty programme was not available to InterCity to compete with the many 'Air Miles' offers.

In January 1992, Chris Green came to InterCity as Managing Director determined that the InterCity brand and image would continue to strengthen and develop. A key area for development was in the customer service arena. In 1988 Senior Conductors had been introduced, whilst the 1989 strategy study proved that the onboard catering service was a necessary and integral part of the InterCity product and needed significant upgrading.

Chris felt that InterCity was still lacking the personal touch that airlines regularly achieved. He therefore gave customer service a new and forceful impetus in order to create a more welcoming, caring and accessible image. This was achieved through the introduction of the customer welcome teams, the telesales operation and the launch of the 1993 InterCity Shuttle on the shorter distance, high frequency routes. Similarly, new colours (claret and blue) were used to emphasise the new, warmer, more approachable image that InterCity wished to create.

'Welcome'

To support this new direction, a radically different advertising campaign was planned and top advertising agencies were asked to pitch for the business. Saatchi and Saatchi once again won the contract with the simple word 'Welcome' and the 'Welcome to a City – Welcome to InterCity' campaign. It emphasised customer service but it also built on the slightly surreal 'train magic' approach of 'Relax'. It proved to be another highly successful campaign with follow-up research showing that customers really recognised that InterCity was becoming a more friendly and welcoming way to travel.

The brand in an uncertain future

During 1992, it became clear that the Government's railway privatisation plans would have a significant impact on InterCity both as a business and as a brand, although the Government repeatedly emphasised its commitment to that brand as a national asset. British Rail had agreed to continue to use the InterCity brand as long as the routes involved were managed by the Board. Beyond that it seemed likely that franchised routes would wish to use InterCity as an endorsement of their own emerging services. One thing, however, does remain clear. The InterCity brand had indeed become a major success and to this day remains a real credit to the creativity and hard work of the many people who had developed it.

ABOVE Your carriage awaits: InterCity Special Trains was set up in 1985 under David Ward's leadership. Operating high-quality charter services for the railway and for private companies, it provided traditional Pullman-style service on board. Business charters were regularly run to Ascot, the Cheltenham Gold Cup and the Grand National. *David Ward*

93001

Chapter 5
BETTER BY DESIGN

ABOVE By 1991, the 160mph IC250 was just waiting to be built. *Authors*

It was the much maligned Dr Beeching who wrote an article in the 'Financial Times' in April 1964 announcing that the Design Panel was engaged upon the development of an extensive new BR corporate image. A year later in 1965 the new Corporate Identity was launched and proved to be one of the most extensive and successful post-war design initiatives. It brought a strong sense of order and uplift to trains, road vehicles, uniforms, stations, signs and marketing.

With a stimulating mixture of external and internal talent, the Design Panel operated continuously from 1965 to 1994 and had its foundations in Sir Brian Robertson's 1956 Design Panel initiative. It was responsible for spotting opportunities for innovative design in such varied projects as the exterior shape of the High Speed Train, the glorious reconstruction of London Liverpool Street station and, for the InterCity story in particular, the challenge of the emerging InterCity brand application.

Early BR corporate identity

In 1966 the emphasis was on creating a single corporate identity for British Rail since, at that time, InterCity was no more than a brand name for the newly-electrified London Euston to Liverpool and Manchester services. The corporate identity was crowned with the genius of the double arrow symbol which came to have European recognition as a symbol for railways. A specially-designed Rail Alphabet was introduced which was to stand the test of time for both clarity and style. It has been widely copied – inside and outside the transport industry.

It was undoubtedly helpful to the emerging InterCity that the clutter of regional liveries based on bygone days should be swept away and replaced by a national colour scheme. This not only brought acceptance for network branding but actually gave InterCity an early sub-brand. Whilst multiple units and locomotives were progressively painted in a new rail blue, express trains were picked out from 1966 in a more dashing and streamlined colour scheme using a striking blue and grey livery. This was a milestone in InterCity's design history since it was the beginning of a nationally branded fleet of long-distance passenger services. Bringing this excellent design into service as part of the prestigious 1966 electrification brought a powerful lesson to the railways that good design was good business.

Locomotive liveries

Over the 28 years from 1966 to 1994, a number of different liveries had been applied to BR's locomotives. Prior to 1966 most diesel locomotives had emerged from the workshops in various shades of green – a throw-back to the days of steam. A few Western Region 'Warship' and 'Western' diesel-hydraulics had daringly entered traffic in maroon, while others wore truly experimental liveries such as golden ochre or desert sand. These elegant applications of colour undoubtedly led to a greater awareness of the value of train liveries in marketing rail travel.

After mid-1966, rail blue was gradually applied to locomotives, either as they were delivered from the manufacturers or as they passed through main workshops for repainting. This changeover to rail blue was a long process with some green locomotives surviving into the early 1980s. Rail blue remained the corporate BR locomotive colour until the mid 1980s when various new schemes were accepted and separate business identities authorised.

Designing the InterCity Brand

The Inter-City name (with a hyphen) appeared on trains from 1966 until the mid 1980s. InterCity Sleepers were branded in 1969 but the major design opportunities were to arrive with the HST and the APT in the 1970s. In 1972, the prototype HST was fully branded in BR corporate style, whilst the production trains retained the blue and grey colour scheme with the Inter-City brand name. However, it was sectorisation in 1982 that strongly developed the InterCity brand and this in turn brought about the appearance of some dramatic new liveries. The APT had been operating in one of the most strikingly attractive liveries ever applied in Britain and in October 1983 this became the basis of the new livery of the emerging InterCity business.

This new livery was based on a light grey with a strong dark grey band through the windows held together by a bold red and white stripe that ran the whole length of the train and locomotive. There were always problems with the front end design of trains as safety agreements required a substantial yellow front to be included in addition to the provision of headlights. The problem was ultimately solved on the HST with an elegant compromise that allowed the red line to wrap right round the cab and run back along the train.

In 1987 InterCity celebrated its 21st birthday with an announcement regarding further refinements in the design of its livery. The new branding was to be developed by the design consultancy Newell & Sorrell who were commissioned to produce a new symbol for InterCity. The brand name from that point in time became INTERCITY in an italicised script whilst the new brand symbol became the swallow. The latter was given a three-dimensional form and the feeling of speed was emphasised by a striated design.

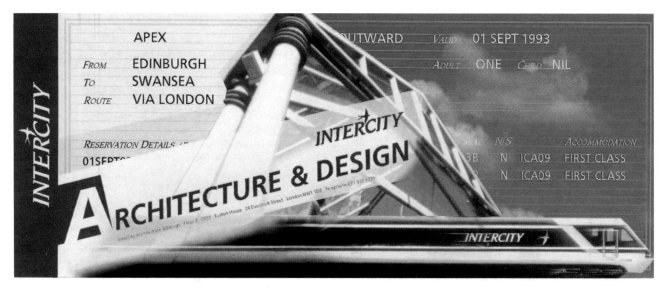

ABOVE Design is the way in which a company presents itself to the consumer. *Authors*

Rolling stock design

Continuous application of good design to the exterior of trains had brought improvement to the point where Britain could claim to have one of the best designed passenger railway fleets in Europe. The evidence could clearly be seen in the progress from the box-like electric locomotives of the 1960s to the West Coast Class 90, to the East Coast Class 91 and finally to the beautiful InterCity 250 where form sadly got ahead of funding in 1992.

The interior of trains had enjoyed similar attention to design detail and full-size mock-ups were regularly used to get every detail right. It took over a year to design the interior of the Mark IV coach, but even a brief glance at the progress from the Mark I designs of the 1950s provided the justification for all the hard work that continuous progress had entailed. The Mark III coach of the 1970s offered a bright, no-fuss interior with high standards of lighting.

By the time of the completion of the East Coast electrification in 1991, the new InterCity 225 was offering a much more sophisticated and reserved interior colour scheme in various shades of grey. Glass partitions and offset central corridors divided First Class coaches into smaller, more intimate bays whilst subdued lights gave a more relaxed atmosphere. Standard accommodation gave a bright and friendly interior with the emphasis on aircraft-type seating arrangements.

Designing for the customer

Design was not only about the more obvious rolling stock products. It was about creating an InterCity house style which flowed smoothly from stations to stationery

and from tickets to trains. As part of the 'Welcome' initiative launched by Chris Green in 1992, design was in the lead again with the decision to upgrade the InterCity brand still further to include more warm and welcoming hues. Focused around a rich claret colour, this was added to the palette to reinforce the reigning classical but cold range of greys and blacks. Because of its associations, claret became identified as the visible symbol for InterCity customer service. The new 'Welcome' teams wore the claret uniforms first and they created a highly-visible impact whilst the new porters at London King's Cross followed as, within the year, did the entire On Board Service staff.

Elsewhere, the message was fully integrated – sometimes in the physical product and sometimes in more general design. New signing included large illuminated running-in name boards to help customers on arriving trains. Clocks, seats, indicators, lamp-posts and Shuttle desks were all highlighted in the friendly InterCity claret. London Euston station was totally upgraded as a major flagship terminal to act as a working model for other main stations and promptly won the 1994 'UK Best Station Award'. The basic design principles were also applied to media presentations and sales literature to reinforce the business quality message. Examples ranged from television advertisements to the redesign of seat reservation labels to match the train interiors. Clarity and simplicity of train time and destination information was essential at busy InterCity stations and the many forms of traditional platform information signs had been replaced as far as possible with specially designed clusters of the much more versatile CCTV information screens. In turn, flap and dot-matrix main departure indicators were being replaced by banks of similar screens.

At that time, and for many InterCity customers, the opportunity to take a snack or meal on the train was very much part of the total travel experience and for some may well have been the deciding factor in favour of rail against the coach or private car. Consequently both the catering product and package had been redesigned to reflect this new quality with a strong InterCity branding throughout – whether on the packaging and labelling of sandwiches or the highly-successful design of carrier bags which brought some care and order to train tidiness.

The InterCity map, showing at a glance all InterCity routes and the main stations served, has gone down in history, along with the HST, as an icon of good railway design comparable to the stylised London Transport Underground map. It had evolved from a complex diagrammatic map into an art form which reinforced InterCity's overall quality image.

Good design is good business

Good design had been at the core of the InterCity brand since its earliest days in 1966. The business was always seen as the stylish, highly acceptable face of British Rail and good design frequently helped it to position itself with its commercial competitors in the market place as a product of quality. Indeed, InterCity's name, image and design have been unashamedly copied throughout the world. It was therefore encouraging that in late 1993 one of the first acts of the new Gatwick Express train operating company was to extend the powerful, InterCity concept of branding to its logical conclusion by providing a unifying colour for its uniforms, its trains and its stations – even down to the replacement of the red line on the trainside with a matching claret stripe. This was very much in the spirit of the 1964 alliance between design and marketing. Dr Beeching would have been proud of the enormous progress made.

ABOVE Air conditioning and bright cheerful interiors contributed to the instant success of the HST. *Authors.*

Chapter 6
FLEET OF FOOT: INTERCITY'S ROLLING STOCK

ABOVE Sweating the assets: in fine external condition power car 43148 is prepared for service at Bristol Bath Road TMD on 1 April 1991.
Bob Sweet

InterCity's character had always been closely associated with its fleet of locomotives and rolling stock and it had always been at the glamorous end of the railway spectrum. The very nature of its business required it to have the most powerful and sophisticated trains. It was interesting to observe how InterCity took over the traditional locomotives of the 1960s and, from the 1970s, evolved them into its own specialist fleet with the High Speed Train, the IC225 and ultimately the beautiful IC250 design.

This demonstrated that InterCity was becoming a more cohesive organisation and was increasingly being driven by cost-effective business management as well as by engineering reliability. Indeed, so successful was the policy that the wedge-shape profile of the HST cab still remains today as one of the most widely recognised symbols of InterCity. It is important, therefore, to consider how the streamlined InterCity fleet emerged from the hotch-potch series of designs resulting from the 1955 Modernisation Plan.

The locomotive fleet

In 1966, the locomotives and rolling stock used on InterCity's services were a decidedly mixed bag and, although steam traction was due to be withdrawn just two years later, around 1,000 main line steam locomotives were still available for use.

The diesel traction fleet consisted of around 2,600 locomotives in 1966. These were used for many types of operation ranging from inter-city trains to humble pick-up freights. Most of the diesel locomotives had been built as a result of the 1955 Modernisation Plan, but some second generation diesel classes were in use by 1966 and these tended to have been designed in less haste and with more horsepower.

For the introduction of the 'New Railway' from London Euston to Liverpool and Manchester, modern electric locomotives were introduced in the 1960s with no less than five mini-fleets built by different manufacturers. These were followed by a much-needed standard locomotive then known as AL6 – later known as Class 86. By the end of 1966, 340 main-line electric locomotives were in service but not all of these were used on Inter-City duties.

By 1982, 3,800 coaches were needed to operate Inter-City services. By 1994, almost the same number of trains was being run with just 2,400 – a reduction of over one third in just over ten years. This was impressive productivity by any standard. Higher stock utilisation was achieved by standardising train formations, improving turnrounds and above all, by investing in DVTs to allow introduction of 'push-pull'

working. These visible changes were also supported by the much less visible 'sweating' of assets at depot level to achieve improved productivity.

Control of the assets

By the 1990s, maintenance schedules were geared to keeping trains in service during the daytime by focusing all possible maintenance on the night hours. An 18-hour working day was commonplace for individual trainsets and routinely involved sets running between 800 and 1,000 miles per day. The best examples achieved up to 1,400 miles a day on the long-haul runs to and from Scotland.

Computer control systems such as Total Operations Processing System (TOPS) and Passenger Operational Information System (POIS) offered new opportunities to get a tighter grip on the passenger fleet. These systems had led to the introduction of precise mileage-related maintenance schedules instead of the previous, somewhat looser time-related maintenance. A conservative estimate was that productivity had improved by at least 10% as a result of stronger asset management. Where trainsets were previously given an extensive monthly overhaul regardless of whether they had travelled ten or thirty thousand miles, the new system only invested in this expensive activity when the full mileage had been achieved.

The POIS system also improved defect management by offering rapid reporting and swift analysis of defects. The introduction of data-link radio messages was a creative development from the Anglia team. It enabled Senior Conductors to give real-time reporting of faults in traffic by using a bar code which triggered an immediate printout at the home depot. The maintenance engineers were therefore ready with the right staff and equipment to carry out repairs as soon as the trains rolled into their depots at night. On the Class 91 electric locomotive, an on-board computer logged any technical problems which had arisen during the day's running and depot staff could take a read-out from this log before the locomotive was serviced. A further development, trialled on some HST power cars, was for this information to be relayed by satellite to the depot.

InterCity did not take direct control of its locomotive fleet until the mid 1980s and prior to this, locomotives were managed on a common user basis controlled by BR's Operations department. The introduction of a dedicated InterCity locomotive fleet, together with fixed-formation train working, brought a new attention to detail which in turn led to increased reliability and an improvement in the 'miles per failure' performance indicator.

ABOVE Sandwiched between power cars nos 43196 and 43107, the unique Inter-City 'Executive' saloon 40513 stands ready to head south from Doncaster. Introduced in November 1983, the saloon was available to those wanting to hold private meetings. In 1984 the charge for each passenger would have been £200 single or £300 return plus the cost of First Class fares plus all related catering expenses. *Bob Sweet*

InterCity coaches

There had been significant improvements in quality since the first Mark I coaches of the early 1950s. The first air-conditioned vehicles were introduced in 1971 and within twenty years all regular, daytime InterCity services were composed of air-conditioned stock. The benefits of air-conditioning were noise reduction and a controlled environment for the customer with energy savings for InterCity.

Other improvements over the years included the replacement of steam-heated by electrically-heated coaches; the replacement of vacuum braking by air brake; and the introduction of disc brakes which were critical in the move towards much higher speeds. From the 1950s to the closure of the InterCity business, bogie design had developed from the BR1 basic bogie with its plain bearings and 90mph top speed through to the air-suspended 125mph BT10 and the 140mph Swiss-designed bogie fitted to IC225 vehicles. Each step in the development had led to improved riding qualities and a reduction in costs.

InterCity coaches needed a heavy overhaul about every ten years and this provided the opportunity to refurbish the interiors, both in terms of decor and materials for the benefit of customers. A refurbishment of the Mark III fleet took place over the 1984-90 period and a more radical refurbishment was being developed for the late 1990s.

Developments in high speed trains

The fleet of 125mph HSTs had always been central to InterCity's commercial performance. In the 1960s the pursuit of higher speeds on existing tracks gave its engineers two demanding technical challenges. Firstly, Britain had to enter the high speed railway market with diesel power because only one of the five InterCity routes was at that time electrified. Secondly and more fundamentally, the new high speed train would have to run within the constraints of the existing infrastructure. The British railway network was the first in Europe to be completed and its main alignments were generally determined well over a century ago, long before railway engineers had begun to plan for today's very high speeds.

In June 1972 the prototype InterCity 125 had been rolled out. This train epitomised what railway engineers regarded as the key to success when applying technical innovation to meet the ever-growing demands of the commercial market place. The philosophy was best summed up in the motto – 'keep it simple, build it fast'.

The world's fastest diesel

The InterCity 125 took available technology and created an entirely new package which represented a step-change in passenger rail travel. From the outset the train adopted air suspension, improved braking and electronic traction control for smoother levels of acceleration. The train was designed as a fixed formation unit with a power car at either end. The enormous success that followed the train's introduction is now history. The production InterCity 125s inaugurated the world's fastest diesel-powered rail services in 1976.

Having proved the commercial benefits of high speed with InterCity 125 and with 110mph electric traction on the West Coast, InterCity was able to show that electrification of the London-Edinburgh route would produce the required 7% return on investment demanded by the Government at the time. In June 1984 East Coast electrification was authorised and important strategic decisions had to be taken on locomotives and rolling stock which would be in service until at least 2020.

The analysis considered ways of reducing the capital cost of traction by adopting the concept of a non-powered DVT at one end of the train, whilst the locomotive stayed at the other end. The train could then be driven from either end but with only one locomotive which would be remotely controlled when pushing.

Productivity of the assets was a second key issue and after considerable debate it was decided that the traction unit should be detachable for use on other services such as parcels and overnight services. As it had become a locomotive again, the new type was given the classification Class 91.

Maintaining operating flexibility was the third major area of analysis and although the train was to run in fixed formation for push-pull passenger duties, a decision was taken not to purchase articulated coaches where adjacent coaches share a common bogie, as in the case of the APT and the TGV. This meant that defective coaches could be more easily removed, so reducing the risk of having to cancel a complete train.

Thanks to the APT project, preliminary work had already been carried out by the Mechanical & Electrical Engineering Department on a new generation high speed train for the East Coast. The new train was to be

even more versatile than the InterCity 125 and included a body profile which would give it tilt capability for the future. The new train was born and finally christened 'InterCity 225' to emphasise its 225 km/h (140mph) design speed.

In putting together the business and technical specifications for the new train, the aim was neither to procure the fastest, most technically advanced train nor was it to build the most luxuriously appointed train. The challenge was to improve on the already highly successful East Coast HSTs at an affordable price and within a relatively short timescale. The InterCity 125 was already the fastest and most successful diesel train in the world. Product development had therefore to be calculated on a step-by-step basis rather than by quantum leap. Coming in the wake of the ill-fated APT, British Rail could not afford another commercial failure with the InterCity 225.

One significant outcome of the APT experience was the extension of engineering knowledge on a number of fronts, such as vehicle dynamics which enabled performance specifications to be significantly improved. Additionally, important lessons were also learned about project management particularly in respect of tighter control and clearer accountability.

East Coast IC225

InterCity 225 was made a free-standing project with its own Project Director, David Rollin, who was directly responsible to InterCity's Managing Director. The project also had its own engineer who was responsible for all technical matters and who, in turn, reported directly to the Project Director. These fundamental decisions gave the project a sharp focus of responsibility which was a major ingredient in its final success.

British Rail's overall procurement policy was also changing as the InterCity 225 went out to tender. Traditionally BR had designed its own locomotives and rolling stock which were then manufactured in its own workshops. Specifications and procurement of bought-in material such as traction equipment was also handled by BR, as was the management of the project. Due to its inherent weaknesses, this arrangement had become increasingly out of step with the requirements of the BR businesses whose primary concern was with the commercial performance of the InterCity 225. The time had come to break the mould. For the first time in many years it was decided that a complete project would be put out to competitive tender.

Potential suppliers bid not on the basis of BR's design as had happened previously, but on a common performance specification. The successful bidder then

ABOVE The pre-production APT arrives at Euston after its inaugural run on 7 December 1981. *Authors*

ABOVE Class 91 locomotives provide elegant power for East Coast trains. *Authors*

ABOVE Introduced for the birth of InterCity, the Class 86 electric was for many years the mainstay of the West Coast route. This example, painted in corporate Rail Blue, leaves Crewe in 1985. *Gavin Morrison*

became the main contractor responsible for delivery to time, budget and specification under the management of the BR Project Director and his team. This radical rethink of procurement policy was taking place at the same time as wholesale change in the railway supply industry. BR was preparing to sell its manufacturing organisation British Rail Engineering Limited (BREL) to the private sector and, during the lifetime of the InterCity 225 project itself, that company itself went through a period of international merger.

The task of directing a £150m capital investment project could not have been accomplished without the Board empowering the project team to act independently. From the outset, the team had this authority. Thus the InterCity 225 project pioneered a new and clearly effective style of business-led project management. Fundamental ingredients to success were a clear project definition with measurable objectives; a dedicated yet accountable project team and a number of disciplined and simple systems of control. As

custodians of such large scale capital investment the project team's priority throughout was the identification and management of risk in three areas; technology, timescale and contracts.

Contracts were placed for 31 trains to cover 27 East Coast rosters and allow for maintenance. Orders were placed with GEC in January 1986 for the Class 91 locomotives at a total cost of £35m and, in December of that year, with Metro-Cammell (now part of Alstom) for the Mark IV coaches. The latter included an option to purchase additional coaches to strengthen train formations – an offer which was taken up in October 1989. After a period of shakedown trials and endurance running, the first InterCity 225 entered service on the London to Leeds route from 2 October 1989.

Part of the track testing programme involved a 10% overspeed test. Early one Sunday morning, and in torrential rain, an InterCity 225 train reached a top speed of 162mph and, perhaps more significantly, achieved 145mph travelling up Stoke Bank between

Peterborough and Grantham whereas 'Mallard' had set the world's record for steam traction going down this particular bank! When electrification was completed throughout in 1991, a record non-stop run from London to Edinburgh took place on 26 September with a total journey time of 3 hrs 29 mins. This powerfully demonstrated the potential of the route.

InterCity 225 took two years to rid itself of its teething problems but once that goal was achieved, the 225 project team was then gradually freed-up to develop their next challenge: the new 160mph InterCity train.

The Intercity 250

In December 1989 InterCity completed a comprehensive Strategy Review of the West Coast. This set out five basic options for the 1990s. Using the best London-Manchester time as a benchmark for the service group as a whole, the options that emerged were as follows:

1. Do nothing and keep a 2 hrs 30 minutes London-Manchester journey time.
2. Accelerate and improve the reliability of the existing 110mph trains, reducing the journey time to 2 hrs 10 minutes.
3. Add some new trains capable of 140mph with some relaxation of constraints on curves to achieve a two hour journey time.
4. Renew or upgrade infrastructure for 140-160 mph trains with minor re-alignment to remove some speed restrictions to give an overall time of 1 hr 50 minutes.
5. Build a new high speed line from the Crewe area to within about 30 miles of London to cut the time to 1 hr 35 minutes.

In the absence of serious capacity restraints, InterCity concluded that in the prevailing political climate, no financial case could be made for investing in a new line. Moreover, it could take up to 15 years to plan and build. At the other end of the scale the 'do nothing' option did not really exist because much West Coast signalling and track would have to be renewed in the 1990s anyway. The debate therefore focused on the middle three options which gave a range in journey times from 2 hrs 10 minutes to 1 hr 50.

The key rolling stock decision was that the West Coast must get a new fleet of high performance trains if its market share was to improve. A major leap forward in speed and quality had to be achieved which would tip the competitive balance in favour of rail. The business impact of new trains had already been demonstrated

in 1966 by the introduction of first-generation electric services to Liverpool and Manchester, and subsequently by the InterCity 125 and the InterCity 225. The rate of business growth, measured by both passenger volume and income, rose markedly following these events. The development of InterCity 225 demonstrated that better quality and reduced unit costs were also possible through improved train design.

A train capable of higher speeds was clearly essential for achievement of the journey times being considered on the West Coast. However, conclusions of some strategic importance were emerging from the examination of rolling stock issues. Firstly, the technical risks associated with specifying a train for speeds in the 140-160mph range were low. The technical changes required for a high speed electric train had been incorporated in the InterCity 225 for the East Coast which had already achieved 162mph in trials. A train with a single source of power was still seen as the best way forward.

Secondly, the business risk would actually lie in specifying too low a speed capability for the train since this would then condemn the West Coast to operate below its potential for the next 25 years. In all, the balance of financial risk favoured the specification of a train capable of 160mph. Thus the InterCity 250 concept was born. It was a truly evolutionary train with technical specifications derived from feedback on the best technical features, operating lessons and customer experience not only from InterCity 125 and 225, but also from European sources such as the German ICE train.

In December 1990 approval was given for the tender process to proceed and invitations to bid were released in March 1991. Following a rigorous tender evaluation exercise, a request for permission to purchase 30 InterCity 250 trains was put to the Board in December 1991.

Sadly, with the UK recession biting hard into InterCity's profits and, with uncertainties arising in the shape of privatisation, funding was not forthcoming and the IC250 project was abandoned soon afterwards. West Coast had been left to operate a fleet of locomotives and coaches built predominantly in the early 1970s to cater for the far more demanding consumer standards of the 1990s.

Leasing concession

In his 1992 Autumn Statement, the Chancellor announced a Treasury concession allowing British Rail to lease rolling stock to the value of £150m over the next three years with only repayments counting against

BR's External Financing Limit. Under this concession BR had invited competing tenders for new trains, the competition being between InterCity 225 and Class 465/3 dual voltage Networker commuter trains for NSE's Great Northern and Kent Coast routes. Both tenders were for follow-on builds from GEC Alsthom and ABB Transportation respectively. Ironically by this time InterCity's Director, Fleet, was Brian Clementson who had developed the Networker.

The InterCity case was based on the upgrading of ten Pullman and other high earning services to InterCity 225 with a consequent cascade of Mark III coaches to displace the older fleet operating London to Birmingham services. The essence of the Government's requirements was to transfer risk to the private sector which would, if necessary, absorb the consequences of under-performance. Various options – such as

outright purchase and various leasing schemes – were considered. Despite reassurances from GEC Alsthom that they had been applying a very sharp pencil to their bid, the resultant offers failed to produce any return on the investment for InterCity.

Consequently, the business was unable to put forward a commercially viable leasing deal and the InterCity option was withdrawn from the competition – the West Coast modernisation had suffered yet another body blow.

It had been a long journey from the Mark I coaches of the 1950s to the InterCity 250 of the 1990s. InterCity owed its engineers much on this journey and they will be remembered not only for their technical skills but for their support in cutting costs and for carrying out so much of their work during the unsocial hours of long nights in depots.

ABOVE With no fleet improvements of the horizon, the West Coast Main Line faced a bleak future in the early 1990s. *Authors*

Chapter 7
CATERING FOR THE CUSTOMER

In 1879 the first restaurant car ran on British tracks. For 115 years the quality of railway food has been an area of lively public interest. By 1994 the food and drink served on InterCity were arguably the best and most cost-effective anywhere in Europe. While many railways were changing over to airline-style tray meals with dishes being reheated on board, InterCity had retained a classic service in dining cars with meals freshly cooked in the train's kitchen.

On Board Services had become a diverse £40m a year business by 1994 and was run by Terry Coyle who was previously with British Airways. Its portfolio included Pullman and Silver Standard on key business services, full-meal service on many other trains, takeaway buffets/trolleys on all others, lounge car and room service on the overnight Sleepers and catering on Special Trains. On the latter, classic at-seat dining was an essential part of the offer for VIP private charters and for Day and Weekend Land Cruises. In addition, OBS won contracts to supply buffet or trolley services on some Network SouthEast routes and catering on the prestigious Venice-Simplon-Orient Express.

Improving standards

Keeping catering in-house was a good decision for it enabled InterCity to maximise its potential as an essential part of its total on-board service concept. As such, it was vitally necessary to meet rising customer expectations. In the 1980s intensified competition on short and long-haul air routes led to many improvements, the most important of which was the creation of Club or Business class travel. These new categories brought into place new standards of customer care. In turn, these became the standards by which business travellers would judge InterCity. At the same time, standards for leisure or budget-priced travellers were also being enhanced.

As a result, during the mid to late 1980s InterCity embarked on defining clear service standards for its evolving travel brands – Pullman, First Class and Silver Standard as well as for the large number of customers using the buffet and trolley services. In terms of improving standards on-board, the merits of using in-house catering as opposed to using outside catering companies had been an on-going debate. At this time, train catering in most European countries – notably France, Switzerland, Belgium, Spain, the Netherlands and Italy – was being provided by separate catering companies with the railway subsidising the operation. Only in Germany, where Deutsche Service Gesellschaft (DSG) had a role similar to that of the former British Transport Hotels, was catering provided under railway

ownership. Based on the quality of service of InterCity trains in Britain and Germany being delivered at the time, evidence suggested that an in-house operation did actually provide a better and more consistent standard of service for the customer.

The modular approach

When it was formed in 1982, one of the early issues that had to be tackled by the new InterCity organisation was the future role of on-board catering. Given a clear business focus, the new regime began to build on the value of catering as a marketing tool. Plans included the re-launch of Pullman as the InterCity flagship for the business market; the introduction of Pullman Lounges at key stations and increased use of trolleys to provide at-seat service both in First Class and Standard accommodation. Given a clear view of its future role, Travellers Fare worked in close association with InterCity in the short period before OBS was formed and recognised that the time was right for a major re-appraisal of new technology. External consultants were engaged and their report paved the way for the changeover to what then became known as modular catering.

By using prepared loading systems similar to those operated by the airlines, it was possible, firstly to open buffets more quickly and for longer periods of time during each train journey and secondly, to have at-seat trolleys stocked and ready-to-go to serve all passengers at the beginning of the journey. Thirdly, restaurant services could feature a wider range of portion-controlled dishes than the current system allowed.

A further key benefit related to the refrigeration chain of supply from the depot to the vehicle which was necessary to maintain the quality of the product. The new modules were refrigerated by direct power in the depots, with the temperature maintained initially by eutectic (chilled) plates and latterly by refrigerated modules between shorebase and train.

Cook-chill

Whilst French Railways had opted for all aspects of airline-style catering including cook-chill hot dishes, InterCity wanted to maintain service flexibility, particularly with regard to a silver service breakfast. For many, it was still the factor that determined the choice of rail or an alternative mode of transport. Defying both economic and health trends, InterCity breakfast sales continued to grow to a level of around 600,000 per year, over half of all meals served. Given its importance, InterCity was not prepared to risk changes to its breakfast specification. While it was perfectly possible to produce good quality cook-chill lunch and dinner items such as coq-au-vin or braised beef, it was conversely very difficult to re-heat a fried egg or toast.

Accordingly, InterCity decided to go for the basic modular system with a range of cook-chill courses, but retaining the ability to cook certain critical items such as eggs, bacon, sausages, steaks and chops in the train kitchen. Equipment for this purpose, together with an automatic toasting machine capable of producing 600 items an hour, was included in the kitchen design. The traditional table layout was replaced by a tray, but the food was still silver-served onto china plates.

In the light of a trial carried out on the West Coast between 1985 and 1987, two important adjustments were made. Firstly shore-base operations, previously in the hands of a third-party contractor, were returned to the more efficient control of OBS. Secondly, prepared meals were replaced by fresh portion-controlled food made possible by recent advances in the industry.

Modular catering was not just about changing food preparation methods, it was far more than that. It offered trolleys designed for specific tasks – chef's fridge, bar fridge, food module and trolleys for use throughout the train – all of which could be loaded onto a train in a matter of minutes.

Throughout the 24 hour period, Euston and the other West Coast shorebases were preparing the modules for the train staff when they reported for duty. Staff on board were now freed from traditional, time-consuming tasks such as washing up. After all, a large industrial machine could do a much better job in the shorebase.

Computerisation of sales and store accounting, an integral part of the modular concept, had also reduced unproductive time as well as improved stock control. Freed from these tasks, on-board staff had more time for sales and service. For far too long, a successful introduction of train trolleys – a normal feature of continental trains and aircraft – had eluded Britain. They had now become an essential part of the InterCity product and this had achieved two long desired objectives; sales had increased and customers were getting catering services at their seats.

Training and Selection

With the development of detailed service specifications on all InterCity trains, the OBS contribution to new customer care initiatives had gained momentum. A new organisation was created to deal with these new challenges. Staff recruitment and training methods were revised. New training methods were introduced including a training school based on a mock-up of a catering car.

One of the difficulties of providing staff was to find individuals who could not only manage the food, but who could also truly manage the provision of on-board service. A new on-board management role, namely that of Purser, was created to complement the tasks of the Senior Conductor.

Almost in profit

In a period of seven years, train-catering turnover had risen to £40m per year whilst the internal subsidy had been reduced to 0.06% of InterCity income. The high £12.3m subsidy for 1988/89 included the cost of changing from classic to modular catering and other costs associated with shore-base management. OBS very nearly did the impossible by breaking even in 1991/92.

In 1989/90, the benefits of modular catering had started to bear fruit. Trolleys had begun to increase on-board market penetration and there was a general upturn in InterCity business. The subsidy had been reduced to 9%, the lowest in Europe. The support moved up to 14%, following a decision to give complimentary tea and coffee to Pullman passengers and complimentary light breakfast trays to customers travelling First Class in Sleepers. Complimentary tea and coffee service required an extra steward and, in a train environment, the life of a china cup is about 10 trips. To put OBS figures into context the subsidy for catering on French Railways at the time was around £29m. In contrast for InterCity it was around £6m.

Menu Innovation

Significant advances had also been made in the range of food products offered for sale. The OBS marketing team had been strengthened by the addition of an executive chef recruited from outside the railway industry. New ideas began to be developed. Revamped restaurant menus were introduced with an international emphasis replacing the traditional joints of meat for so long a feature of train meals. Roasting joints for an unknown number of customers often led to unacceptable levels of waste and dishes based on pre-portioned, extended life, products were developed.

Also, new products on the market made it possible to upgrade the quality of soups and introduce sauces (hollandaise, onion, wine, etc) hitherto difficult to make within the confines of a small kitchen. Reflecting trends in public taste, menus were now becoming much more cosmopolitan. Summer and winter menus were rotated on a four-weekly cycle, and all chefs attended a training course at Westminster Catering College, prior to the introduction of new menus.

ABOVE A contrast in Buffet styles: 1960s ... *Authors*

ABOVE ... and 1990s. *Authors*

ABOVE In 1993 Chief Steward Tony Pullin poses with his team wearing the new Inter-City uniform.. *Authors*

Using its purchasing clout, OBS was constantly looking out for new ideas and food items to meet changing public tastes. Planning menus for production in a small train kitchen was an on-going challenge. Each menu had a red and white meat dish, a fish dish and a vegetarian option, but the complete menu had to make use of every piece of equipment in the kitchen. For instance, there had to be a grilled item, a stove top and an oven item. If all menu items were grilled dishes, the kitchen would not be able to cope. Also, the menu had to be capable of being cooked by two different methods to safeguard against failure.

Over the years, the 'Great British Breakfast' had become a major feature of early-morning, business travel. Despite rises in prices and against all contemporary health trends, sales of this meal had continued to grow. While there was not a lot that could be done to change breakfast, OBS had still managed to bring in a number of innovations. Smoked Scotch salmon with scrambled egg was, for example, was offered as a main course on Pullman services as an

alternative to the traditional grill tray and kippers.

Major improvements to the Buffet range

In terms of revenue generation and the number of customers that could be reached, the train buffet and trolley service generated two-thirds of receipts and, naturally enough, was very important to InterCity. Trolleys accessed the entire train reaching many customers who preferred at-seat service and doubling demand on many routes. A significant market had been opened up, generating revenue and helping to reduce unit costs. Many new products had been added, the most important of which was the sandwich range. In the pre-modular period, all sandwiches were made on-board in the buffet from materials supplied from the depot. Given the time taken to load and stock a restaurant car, there was often a long delay before sandwiches could be made and put on sale. Quality, moreover, was often inconsistent.

Large retailers, including Boots and Marks & Spencer, had begun selling a range of pre-packed sandwiches bought-in from specialist suppliers. Sealed in special packaging, they retained quality and product integrity for up to 36 hours. They were ideally suited for InterCity. Following a successful test on the West Coast, OBS changed over to bought-in sandwiches in 1986. The higher buying-in cost was more than offset by the dramatic rise in sales from two to six million sandwiches a year. A national promotion of 'Celebrity Sandwiches', with fillings designed by then well-known figures such as Sir Clement Freud, helped to boost sales and finally lay to rest the old jokes about stale sandwiches.

Another success had been the development of hot takeaway meals served over the buffet counter. Advances in food technology had led to the development of complete meals, stored and served under refrigerated conditions which could be quickly re-heated in a microwave oven. All large stores had extensive ranges of these products. Here too was an opportunity for InterCity. Complete meals – such as chicken curry, braised beef and dumplings and vegetarian lasagne – would be offered for sale and at prices affordable by the large number of budget-conscious customers whom InterCity regarded as an important part of its market.

All products were now branded under a family InterCity identity covering a wide range of new products such as Danish pastries, American cakes, Flapjacks, low-calorie snacks and other healthy options to satisfy the latest eating trends.

Universal, all-purpose vehicles

Over the years, InterCity had come to prefer an all-purpose catering car consisting of a small seating area and a centrally-positioned kitchen leading to a small, takeaway bar at the opposite end of the coach. This enabled staff and equipment to serve both the restaurant and the buffet. In a normal train formation, the seating part of the catering car would be next to an adjoining First Class coach which could also be used for meal service on busier trains. This was the standard configuration for all InterCity meal services.

When the 1C125 was first introduced, in 1976, it was originally intended to have two separate catering cars in each eight-coach train set: a full kitchen car with twenty four First Class seats (TRUK in railway parlance) and a buffet car (TRSB) with thirty six Standard seats marshalled in the Standard end of the train. In the light of experience, it became apparent that two separate catering cars in an eight car train were more than were needed on most services. A more flexible car was introduced based on a seventeen seat saloon together with kitchen and buffet. Most of the TRUKs were converted to modular cars for the West Coast. However, because of the need to serve a large number of breakfasts in a short time span, some Pullman services still had two separate catering cars until 1992.

Two other types of InterCity catering car should be mentioned. To provide a full, at-seat service on the very successful charters sold by Special Trains, some old Mark I catering cars, with high-capacity kitchens capable of producing 150 main meals for one sitting, were extensively refurbished and retained in service. Apart from the Manchester Pullman stock built in 1966 for the 'New Railway', no Mark II catering cars were built. To meet the need for a small catering car for Midland Cross Country and overnight services, some Mark II coaches had a small buffet area incorporated – those used on overnight services had lounge-style seating.

Prior to the end of InterCity on 31 March 1994, the OBS organisation was route-based with the largest, located on the West Coast with a staff of around 450. The West Coast shore-base was at London Euston with smaller bases at Wolverhampton, Manchester, Liverpool, Preston and Glasgow. Smaller supply points were also provided at Holyhead and Inverness. Staff covered specific trains and were kept to their regular services wherever possible in order to know their customers better. The composition of each catering crew even varied according to the level of business and covered a series of trains on a work programme known as a 'circuit'. Minimum staffing for a restaurant and buffet service was three with up to ten for a busy Pullman. To minimise stocking and destocking work, every effort was made to keep staff on the same train set throughout their working day, but there were inevitably some long days.

On-Board Contract Services

Under privatisation, the twenty-six train companies were free to choose whether they wanted to operate their own on-board services or whether they wished to contract out the work to specialist firms such as OBS. In 1994, On Board Services already operated on some Network SouthEast services, on Special Trains and on the Venice Simplon-Orient-Express. The company would also take over the shareholding in the new Cross Channel Catering Company which was formed by InterCity in association with Wagon-Lits and Sabena to provide on-board service on the Eurostar trains between London, Paris and Brussels. What subsequently happened will be covered in more detail in Chapter 9 'InterCity in Transition'.

Chapter 8
DELIGHTING THE CUSTOMER

There can be no doubt that one of InterCity's real success stories was the massive improvement in the quality of service both on trains and at stations. The combination of a unified InterCity organised around a powerful marketing brand had provided the catalyst for a series of customer service initiatives in the late 1980s and early 1990s. Having broken through the profit barrier in 1988, InterCity had developed a business strategy to maintain a sound financial position at a time of deepening recession, falling demand and plummeting investment. The strategy agreed was one of providing enhanced customer service. In short the vision for the 1990s was one of 'delighting the customer'. A number of examples of best practice are given below to illustrate the great strides that the business had made in achieving that vision.

By 1990 InterCity was already well into a process of radical change that was to make it a market rather than a production-led business. Leisure customers – the most significant in volume terms – were judging InterCity by the improved standards of customer service offered, not only by the airlines and coach companies but also by retail stores such as Boots, Marks & Spencer, Sainsbury and Tesco.

A total travel experience

To develop its full potential as the most civilised means of long distance travel, InterCity had to re-orientate its thinking so that its activities reflected a market-led organisation. InterCity no longer sold trips by train but provided a total travel experience. This had meant thinking about customers' needs, not just when they arrived at stations to buy tickets, but when they were sitting at home planning to make a rail journey. How did those customers want to make initial contact with the business? Was the telephone information provided adequate and welcoming? Was the route to the station well-signposted? Were secure and well-lit car parking spaces available? Furthermore, was help needed and available on the actual station before the journey itself? Almost half of InterCity's customers travelled only once a year. Customer research showed that coping with the complexities of a busy station and searching for the right train was a daunting prospect for many would-be travellers.

Leading from the top

It was increasingly clear that a total rethink of InterCity's customer service policy for the 1990s was required. Strong leadership needed to come from the top and the newly-formed Directors' Group committed itself to a series of strategic conferences to think through the issue of maintaining market share with minimal new investment. The option that emerged was probably one of the toughest for InterCity to manage. It recognised that there would be no hard investment-led solutions for at least five years and that the only hope for improved market share lay in switching its efforts into the softer areas of customer service. InterCity would have to go through the sort of radical culture change that British Airways had experienced in order to convert itself from a product-led organisation into a customer-driven one. This involved convincing some 30,000 InterCity staff of the need for change and then training them to meet that challenge, all within the space of just two years.

In 1988 a key initiative had been developed which had helped to provide a firm basis for the development of customer service excellence within BR. The 'Quality Through People' initiative (QTP), was launched by the British Railways Board, with the aim of bringing about major changes in railway culture. By providing a framework for process-driven, ground-level initiatives it focused particularly strongly on empowerment and teamwork. Brian Burdsall, Director QTP, was adamant that customer care improvements should be devised and delivered by ground level staff so that they would result in real ongoing change rather than be seen as a 'spray-on' initiative.

InterCity's continuing strength and development in the market place depended on being able to convince its managers and staff that only radical improvements in customer service would keep passenger loyalty. There can be no doubt that InterCity's customer service revolution could not have taken place without the benefit of its strong commitment to Total Quality Management allied to the successful completion of its re-organisation. Under this, station and on-train staff came to work together, providing a much more focused approach. From 1990 onwards, the business emphasis began to move away from the provision of new hardware towards strongly focused people initiatives.

Introduction of Senior Conductors

A second major break with the past had occurred in 1989 with the introduction of the 'Senior Conductor' role. The traditional Guard's responsibilities had been primarily based around revenue protection and safety. They did not work exclusively for InterCity and they could be handling InterCity services one day and marshalling coal or aggregate traffic the next. Eight hundred and fifty new Senior Conductors were carefully selected. They were given new uniforms and equipment and worked with managers dedicated to helping them fulfil the requirements of their new role.

All Senior Conductors attended specially designed programmes to prepare them for the greater responsibility and freedom of action which they were now starting to enjoy. For example, if a train was badly delayed, the Senior Conductor could authorise complimentary drinks or refreshments for customers. Where appropriate they were empowered to organise taxis to get passengers to their ultimate destinations if the situation warranted such action. These additional responsibilities motivated staff and were much welcomed by customers. However, the length of time it took to achieve this cultural change should not be under-estimated.

In the past, guards had tended to sit out of sight in guards' vans. They were trained to respond to operating incidents rather than to be particularly concerned about passenger needs. These new ambassadors for the business were selected from a traditional pool of guards but the selection process ensured that those most dedicated to meeting customer requirements were chosen. One of the biggest breakthroughs in their development came when senior managers started to listen to the problems that new Senior Conductors had to face every day. They felt, for example, that once their trains were on the move that they were totally isolated from key decision makers on the ground. Often, they felt powerless and embarrassed that they could not help their customers more.

The 150 year old problem of train staff being cut off from train service Control was solved by the end of 1993. InterCity provided the Senior Conductors with bleepers and radio phones and set up shore-based Customer Service Controls. The Senior Conductor had up-to-the-minute information on what was happening and was able to pass particular customer problems back to Control for resolution. This initiative completely transformed the Senior Conductors' ability to seize the initiative in serving their customers. The Senior Conductor had become a champion for the customer and an ambassador for InterCity.

Delighting the customer

On his arrival in 1992, Chris Green stressed the clear hierarchy of customer needs with safety and reliability remaining the foundation stones of passengers' requirements. Only when an organisation had fully addressed these needs could it then move on to the higher consumer needs of cleanliness, information and customer service. InterCity was beginning to perform well at the basic needs' level and was ready to progress to working with the equally difficult higher needs.

In 1991 market research had identified InterCity as being a good product but one which had inconsistent presentation. In order to meet this challenge, the business had decided to bring in external expertise in customer service and had appointed Graham Smith, formerly British Airways General Manager for Scotland. He proved to be a lively and creative crusader for the consumer and played a strong role in a new Customer Service Council. This was made up from a complete cross-section of individuals throughout InterCity from members of Directors' Group to station retail and depot engineering staff. The in-house enthusiasm, energy and experience of staff was channelled through a number of seminars to solve many of InterCity's own problems in an approach very strongly influenced by the team-based QTP process.

The Trail to the Train

The in-house work developed 'The Trail to the Train' concept which helped to identify difficulties encountered by customers while travelling by InterCity. These difficulties needed to be removed. A number of exciting solutions were found for problems encountered at each of the stages and the degree of success was tracked through three-monthly customer opinion polls conducted by external market research professionals. These picked up the strengths and weaknesses that were of concern to customers. The research enabled the business to track the 'Quality Gap' between the level of importance customers attached to a certain service and the levels of satisfaction they were receiving from that service.

By early 1994 it was clear that InterCity was well on the way to meeting many more of its customers' needs. This was undoubtedly due to the hard work and enterprise of the dedicated teams that had worked on the problems identified in 'The Trail to the Train'. Their achievements are best explained through a number of examples.

Telephone Enquiries

The first point of contact with the customer was of vital importance, and at that time, customers increasingly expected to do business by telephone. In 1993 InterCity answered 1,800,000 phone calls a month – on average, one call per second for the two shifts available. Detailed analysis revealed that a better and more consistent standard of service could be offered through larger Telephone Enquiry Bureaux (TEB) and so the total number of TEB was therefore rationalised to a total of twenty across the UK. Significantly greater use was then made of part-time staff and of computerised timetables and telephone answering equipment.

The new enquiry offices were still labour-intensive and telephone operators were often required to respond to 25 calls per hour throughout their shift. The future lay in operators answering less calls but converting more of those calls into a sale. Thereafter the trend was towards new telesales offices equipped to answer enquiries, issue tickets and make reservations. Recorded tapes increasingly helped to answer routine enquiries.

Car Parks

InterCity knew that it would never increase its market share without being able to welcome the car to the station. In the 1990s much scarce investment was diverted into providing extra car parking at motorway 'Gateway' stations such as Luton, Watford, Reading and Stevenage. Increasing attention was also paid to the security of cars which were often left unattended for long periods. In 1993 InterCity adopted the new AA Silver and Gold Secure car park standards and this involved further investment in CCTV surveillance, better lighting and more patrols.

Telesales

Research had shown that the point of maximum customer stress occurred in the ticket queue just before departure. The customer-friendly solution did not lie in providing still more ticket windows. It emerged that the best way to book a ticket was to avoid the ticket office all together.

Many customers actually wanted to buy their tickets from the peace and quiet of their own home or from the convenience of their own office. This had been achieved in a pilot exercise carried out at Reading which was so successful that it had led to the immediate investment in a £2m Telesales office in Newcastle. This opened in November 1993 and was staffed by a team of highly motivated, committed people. Customers phoned 0800 450 450, quoted their credit card numbers, discussed their journey opportunities and then received their tickets by first class mail.

The successful move to Telesales could not have been accomplished without significant investment in new ticketing issuing machines. InterCity, in association with European Passenger Services, had invested nearly £17m in a new ticketing system called 'Tribute'. This gave travel packages which, combined with telesales, provided a state-of-the-art purchasing system.

Customer Welcome

One point that had been raised at the Customer Service Council was the tremendous difference in the initial reception customers encountered when they first made use of an airline as opposed to that provided by InterCity. Railways had always prided themselves on letting customers process themselves through a station, but airlines put their most presentable and customer-friendly staff up-front to greet and guide arriving customers.

The idea emerged of highly visible 'Welcome' teams on the concourses of major stations. Over 90% of InterCity customers passed through just twenty stations, and by monitoring these stations InterCity very quickly gained a good deal of evidence about the worth of this particular initiative.

Within six months, the business had established excellent training programmes and had selected well-qualified teams for all the major stations. Individuals were selected because they wanted to work in a close customer environment and came from both outside and within the railway industry. They gave InterCity a warm heart and achieved a more positive customer response than any other initiative. Their bright claret uniforms were synonymous with friendly customer service at stressful points on customers' journeys.

Platform Zoning

Unlike European countries, Britain had never been particularly good at identifying the formation of trains to passengers waiting for them to arrive.

This had proved to be another stress point for customers and in 1994 a system of dividing the platform areas into zones was taken as best practice from German railways. January 1994 saw the start of the installation of illuminated colour cubes on InterCity platforms showing a Gold Zone for First Class passengers, and blue and purple zones for Standard. Station Welcome teams, public address and special posters then advised customers where to stand for their specific coach. The best consumer ideas were often the simplest.

Train Environment

InterCity had a dedicated team of fleet engineers who worked around the clock, seven days a week, to keep the trains safe and reliable. The challenge had been to get them to spread the focus of their attention from the technically exciting engine rooms and inspection pits to include the customer environment inside the train.

The change was achieved in a series of brainstorming conferences where engineers, customer service people and catering staff all worked together. The work started by sharing the results of local customer opinion surveys with the staff. These showed general satisfaction with InterCity reliability but dissatisfaction with attention to detail over internal matters within the coach such as air-

ABOVE A customer welcome. *Authors*

conditioning, payphones, headrests, lights, interior door failures and, above all, the defects in catering equipment. All of these missing details resulted in a loss of customer support however punctual the train might be.

Each depot then went away to find its own solutions to a common problem. Some set up specialist teams; others put items out to contract and some made ingenious technical modifications. The important point was that the InterCity business had now achieved a reliable level of customer environment by sharing a problem and delegating the solution. Many would not have believed that a seemingly traditional part of the InterCity business could have changed so quickly. For example, better reliability in the train kitchen equipment brought an immediate return in more motivated stewards and stewardesses.

InterCity Shuttle

The InterCity Shuttle concept was introduced in May 1993 to bring all the strands of the new customer service initiatives together. Routes were selected in the high frequency, middle distance range such as Euston to the West Midlands and St Pancras to the East Midlands. These services tended to have trains with few customer or meal services but were vulnerable to

motorway competition. The principles of the shuttle service changed this and customers found:

• Welcome teams on the concourses of all principal stations served;
• Dedicated Shuttle desks provided as 'check-in' points;
• Ticket checks were eliminated at the barriers whilst the on-train team provided a trainside welcome;
• Trains were platformed and available at least 20 minutes before departure;
• Buffet cars open when they joined the train and stayed open throughout the journey and the turnround;
• Catering trolleys moved up and down both Standard and First Class throughout the journey.

Silver Swallows

It was always a problem in a large industry to say thank you to the unsung heroes and heroines who kept the railway running against all the odds.

InterCity hit upon the idea of awarding a Silver Swallow in the form of a lapel badge as its commendation for excellence. Around 300 were issued each year, averaging about one per cent of total staff.

Staff could be sponsored by customers, managers or supervisors and the citations certainly made humbling reading. A stewardess who rescued a customer who had fallen off a platform just as a train was running in; a driver who kept his train running despite suffering injuries from a brick thrown through his window; countless examples of individual kindness including driving customers home after they had missed late trains or even putting tourists up for the night.

The staff who wore the Silver Swallow were indeed the elite of the InterCity teams.

Changing the top team culture

The transformation from a top team seeking engineering solutions into a Directors' Group that wanted to make the customer the centre of all activity clearly did not happen overnight. The key was convincing a loyal but sceptical workforce that top management was really committed to making change. The consumer initiatives did not begin in isolation. They resulted from long and searching debates at Directors' Group over the strategic direction that InterCity should take in the 1990s. This direction was eventually expressed in the form of a single vision supported by detailed strategies, group values and behaviours.

To have any chance of bringing about lasting change, the InterCity Directors' Group had to forge a clear vision of its own. It had to be seen to be pursuing courses of action that were demonstrably different in behavioural terms from the old railway whilst, at the same time, delivering the service levels and bottom line requirements of the new railway.

Given that all members bar three of the Directors' Group were from a railway background, it was clear that some difficult changes and choices would have to be made. Barry Woledge joined from British Airways as Human Resources' Director and provided vital experience of major cultural changes achieved in other large organisations.

Vision, Strategy and Values

InterCity formulated the Vision, Strategy and Values which were to become the cornerstone of cultural change during the 1990s through a series of residential development sessions. The VSV as they became known, were tested at a conference where InterCity's senior executives were asked to feed back their comments. Questions raised from this conference led Directors' Group to create an Empowerment Group to look at the whole issue in more detail and from that process the InterCity Behaviours were born.

Public expressions of change

Making the Vision, Strategy, Values and the Behaviours live so that they actually became part of people's way of behaving was vital to the success of InterCity. Directors had to show their commitment as role models to staff and both the VSV and the Behaviours were widely distributed throughout InterCity. A group of staff from all levels of the organisation was encouraged to develop guidelines for railway managers, concerning the help and support that they could give to on-train staff in the course of severe delays or other emergencies. Actions ranged from manning telephones to commandeering managers' mobile phones for customers to use throughout the train. InterCity was not only seeing things differently from other organisations – it was actually behaving differently as well.

Empowering for results

It was always recognised that empowerment brought additional accountability. To this end leadership style changed to fit the new values. Key financial issues such as the management of profit and loss accounts were devolved to the routes. In turn, routes and functions were asked to manage cost, revenue targets, safety and Passenger's Charter targets. InterCity HQ had to let go by delegating but not by dumping.

In addition, the individual performance management methods used by InterCity were radically altered. A new approach was taken which ensured that the personal performances of leaders and managers were measured against hard objectives. In addition, the behaviours needed to sustain a successful customer service business, the 'how' of the job, were also closely identified and developed so that the business could be sure that not only were managers performing well but they were also behaving well both towards customers and staff.

Repeat business

This era of customer service development was one of the toughest periods in InterCity's history, but it was also an extremely rewarding time for both productivity and people. Putting customer requirements first demanded a thoroughly committed and almost evangelical belief in ensuring that the business and all of its people were fully aligned to adding value to every encounter between staff and customers. Satisfied customers had a tendency to become repeat customers and repeat customers made the difference between profit and loss to a highly competitive business such as InterCity.

Customer service success

Helpful staff tended to be confident and competent people in their own right. These were the very people who, in turn, secured satisfied customers in their daily encounters. Nevertheless, however satisfied and able the staff, they too needed support and they needed to have their difficulties acknowledged. They also needed to know that help was there when they wanted it, especially if they were in the front-line of customer service day in and day out. In a service business, 'service' and 'business' should not be separated. It was not by chance that profit rose strongly in the 1993 recession just as InterCity began to get its customer service right. Consistent and clearly-defined standards were essential to an InterCity brand under extreme competitive pressure.

By the early 1990s giving 'added value' to all staff and customer encounters had started to become an integral part of the InterCity business culture. There was no doubt that the cold realities of the deep recession from 1990 to 1994 had forced InterCity to face up to a radical improvement in its customer service. In the strong economy of the 1980s energies had been diverted to investment in physical assets. In the insecure 1990s, the challenge of survival in the market place and the uncertainties of privatisation ensured that InterCity diverted its energy back into innovative investment in its people.

Chapter 9
INTERCITY IN TRANSITION

ABOVE The InterCity spirit lives on. DVT 82231 rests at Peterborough whilst on a high-speed test run from King's Cross to Newcastle on 2 June 1995. *Colin J. Marsden*

Organising for Quality

In January 1992, when Chris Green was appointed Managing Director, InterCity was at its peak – yet only months later he would be standing by the company's Press Office television, listening to John McGregor, Secretary of State for Transport, announcing the Conservative Government's intention to privatise the entire rail network. His first feeling was one of irony. It had taken British Rail almost half a century to find an effective organisational structure – and now it was to be blown away in yet another massive restructuring of the industry.

The new internal BR organisation was called Organising for Quality – OforQ for short – and it meant that, for the final two years of its life, InterCity had a totally integrated business with its own balance sheet and ownership of the assets it needed to run a railway. These ranged from its 34,000 people to its £2 billion asset base. Here was a state business with a turnover of almost £1 billion that was ready to compete with motorways and airlines to provide a profitable long-distance rail service. In railway terms, it was a vertically integrated business with the ability to control its destiny within the wider BR umbrella.

Chris and his team decided that whatever the outcome of privatisation, it must be right to continue growing the InterCity business – so their energy was focused on train refurbishment, customer-service training and aggressive marketing. InterCity's profit had exceeded £100 million before the recession hit and it was determined to remain in profit, despite the economic downturn. At privatisation in 1994, the team were indeed able to demonstrate that InterCity had stayed in profit for every year since 1988.

The integrated OforQ structure also unlocked new productivity initiatives, which helped to keep InterCity profitable in the economic downturn. The new organisation gave InterCity the authority and means to cut a further £54 million off its cost base to keep the business in profit. Eighteen long-distance services were removed from the timetable and 3,600 staff left the business under voluntary redundancy between 1992 and 1994, whilst investment in track renewals was cut still further. The delayed track renewals triggered more speed restrictions and these were managed by adding extra time into train schedules to maintain punctuality at around the 85% mark.

Organising for privatisation

InterCity's next challenge was to try to shape the emerging railway privatisation. The senior team was forward-looking and was not against privatisation in

principle. An early idea was for InterCity to be split into a train company with a parallel infrastructure company, but this proved impractical. Then, with the British Railway Board's (BRB) support, the full InterCity Director's Group met John McGregor and his advisers in 1993 to propose that InterCity should be sold or franchised as a single train company, with Railtrack providing the infrastructure support. Their case was straightforward: InterCity was one of the best-known brands in Britain, with an 82% brand awareness that had taken a quarter of a century to develop. It was a well-defined business with a highly successful track record in profit, performance, marketing and quality delivery – so why not sell it as a going concern?

However, after discussion, the response was equally straightforward. John McGregor recognised all of InterCity's strengths but felt that the business was just too big to privatise as a single £1 billion-turnover company. It had become a victim of its own success. The Government believed that the key lesson from earlier utility privatisations was that future sales should be built around selling smaller units to attract a wider ownership. There was a real fear that there would not be enough bidders for an InterCity sale or even for a single franchise.

From that moment it was clear that the InterCity routes were going to become free-standing train operating companies which would be franchised to the widest possible market. The success of the InterCity team was not in doubt however, and the directors were actively encouraged to lead management buy-outs for the new franchises. The future was now clearer, and the InterCity team moved onto Plan B – to preserve InterCity as a marketing brand. InterCity suggested that if the routes were to be franchised individually, then the new owners should at least be required to

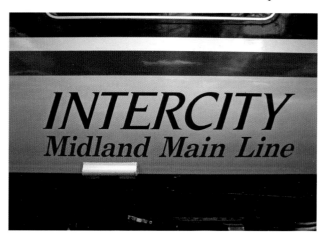

ABOVE InterCity-style Midland Main Line logo on coach 40754, 17 October 1994. *Colin J. Marsden*

endorse their services with the InterCity brand and use it for joint marketing activities. They emphasised that new brands are expensive to establish and that InterCity's high brand awareness had taken more than 25 years to develop.

They were encouraged by a letter from Roger Freeman, Minister of Transport, to Chris Green on 2 February 1993 that said: 'We will want to preserve the InterCity brand name. That will facilitate joint marketing in the manner of the Regional Electricity Companies.' The Board supported a decision to set up a shadow company led by John Cimelli, InterCity's Marketing Services Director, which would own the brand and offer support in advertising campaigns, in Railcards and in national travel centres and telesales offices.

The company was to be called the Travel & Rail Marketing Co, and it began operations as a shadow organisation winning a bid for an advertising campaign sponsored by the seven shadow train units to promote 'InterCity' Railcards. This was a major success, but it was to be the last InterCity advertising campaign. Whilst there was considerable goodwill for keeping the InterCity brand alive, the proposal was ultimately rejected because many of the potential corporate bidders such as FirstGroup, Stagecoach and Virgin had strong brands of their own which they wanted to apply to the rail industry.

ABOVE Sampling the delights of the new catering trolley, Managing Director Brian Scott helps to launch the Great Western train company at Paddington on 15 October 1996. *Colin J. Marsden*

The issue of branding was to be raised again by some of the new train company managing directors when they became franchises, but they were again met with an apologetic statement that the application of InterCity branding could only be applied on a voluntary basis and would not be imposed onto the new owners. Chris Stokes, Deputy Director, OPRAF remembers that his team reached this conclusion 'with regret' and confirms that they could not risk deterring new bidders with strong brands of their own. The proposals were dropped, but the one positive result from this outcome was that ATOC was persuaded to take ownership of the future management of Railcards and the DfT took formal ownership of the InterCity brand name, which it still owns today.

Managing the transition

The writing was now on the wall, and the InterCity team did not have long to wait before the controversial Railway Act took effect on 1 April 1994 at which point InterCity ceased to exist as an integrated business. Its headquarters closed with some 655 staff having to find new roles either beyond the railway or within the emerging internal organisations. The recently integrated OforQ structure rapidly unravelled, with a newly privatised Railtrack taking the infrastructure and the emerging rolling stock companies – the ROSCOs – taking the train fleets. Train Operators now needed a licence to operate on Railtrack's infrastructure and a contract to secure their track-access rights.

ORR

A new Office of the Railway Regulator was created, led by John Swift QC, an expert in competition law. He appointed Gordon Pettitt, ex-Managing Director Regional Railways, to provide experienced advice to his new team and Gordon remembers having to explain the limited reality for head-to-head competition on a tightly planned railway network. He was also witness to the huge problems that the legal teams – both BR and Government – had in helping to design and implement the complex and wide-ranging changes that were needed to deliver privatisation against a ticking clock.

OPRAF

The new Office of Passenger Rail Franchising – OPRAF – assumed responsibility for the shape of the future franchises, and a powerful team was created with the combination of Roger Salmon from the external commercial world, and Chris Stokes, an experienced railway director who had worked in all three of the passenger businesses. They formed a close link with the BR teams who were breaking up the existing railway into over one hundred 'shadow' companies in preparation for competitive tendering.

Following the split of the Anglia & Gatwick and Midland & CrossCountry routes, there were now seven ex-InterCity routes in place of the original five. They became shadow train companies with an experienced BR director in the lead as they entered a period of frenetic activity in which their directors found themselves doing three jobs simultaneously. Their day job was to run the routes safely and professionally: their evening job was to become shadow train companies and help prepare the mountains of legal documents needed in the brave new world – and their night job was to prepare their own management-buyout bids if they so wished.

ATOC

The shadow train company directors were then required to establish an Association of Train Companies (ATOC) which, after privatisation, would be responsible for common passenger activities. Ironically enough, this was very similar to the proposed InterCity Services' Company, but was to be owned and supported by all train companies, with the emphasis now on joint

ABOVE Running 'wrong line', the 0945 (Sun) Aberdeen-London King's Cross HST crosses the Forth Bridge on the structure's centenary day – 4 March 1990 – with power car No 43076 leading. *Brian Morrison*

systems rather than joint marketing. This association would manage National Rail Enquiries, the Railcard Schemes and the Railway Settlements Group. The Railway Settlements' Group was a core activity which allocated ticket income between the 26 new companies on an agreed basis. The process had been developed by British Rail into very sophisticated algorithms for apportioning ticket income to its business sectors and was well ahead of the rest of Europe. It can safely be said that without this sophistication the complex railway network could not have been broken up into either sectors or franchises.

Franchising

The scale of the changes required between 1994 and 1997 was incredible, and still represents the most radical restructuring of any railway system in Europe. Even the Government of the day did not expect to get more than 51% of the railway into private hands in the three years before the next election in 1997.

It is a tribute to the experience and commitment of the senior BR management team that they enabled the Government to deliver the entire railway network into

the private sector just one month before the election deadline. There was no way that any external team could have achieved this feat within the timescale. Richard Brown, now Chairman of Eurostar, believes that it was a very smart move by Government to allow the shadow teams to compete for their own management-buyout bids, as it locked them into the process and energised them to get their franchises out to tender before the next election.

The result of all this concentrated energy was that the ex-InterCity team prepared the seven shadow companies for franchise in record time and OPRAF started tendering the least-complicated companies first to 'get some wins on the board'. Table 9.1 shows the rapid sequence of events that took place. Great Western was the first InterCity franchise, quickly followed by Gatwick Express, East Coast, Midland Main Line and Anglia. The two more complex franchises, CrossCountry and West Coast, were kept to the end of the process but they too were still both franchised by March 1997 just before the deadline for the May general election.

One especially controversial issue was to be the future of the Anglo-Scottish Sleeper services. These were finally transferred from the ex-InterCity West Coast route to the new ScotRail franchise on the basis

ABOVE No 43146 is seen on the rear of one of two HSTs leased from Angel Trains to operate the Eurostar services from London to Manchester and Edinburgh. Leaving from Waterloo at 1245 on 5 February 1996, this departure is bound for Scotland's capital city. Returned to the lease company at the end of March 1996, both sets subsequently went to work for Great Western Trains. *Brian Morrison*

that their main market originated in Scotland. The services were rationalised into two subsidised services, with a Highland service that divided to serve Inverness, Aberdeen and Fort William, and a Lowlands service that split to serve Glasgow, and Edinburgh. The West of England sleeper was to remain with the Great Western franchise.

Business sales
The InterCity Special Trains unit was one of two interCity units which were sold rather than franchised. Its Managing Director, David Ward, ran the unit for InterCity until the completion of the trade sale in 1995. The Royal Train was transferred to EWS Freight to ensure its long-term stability, whilst all the remaining locomotives and coaches were sold to Pete Waterman, who set up a new operation based at Crewe. The story of Charter & Special Trains is told in more detail in Factfile F.

ABOVE No 312717 departs from Harwich International on 31 January 1996 forming the 1304 Manningtree-Harwich Town. Alongside, InterCity Anglia No 86246 *Royal Anglian Regiment* is scheduled to depart with the 1905 boat train to London Liverpool Street *Brian Morrison*

BELOW Providing the rare sight of Gatwick Express stock at London St Pancras and brought in as part of the MML franchise handover to National Express, No 73210 *Selhurst* heads five GatEx coaches and No 73208 at the rear end of the rake on 29 April 1996 *Brian Morrison*

Table 9.1: InterCity franchising

Year	Activity
1993	InterCity business sector ceases to operate from 31 March 1993
1994	Railway Act takes effect from 1 April 1994 Ex-InterCity shadow train companies prepare for franchise
1995	Special Trains unit sold to Pete Waterman: March 1995 On Board Service unit sold to Management Buy Out, March 1995
1996	Great Western franchise starts trading (GW Holdings), 4 February 1996 East Coast franchise starts trading (Sea Containers), 28 April 1996 Gatwick Express franchise starts trading (National Express), 28 April 1996 Midland Mainline franchise starts trading (National Express), 28 April 1996
1997	Anglia Railways franchise starts trading (GB Railways), 5 January 1997 CrossCountry franchise starts trading (Virgin Group), 5 January 1997 West Coast franchise starts trading (Virgin Group), 9 March 1997 Last BR train runs (Glasgow–Euston sleeper), 31 March 1997 General Election: Labour replaces Conservative Government, 1 May 1997

ABOVE Captured in its post-privatisation state, the Royal Train – headed by Class 67 No 67005 – returns to Wolverton depot on 23 February 2004. *Bob Sweet*

The second unit to be sold was the On Board Services (OBS) operation which provided a vital service to InterCity in supplying all its trains with food and drink through a network of cold stores. Terry Coyle, InterCity's On-Board Director, led a successful management buy-out in 1995 and in the same year became Managing Director of the renamed European Rail Catering Services. In 1997 the company was bought by the Swissair group, but after that company suffered financial difficulties in 2001 it was acquired by Compass Group plc the following year. It was again sold in 2006 to the private equity firm EQT Partners and it currently trades as SSP – 'The Food Travel Experts'. Terry Coyle remained a director until 2003 and, at the time of writing, Rail Gourmet is still serving all the long-distance operators with the exception of CrossCountry.

InterCity privatised

Britain's railway became fully privatised on Monday 1 April 1997. The new Great Western train company was tipped to the post by half an hour in becoming the first company to run a private train. It was beaten by South West Trains, but Richard George – the new Deputy Director at Great Western – remembers that

ABOVE Privatisation is approaching as staff at Gatwick Express show off their new uniforms on 15 December 1993. *Colin J. Marsden*

BELOW The re-branded Gatwick Express ticket office catches the eye of travellers on 15 December 1993. *Colin J. Marsden*

ABOVE The City Line Rail Link bus illustrates the customer benefits of regional rail/bus ownership at Bristol Temple Meads on 30 September 2002. *Colin J. Marsden*

LEFT Staff in their stylish new uniforms herald a new era as they stand in front of a newly branded HST at Bristol Temple Meads to launch Great Western Trains on 30 September 1996. *Bob Sweet*

this was no bad thing, as its first train was the 01.55 from Fishguard to Paddington, which unfortunately began its journey on that date as a replacement bus to Swansea due to planned engineering work!

The ex-InterCity teams had not only helped to create the new structures for the private railway but – wherever they were allowed to – they also provided a smooth transition for their new owners into this uncharted and complex context. In retrospect the years 1996-2000 can be seen as something of a honeymoon period during which performance improved and passenger numbers grew as private investment started to flow into cash-starved railway businesses. However, the rail industry had a difficult journey ahead and it was to experience new depths of despair before emerging as a more mature and successful industry.

Table 9.2: The transition

British Rail 1994		Private franchise 1997	
Train Unit	**Director**	**New owner**	**Managing Director**
Anglia	Andy Cooper	GB Railways	Andy Cooper
CrossCountry	Chris Tibbits	Virgin Group	Brian Barrett (CEO)
East Coast	Brian Burdsall	Sea Containers	Christopher Garnett
Gatwick Express	Rob Mason	National Express	Mac McIntosh
Great Western	Brian Scott	GW Holdings	Brian Scott
Midland Mainline	Richard Brown	National Express	Richard Brown
West Coast	Ivor Warburton	Virgin Group	Brian Barrett (CEO)
Charter Trains	David Ward	Pete Waterman	(Sale)
On Board Services	Terry Coyle	MBO	(Sale)

Table 9.3: Long-distance passenger subsidy

1998 prices	Total subsidy (£)		Subsidy per passenger mile (pence)			
	1998/99	**1999/2000**	**1997/98**	**1998/99**	**1999/2000**	**2000/01**
CrossCountry	101.4	86.8	9.3	7.4	5.8	5.4
West Coast	70.3	59.1	3.7	3.4	2.8	2.7
Great Western	55.5	48.6	4.3	3.9	3.3	2.9
GNER	37.4	17.6	2.5	1.7	0.7	0.2
Anglia Railways*	26.9	23.6	10.1	6.8	5.2	3.8
Midland Mainline	2.5	0.9	1.6	0.4	0.1	0.1
Gatwick Express**	– 8.2	– 10.3	– 6.7	– 6.7	– 8.7	– 10.0
Long-distance	285.8	226.3				

* Anglia subsidy includes East Anglia branches ** Gatwick Express was the only ex-InterCity TOC not in subsidy

Sources: **OPRAF Performance Bulletin 1999 and SRA Performance Trends 2000**

Summary

InterCity made the transition from a successful business sector within British Rail to seven independent train company franchises in just three years from 1994 to 1997. The InterCity Directors had tried to get InterCity sold or franchised as a single business – and when this failed, they had then tried to keep the brand alive through an InterCity Brand association. Both initiatives were to prove incompatible with the needs of the new private owners.

Only when these final hopes were extinguished did the team put its energies into developing InterCity's legacy through the successful franchising of the seven long-distance companies. Chris Green, now retired, believes that the positive energy and experience of the InterCity team, together with the effectiveness of OPRAF, made the crucial difference between a 51% and a 100% franchise delivery by March 1997.

It was, however, a surprise for the ex-InterCity teams to find that under the new financing regimes their routes went back into subsidy in 1997. Table 9.3 shows that InterCity needed a subsidy of £285 million in 1998/99 under the new track charging agreements and Gatwick Express and Thameslink became the only train companies in Britain to remain in profit. The aim was to eliminate this unwanted subsidy in the ex-InterCity train companies and this was being achieved until the industry entered a very difficult and disheartening period in the early years of the 21st century.

Chapter 10
EAST COAST

Two very different franchises

There has always been healthy competition between Britain's two main lines from London to Scotland and the competition is still alive and well in the 21st century. Both Christopher Garnett and Chris Green confess to having kept a close eye on each other's operation when they found themselves heading up the new GNER and Virgin West Coast franchises respectively. It was a classic red-versus-blue business game scenario, which was even matched by their brand colours.

However, the new owners found that they had inherited two very different train companies which were operating on totally different investment cycles. InterCity East Coast entered privatisation ripe for development after its £0.7 billion route upgrade. InterCity West Coast was due to follow with a similar £0.8 billion upgrade, but Whitehall froze the investment pending privatisation, by which time both its trains and infrastructure were in desperate need of renewal.

The next 20 years were to see a rollercoaster of events on both routes which would dramatically reverse their positions.

East Coast

InterCity's East Coast route had been led by Brian Burdsall, who had prepared the business for privatisation as its Shadow Director from 1994 and then went on to lead a subsequent management buyout bid. However the new franchise was awarded to Sea Containers in 1996 when Christopher Garnett was appointed CEO of a new GNER train company, with Jonathan Metcalfe as Chief Operating Officer.

GNER: A stable start

East Coast bidders had been offered a seven-year franchise on the basis that the newly modernised railway would not need to fund major investment. GNER's bid committed it to increase passenger numbers by 6%: to live within a subsidy of £67 million: to increase train services from King's Cross to Newcastle and Leeds to half-hourly all day: to invest £28 million in business lounges, stations and car parks – and to consider Parkway stations at Musselborough (A1), Doncaster (M18) and Hadley Wood (M25).

Christopher Garnett took time out after winning the franchise to meet his staff and to travel on his new services. He concluded that

he was 'inheriting a well-run business from InterCity' and that GNER's added value should be to develop the 'soft' areas such as marketing, customer service and catering. He retained the experienced former BR team and harnessed the operating skills of people such as Richard McLean to run a high performance railway. An early priority was a major rebuild of the troublesome Class 91 locomotives and Mk4 coaches, which would double their reliability within five years.

GNER kept the InterCity livery on its trains and stations for a year and took its time in identifying its own strong but traditional brand. The first fully branded train was finally launched in 1997, resplendent in a deep blue livery. Jim Sherwood personally chose the

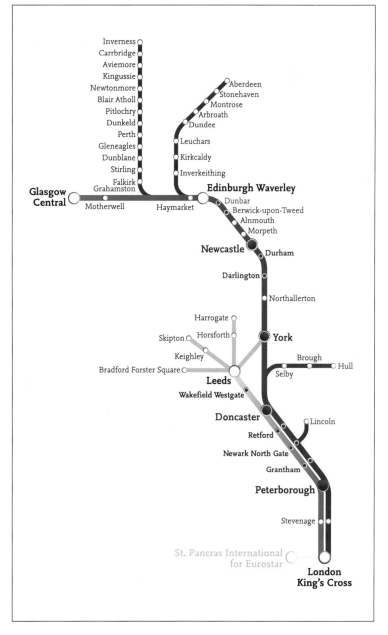

ABOVE East Coast route map 2012 *East Coast Main Line Co Ltd*

ABOVE Following the completion of the East Coast electrification, HM the Queen and Sir Bob Reid, Chairman, BRB, alight from Class 91 No 91029 at King's Cross on 28 June 1991 after naming the locomotive *Queen Elizabeth II*. *Colin J. Marsden*

ABOVE GNER launches its new logo on 28 January 1997. In attendance are, from left to right, Sir George Young (Secretary of State for Transport), Jim Sherwood (Chairman, Sea Containers) and Christopher Garnett (CEO, GNER). *Colin J. Marsden*

'the Route of the Flying Scotsman' motto, which was applied to each coach, along with a new GNER crest.

The brand unashamedly focused on traditional up-market comfort. It was matched with luxurious business lounges, smart new GNER uniforms and beautifully designed GNER china crockery in the restaurant cars which maintained InterCity's mission for 'fast and civilised' travel. The delivery of a quality brand was underpinned by a significant investment in staff recruitment, as shown by the creation of a new post of Customer Services Manager which was put in place to ensure that the customer experience was well managed whether at the restaurant car, the buffet or the catering trolley.

The restaurant car was the hallmark of the GNER franchise, and the company would become the last to maintain the InterCity tradition of a full meal service of breakfast, lunch and dinner on the majority of its services. This service range was maintained to the end of the first franchise, despite declining demand and rising subsidy. Christopher Garnett felt strongly that it was an essential ingredient in competing with the domestic air market. He opposed copying airline catering and felt that GNER should celebrate the 'rail difference', as he introduced fresh food, more interesting menus and higher staffing levels.

GNER used its early stability to develop staff pride in the new-look East Coast through comprehensive marketing and customer service training. Jim Sherwood's track record in prestige hotels and 'land cruise' trains made Sea Containers the ideal company to take on this role, and GNER took InterCity standards to new levels of customer service. Jonathan Metcalfe, then Passenger Services Director, remembers GNER spending as much on its customer service training as on marketing in this period, and the high levels of staff morale that resulted were to keep the company going through the crises that lay ahead.

GNER's final initiative in these early years of stability was to raise its marketing game. It was to become an early player in developing yield-management techniques and in bringing in external expertise to help maximise its income. InterCity had left a legacy of early yield management in its budget Advanced Apex fares which guided passengers to its

ABOVE GNER belts out a novel InterCity message to motorists on the A4 near Earl's Court in 1998. *Antony Guppy*

RIGHT A train attendant demonstrates GNER's customer-service style as she waits to greet passengers joining her train. *East Coast Main Line Co Ltd*

emptier trains through compulsory seat reservations. GNER now started to follow the budget airlines in majoring on very low headline fares to encourage passengers to book in advance. It also became the first company to introduce a loyalty scheme for First Class passengers – a venture that had eluded InterCity.

The original assumption of a 6% growth over the franchise life was to prove hugely pessimistic when GNER achieved a 21% growth in the first three years and overcrowding became the issue. The new half-hourly service to York had been achieved by tightening train diagrams, but this still left Leeds with an hourly service and by 2000 the company had considered buying 'Pendolinos' and even converting Mk3 sleepers. It finally decided to lease four Regional Eurostar sets to

introduce its 'White Rose' services to Leeds and York. Even this was only an interim solution until 2004 when it leased extra HSTs from CrossCountry, using them first to increase its train fleet and then to lengthen the entire fleet to nine cars.

BELOW Regional Eurostar No 3301 streaks through Essendine. *Antony Guppy*

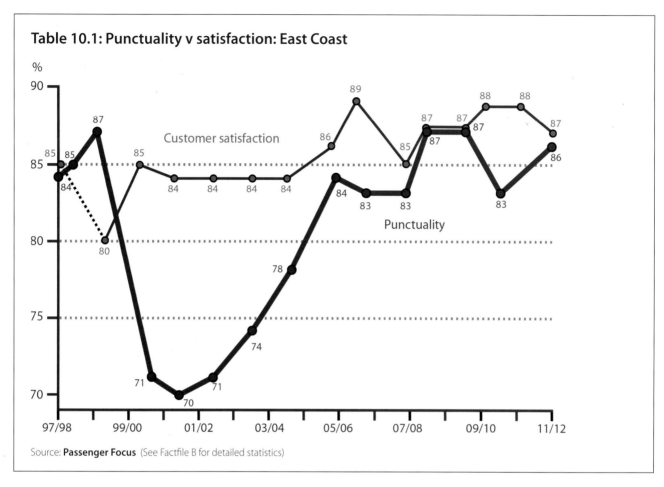

Table 10.1: Punctuality v satisfaction: East Coast

Source: **Passenger Focus** (See Factfile B for detailed statistics)

Operational instability

Railways have complex production lines which only work well in long periods of stability. GNER was to enter a traumatic period when it was de-stabilised by no less than three high-speed derailments all of which had a serious impact on its safety reputation, performance and morale. The 1998 derailment at Sandy was due to a wheel fracturing on one of its own trains, but it was to be blameless at both Hatfield in 2000 and Great Heck in 2001.

The Hatfield derailment was caused by the disintegration of a rail overdue for renewal. This event triggered almost a thousand precautionary speed restrictions across the nation – with long-distance passenger operators taking the most pain as their 125mph trains were reduced to constant 20mph crawls. The situation was made even worse by severe flooding across Britain a month later, which rendered many routes almost impassable and caused the shadow SRA to suspend the performance regime until emergency timetables could be introduced in January 2001. Sir Alastair Moreton, Chairman of the Strategic Rail Authority, famously christened this period 'the industry's collective nervous breakdown'.

Table 10.1 shows the spectacular drop in punctuality

from 2000, but it also shows the exceptional level of customer understanding and loyalty recorded in a satisfaction score that never dropped below 84% through a period of appalling performance. No other long-distance company was to earn such a round of applause in this dark period.

Despite the distractions, GNER still found time at the end of its first franchise to conceive an inspired makeover for its Mk4 fleet. The fleet was now 15 years old and GNER took the decision to go further than the normal half-life maintenance and invested an extra £70,000 per coach to create higher standards of comfort and design. With over 300 vehicles in the fleet, this meant an investment of £21 million and resulted in the iconic 'Mallard' refurbishment which included plush First Class interiors, extra seats for standard – and Britain's first on-board wi-fi. The first set was unveiled by HM the Queen in 2003 with the programme continuing on into the company's second franchise.

Franchise instability

However, no sooner had performance started to stabilise than GNER found itself reaching the end if its short franchise and senior managers' time and energy were

ABOVE Class 91 No 91122 pauses at York with the 0900 King's Cross–Glasgow on 5 October 2007. *Gavin Morrison*

being diverted into the life-and-death fight to re-bid for their franchise. The company found itself bidding for a welcome 20-year tender, but the competition was hot. A rival bid from Virgin/Stagecoach included a totally unexpected offer to build a section of new high-speed line through the Fens, and this caused the SRA to re-start the bidding process once more, leaving GNER with a tight two-year extension to its existing franchise.

The two years 2003-5 were spent in preparing yet another bid, but this time only for a 10-year franchise. The distraction was enormous and punctuality languished as the competitive tendering process took its toll. Christopher Garnett still has a vivid recollection that: 'GNER seemed to be in perpetual re-bidding mode from 2003 onwards'.

Table 10.2 shows that sadly, this franchise instability was to continue, with no less than five franchises in place on the East Coast between 1996 and 2013[1], whilst the route was also deemed fair game for the only sustained open-access competition in Britain.

GNER won the 2005 franchise with the support of a strong 'Save our Railway' campaign but the competition was tougher the third time around and GNER had to commit to a £1.3 billion premium which was heavily dependent on growing income in an expanding economy. It also committed to introducing a full half-hourly service between Leeds and King's

[1] Including Directly Operated Railways 2009–15

Table 10.2: East Coast into privatisation

Timeline	
1996	First franchise, 1996-2003 Sea Containers wins bid: GNER brand
2003	Second franchise, 2003-23 Tenders aborted by SRA GNER two-year extension 2003-5
2005	Third franchise: 2005-15 GNER wins franchise again
2007	GNER hands back franchise to DfT Management contract until re-franchise
2007	Fourth franchise: 2007-15 National Express wins bid
2009	National Express hands back franchise
2009	Fifth 'franchise', 2009-15 Direct railway operations
2013	Sixth franchise: 2015

Managing Directors	
1994	Brian Burdsall, MD BR East Coast
1996	Christopher Garnett, CEO GNER
2006	Jonathan Metcalfe, CEO GNER
2007	David Franks, CEO East Coast (National Express)
2009	Susan Goldsmith, CEO East Coast
2010	Karen Boswell, MD East Coast (Directly Operated Railways)

ABOVE GNER celebrates the arrival of the first refurbished Mk4 'Mallard' stock as DVT 82202 breaks the banner at King's Cross on 9 November 2005. *Brian Morrison*

BELOW Secretary of State for Transport Alistair Darling and Christopher Garnett test the First Class 'Mallard' refurbishment. *East Coast Main Line Co Ltd*

ABOVE The ultimate catering experience: tables laid in a 'Mallard' refurbished coach on 12 March 2007; only the customers are missing. *Brian Morrison*

BELOW Customers enjoy their lunch as their train dashes across the Vale of York towards Newcastle on 6 March 2006. *East Coast Main Line Co Ltd*

PREVIOUS PAGE As GNER's franchise comes to an end, Class 91 No 91109 crosses the Royal Border Bridge with the 1530 King's Cross–Edinburgh on 9 August 2007. *Gavin Morrison*

Cross, to giving its 14 HST sets a £42 million 'Mallard'-style refurbishment, to investing £25 million in station improvements and to delivering a record 90% punctuality. But this third GNER franchise was to prove how sensitive long-distance franchises were to sudden changes in income in an industry where the costs were largely fixed by contract. Only a year later, in 2006, a barrage of bad news conspired to destroy GNER's income assumptions.

The first omen was a serious economic recession which curtailed business growth; then came the London bombings which ended the expansion of leisure travel and finally a new open-access operator, Grand Central, reduced GNER's income by a further £10 million per annum when it was allowed to call at York.

Open access
Open-access operators tended to focus on the East Coast, as the West Coast was largely protected from this competition during its route modernisation. Hull Trains had started to run in 2002 and Grand Central began its Sunderland service in 2008. The problem lay in the incompatible nature of franchise and open access. Open access operators paid only the lower variable track-access costs and could withdraw at any time, whilst franchisees paid the additional, and much higher, fixed costs and were committed for their contracted period.

When GNER was bidding for the 2005 franchise, it was initially assured that it could plan its 10-year income and premium to Government on the basis of only competing with Hull Trains. This protection was withdrawn only hours before it signed, following an ORR decision to allow Grand Central to operate. This factor was to create a long-running dispute over calling patterns and a battle for scarce paths (see Factfile E). Grand Central worsened GNER's income and flexibility at a difficult time for the latter's parent company, Sea Containers, which was unable to cover GNER's premium payment commitments as it was itself facing bankruptcy. Indeed, it had even attempted to sell GNER in this period without success.

Christopher Garnett retired in 2006, and Jonathan Metcalf took over as Chief Executive, but such was the respect for GNER that the DfT asked GNER to continue running the company on a management

BELOW Hull Trains demonstrates open-access panache as Class 180 'Adelante' No 180113 departs Hull station on the 1245 service to King's Cross on 9 September 2009. *Gavin Morrison*

ABOVE National Express shows off its new livery as HST power car No 43312 slices along the Selby Diversion at the head of the 0952 Aberdeen–King's Cross on 26 September 2009. *Gavin Morrison*

BELOW Illustrating yet another East Coast livery change, No 43308 displays the new Directly Operated Railways colour scheme at the head of the 0755 Inverness–King's Cross, seen just south of Newcastle on 28 September 2011. *Gavin Morrison*

contract basis until 2007, when a fourth franchise tender would be issued. The DfT maintained funding to complete the HST refurbishment and also to introduce the half-hourly service from King's Cross to Leeds, which brought a quick return in the shape of 60,000 additional passengers.

National Express

GNER did not bid for the 2007 franchise but did take a surprise 10% share in the Virgin/Stagecoach tender at the last minute. However, the new 10-year franchise was won by National Express, which committed to a £1.4 billion premium; a 25% increase in train services; 33% more car-parking spaces; £8 million in gate-lines and £7.4 million in improvements to stations and information systems. The extra train services were to be delivered through a fifth path every hour out of King's Cross, which would in turn allow the Anglo-Scottish services to be accelerated and give Lincoln a new two-hourly service to London.

But National Express had hardly won the franchise before Network Rail announced that it could no longer offer the fifth path due to a huge growth in coal traffic north of Newark together with further open-access aspirations. The issue was only re-opened when David Franks, National Express Group's Rail Director, helped demonstrate that there was room for both the coal traffic and a fifth path from London.

However, the open-access issue was not so easily resolved, and no party could get agreement to change its services on the East Coast without 'Town Hall'-size consultation meetings to ensure a transparent process. The result was that any change became very difficult to implement since East Coast only ran 23% of the total services on the route. David Franks found himself facing the same frustrations that GNER had met when he was unable to get a fifth path for trains that were paying full fixed and variable track costs, whilst freight and open-access operators were often allowed to fill the spare spaces they found at variable cost.

The performance issues were equally difficult to resolve, and David Franks had to double up as both Director Rail for the National Express Group and Managing Director of East Coast. He made punctuality his top priority and focused on a 'return to basics' approach that included significant investment in re-engineering the HST fleet to get performance moving in the right direction. Punctuality peaked at 87% in 2009/10, but it had taken almost 10 years to restore it to the standards achieved by InterCity in 1989.

Within two years of taking over East Coast, National Express hit the same problems as GNER had

encountered. As losses increased, it sold its historic headquarters at York to a hotel operator whilst, at the same time, progressively reducing its dining-car services and cutting staffing levels. The £1.4 billion premium was undeliverable in the slower economic climate and the company's losses had reached £48 million by November 2009 when National Express asked for a franchise re-negotiation. This time, however, the DfT refused to negotiate and abruptly ended the franchise.

Directly Operated Railways

The fifth 'franchise' term was to be a temporary return to state ownership. The DfT had established its own company called Directly Operated Railways (DOR) with the sole purpose of running failed train companies. It was initially chaired by Elaine Holt and then by Michael Holden from 2009. DOR appointed Karen Boswell as the new MD East Coast and gave her just 10 days warning that her team would be taking over the 'franchise' for the next four years until it could be stabilised and re-franchised in 2013. She took advantage of not having the distraction of a bidding process to focus on creating a period of stability to restore performance – but said that she found that in all other respects 'it felt like running a commercial business'.

East Coast DOR inherited the unfinished business of the fifth path from National Express, and Michael Holden had to re-fight the battle by bringing all the parties together and agreeing to compromise on an hourly service alternating between York and Newark. This left Lincoln with only one daily through service to London – but also provided freight capacity between Newark and York. The extra train sets were found by terminating all but one of the East Coast London-Glasgow services at Edinburgh and extending CrossCountry services to Glasgow. The five 'Adelante' units planned for the Lincoln services were finally transferred to the Great Western in 2012.

With restaurant-car losses rising to £21 million per annum it was left to East Coast DOR to withdraw the remaining services and replace them with an at-seat offer to all First Class passengers in 2011. This proved popular with the market and delivered an overall 21% increase in First Class passengers in the first 10 months and a 36% growth in Edinburgh to London business travel. East Coast was now serving 100,000 First Class meals a month – about 10 times more than were served in the former restaurant cars. It also removed the wasted train capacity in allowing diners to occupy two precious seats on the train and also differentiated more clearly the added value of travelling First Class.

ABOVE East Coast DOR shows its style with a unique livery on Class 91 No 91101, seen propelling the 1345 Leeds–King's Cross near Newark Northgate on 28 September 2011. *Gavin Morrison*

East Coast put significant effort into stimulating growth both through marketing and revenue management initiatives. The improvements introduced with the May 2011 timetable included additional services, new destinations and the introduction of complimentary food and drink in First Class with all these initiatives being supported by a high profile advertising campaign. Called 'Welcome to East Coast' the campaign put customer service at the heart of the business and was highly successful in stimulating growth and turning around the decline in First Class travel. The company continued to lead the way in revenue management and was the first train operator in the world to invest in a revenue management optimiser system. These and many other initiatives were rewarded when East Coast won no less than 19 external awards in 2011.

Summary

East Coast clearly performed best in its two brief periods of stability – 1996-99 and 2009-13 – when its many innovative ventures were largely conceived. It was extremely unfortunate to have suffered such dramatic instability in the 10 intervening years. Yet despite the distractions, Table 10.3 shows that its successive leaders managed to increase passenger travel and train frequencies by 40%, whilst improving on the journey speeds, punctuality and passenger satisfaction that it inherited from InterCity. Another challenging era looks set to follow in 2015, when the East Coast franchise is re-let for the sixth time in 17 years.

Table 10.3: East Coast overview

	1997/98	2001/02	2011/12
Punctuality: Annual MAA	84%	70%	86%
Trains run: Weekday trains	93	107	154
Average speed: London–Peterborough	99mph	99mph	101mph
Growth: Journeys per annum	13m	14m	19m
Satisfaction: Overall	85%*	84%	87%

*Year 2000

ABOVE Putting the final touches to the new livery of the 'Flying Scotsman' just before midnight at Craigentinny depot on 22 May 2011. *East Coast Main Line Co Ltd*

BELOW The new-style at-seat breakfast is served on board the 'Flying Scotsman' as it launches the new East Coast timetable on 23 May 2011. *East Coast Main Line Co Ltd*

ABOVE Karen Boswell, Managing Director of East Coast, and pipe band welcome the arrival of the inaugural 'Flying Scotsman' in the new timetable at King's Cross at 0940 on 23 May 2011. *East Coast Main Line Co Ltd*

BELOW Class 91 No 91129 and HST power car No 43120 provide staff with a connection challenge at King's Cross on 16 July 2003. *Paul Bigland*

ABOVE With Manchester as a backdrop, the diverted Birmingham-Edinburgh train headed by No 47828 passes Ordsall Lane in Salford on 5 November 1995. *Gavin Morrison*

Chapter 11
WEST COAST

ABOVE An historic moment on 10 February 1997 as Richard Branson accepts the handover of West Coast from Secretary of State for Transport Sir George Young. *Colin J. Marsden*

InterCity West Coast had been led by Ivor Warburton, who became the BR Shadow Director for its transition and who also led a management bid for the franchise. The tender was subsequently won by the Virgin Group in 1997 and Virgin's bid leader, Brian Barrett, became the first CEO of the new Virgin Trains company with Chris Tibbits as Deputy Chief Executive and Ivor Warburton as Business Development Director.

West Coast's dire investment backlog led to a 15-year franchise being awarded in return for a multi-billion capital programme to kick-start the delayed route modernisation. The scale of the investment risk was recognised in an unusual 'Moderation of Competition' agreement which protected the core route from direct competition for the life of the franchise. Unlike East Coast, West Coast had the stability of both a 15-year franchise with protection from open-access operators – but it was still destined to suffer an even worse period of instability than East Coast.

The Virgin difference

Virgin had a totally different customer service philosophy to GNER. It was not interested in evolving the InterCity brand. It had a powerful brand of its own and wanted to 'make the Virgin Difference' and, unlike GNER, it made an immediate start on re-branding the existing fleet.

For Virgin the whole point of privatisation was to bring a new diversity of ideas to the railway, and it was to be a leading proponent in innovative thinking. Far from developing the InterCity restaurant-car model, Virgin abolished it within a year when it introduced a radical shift to airline-style meals at seat in 1998 – a service available for First Class passengers only. And whilst Virgin's 'Retail 2000' brought investment in new-look travel centres, it was its £10 million investment in Trainline.com that led to the real revolution in electronic ticketing and to a new era of low price fares.

Virgin hoped that the 'wallet-free' airline experience would tempt more domestic airline passengers to travel First Class on rail, but when Chris Green took over as Chief Executive in 1999 he found serious dissatisfaction with the new catering due to inexperienced young staff and sudden shortages of food, drinks and staff. His challenge was to deliver the 'Virgin Difference' in a way that could be sustained in a demanding marketplace.

Table 11.1: West Coast into privatisation

Timeline	
1997	First Franchise 1997–2012
1997	Virgin Group wins franchise
1998	Stagecoach buys 49% shareholding
2002	Virgin on Management Contract
2004	First 125mph tilting timetable introduced
2006	Virgin off Management Contract
2008	Virgin High Frequency (VHF) timetable
2011	Franchise extension
2012	Further franchise extensions
2017	Second Franchise
Managing Directors*		
1994	Ivor Warburton	Dir BR Shadow Train Unit
1997	Brian Barrett	CEO Virgin Trains
1999	Chris Green	CEO Virgin Trains
2004	Tony Collins	CEO Virgin Trains

* Charles Belcher MD West Coast 2003-07

Source **Chris Gibb COO West Coast 2007**

RIGHT Chris Tibbits, Managing Director, Virgin Trains, in full flow on 3 May 2001. *Bob Sweet*

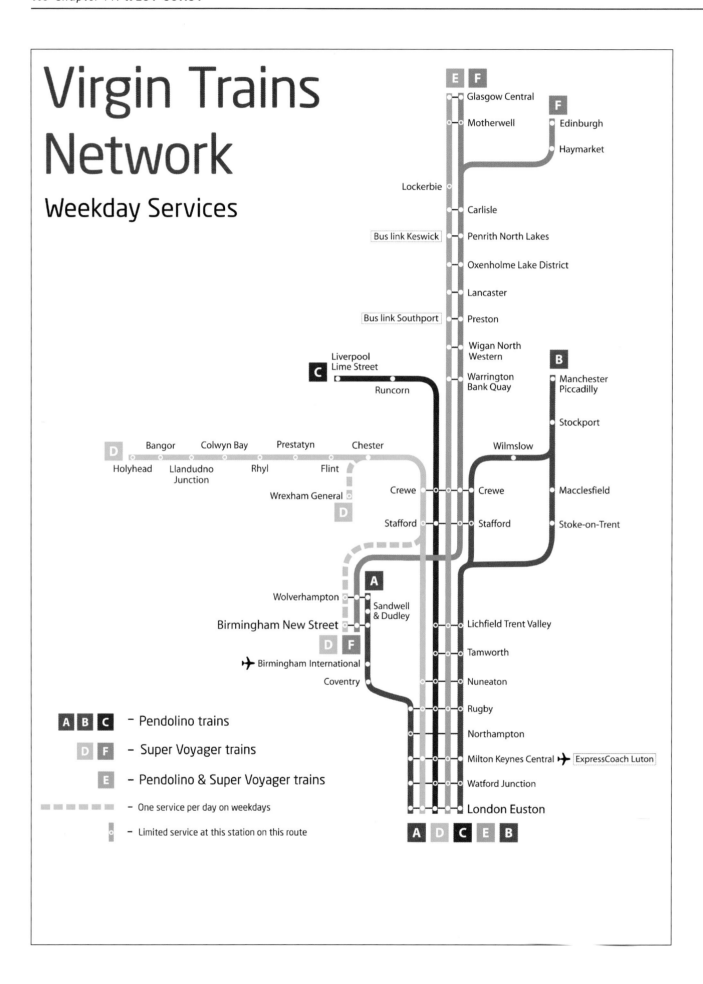

Virgin Trains Network

Weekday Services

E **F** Glasgow Central
Motherwell
F Edinburgh
Haymarket
Lockerbie
Carlisle
Bus link Keswick Penrith North Lakes
Oxenholme Lake District
Lancaster
Bus link Southport Preston
Wigan North Western
Warrington Bank Quay

B
Manchester Piccadilly
Stockport

Liverpool Lime Street
C
Runcorn

Wilmslow

D Bangor   Colwyn Bay   Prestatyn   Chester
Holyhead   Llandudno Junction   Rhyl   Flint
Wrexham General
D

Crewe   Crewe   Macclesfield
Stafford   Stafford   Stoke-on-Trent

A
Wolverhampton
Sandwell & Dudley
Birmingham New Street
D **F**
✈ Birmingham International
Coventry

Lichfield Trent Valley
Tamworth
Nuneaton
Rugby
Northampton
Milton Keynes Central ✈ ExpressCoach Luton
Watford Junction
London Euston
A **D** **C** **E** **B**

A **B** **C** – Pendolino trains
D **F** – Super Voyager trains
E – Pendolino & Super Voyager trains
– – – – – – One service per day on weekdays
– Limited service at this station on this route

He decided to bring in an experienced customer service leader to solve the problem and Brenda Klug was selected for this daunting task following her experience with British Airways. She decided to start again by getting the managers to agree a Mission, Strategy and Values statement for the new company which would have general acceptance. Only then could she develop the Values and Behaviours which would deliver the 'Virgin Difference'.

The original approach taken by the company of simply encouraging staff to use their own intuition was not going to provide the consistent service that high-value business travellers expected. A new recruitment policy was introduced to attract more mature staff with proven customer service experience. Supporting training courses of up to eight weeks were then introduced, in which both newcomers and existing staff learned how to serve customers professionally.

The new 'Service with Style' courses focused on delivering the 'Virgin Difference' and the '10 Customer Commitments' were woven into every aspect of the behavioural training as shown in Table 11.2. They taught specific service behaviours where, for example, 'being there for the customer' could mean helping elderly passengers out of trains or entertaining children on the trains. Brenda Klug's big message was that 'the Virgin people made the ultimate difference – not the hardware'.

Once trained, the final badge of customer service was the issuing of red tailored uniforms in 2003, just before the new 'Pendolinos' came into service. In less

than a month, all 1,500 staff went through the uniform change, and Chris Green remembers being stunned by the transformation: 'overnight people smartened up, behaved differently and showed a new pride in their job'.

Continuous instability

The customer service initiative helped to mitigate the collapse in performance when Virgin paid the price for the 10-year delay in the West Coast upgrade. It inherited a railway where locomotives were breaking down, coaches were losing their air conditioning and where infrastructure was no longer able to sustain the intense train services. Performance had collapsed on West Coast even before the disruptive route upgrading started. Chris Green had been appointed to see Virgin Trains through this transition period, and whilst he realised that he was destined to live through a period of continuous instability, he was later to admit that the job 'had proved twice the nightmare that he had feared'.

RIGHT Virgin launches its new at-seat catering service for First Class passengers on 10 March 1997. *Colin J. Marsden*

He launched an immediate performance drive to restore basic operating disciplines and he appointed Jackie Townsend to a new post of Operations Manager West Coast to restore order. 'Right Time' starts became a company priority after a period when it had become acceptable to delay departures whilst waiting for staff, catering supplies or connections. A recruitment campaign was launched to increase key staff – whilst a speculative venture to recruit and train a cadre of 'Millennium Drivers' to lease to other companies was closed down.

Even the new organisation itself was to prove an unexpected challenge to smooth delivery. East Coast was a single franchise, but Virgin had won both the CrossCountry and the West Coast franchises and it seemed wasteful to duplicate management resources across two companies. The decision was therefore taken to put a single CEO in charge of a new Virgin Trains company with responsibility for both franchises. This made good sense for central functions such as

ABOVE The smart new Virgin uniforms were introduced at Euston on 22 May 2002 to welcome a new era as the 'Pendolinos' finally entered service. *Colin J. Marsden*

finance, marketing and projects, but was to overwhelm the operations' team as it struggled to manage two of the most complex routes in Britain.

Tilting trains

Virgin's visionary bid depended on doubling passenger travel to 30 million journeys per annum by a simultaneous increase in both speeds and frequencies. The new tilting trains represented an investment of £390 million through Angel Trains leasing company, and a further £600million in a 15-year maintenance deal with Alstom. The trains were originally to be called Advance Tilting Trains (ATT), but this was changed to the more sexy 'Pendolino' (Italian for tilting) after a media visit to Fiat's production line near Turin in 1999. Virgin had taken a risk in bringing the tilting train back to Britain, but Fiat's technology worked well, and the tilt proved so effective that most passengers were not aware that they were tilting an extra 8% around the sharper curves. The result was to give West Coast a near-continuous 125mph 'racetrack' from London

LEFT This customer is clearly enjoying First Class Virgin West Coast service on 22 October 2003. *MP92½*

Table 11.2: The Virgin Difference

MISSION
A world-class travel experience by 2003

STRATEGIES

To deliver the mission by:
    Being safe and reliable
    Transforming the railway
    Developing our people
    Offering memorable customer service
    Expanding the market
    Delivering shareholder value

BEHAVIOURS

The 10 Customer Commitments	What they mean
Making it Safe for Everyone	Safety is the responsibility of each one of us – we have to look out for each other and our customers.
Delivering the Virgin Difference	Customers have high expectations of us, because we're Virgin
On Time, Every Time!	We need to role model punctuality in everything we do.
V-smarT in the Public Eye	We are all ambassadors for Virgin and want to reassure customers that we are professionals.
Warm welcomes and fond farewells	It's about turning every encounter into a warm encounter and creating great first and last impressions
Seeing each customer as an individual	Everyone is an individual – behaving in a way that the other person feels unique is true empathy!
Being there for the Customer	It's not just about being physically there – but being there in mind and spirit too.
Information belongs to the Customer	We all like to feel in control of our lives – great customer service recognises this with timely information
Creating the right atmosphere	A little bit of 'emotional connection' can create the right atmosphere – even when things aren't going well
Doing that little bit extra	As long as we don't compromise safety or punctuality, let's go that extra mile for our customers.

Source: **Brenda Klug, Director Customer Service 1999-2004**

to Preston with powerful 5,000hp trains. The only downside was a narrower coach body which led to more cramped interiors – the price for a tilting train running on Britain's limited loading gauge. Virgin also made a bold £50 million investment decision, taken just before the Hatfield crisis in 2000, to lengthen the entire 'Pendolino' fleet from eight to nine cars.

A major distraction, largely unseen by the public, was the problem of getting the new 'Pendolino' trains through the labyrinthine European Safety Case. This was to take two years and proved so complex that Chris Green had to join senior managers from Virgin, Alstom, Network Rail, Bechtel and the SRA every week for two years to co-ordinate a rolling programme of modifications to trains, track, signalling, structures and electrification equipment through a highly-fragmented industry. Even then problems arose in dragging the 'Pendolinos' through non-electrified diversions, and endless problems were to arise before the Class 57 'Thunderbirds' would interface with the 'Pendolinos'.

140mph track

Virgin's big idea was the complete renewal of West Coast track and trains, in partnership with Railtrack and Alstom. Whereas InterCity's modest £0.8 billion West Coast investment would have brought Manchester within 2hr 15min of London Euston with non-tilt trains, Virgin and Railtrack were proposing a much bolder £2 billion investment with a journey time of just 1hr 50min. Table 11.3 shows the contrast

Table 11.3: West Coast upgrade

Proposals	InterCity 1993	Virgin 1997
London/Manchester	2hr 15min	1hr 50min
Track upgrade	125mph	140mph
Investment (Railtrack)	£0.8bn	£2bn
Trains	14 x Class 91 + Mk4 sets	53 'Pendolino' sets
Routes upgraded	Manchester & Liverpool	Whole West Coast
Tilt	No	Yes
Signalling	Conventional	Moving Block ECS
Cascade	Mk3 to West Midlands	None – all new trains
	Mk2 to CrossCountry	None – all new trains

between InterCity's Treasury-driven approach in 1993 involving just 14 new trains at 125mph, and the more ambitious Virgin/Railtrack 140mph plans.

The growth needed to fund extra investment was dependent on a PUG[1] contract delivering 125mph 'Pendolino' services by 2002, together with a further PUG2 contract providing the full 140mph upgrade by 2005. But within two years of signing the contract Railtrack announced that 140mph running was undeliverable and that even the 125mph railway would be delayed until at least 2004. Railtrack was trapped in a legally binding contract which required it to deliver a new 'moving block' signalling system by 2005 for 140mph train running. It had signed the contract even though the technology was not in operation anywhere else in the world on a classic inter-city route. This contract proved to be undeliverable

and the cost of the alternative conventional re-signalling, together with the serious under-estimation of the infrastructure conditions, would reach almost £9 billion. Railtrack could not break the contract and owed Virgin a huge compensation sum for lost income – which came on top of the large compensation which it was paying train companies for the impact of the post-Hatfield speed restrictions. These two factors combined to tip Railtrack into administration.

Financial instability

The period 2002-6 was one of huge financial instability in which all players came close to bankruptcy. Whilst Virgin ultimately held Railtrack, and later Network

[1] PUG1 Passenger Upgrade One: PUG2 Passenger Upgrade 2

BELOW Virgin Trains hosted a special event at Alstom's Old Dalby Test Track on 9 July 2001 when 'Pendolino' set No 390002 gave the first tilting demonstration run for the world's media. *Colin J. Marsden*

ABOVE Doing what it was designed to do, a 'Pendolino' demonstrates the full effect of its tilting action. *MP92½*

BELOW Class 57/3 'Thunderbird' No 57308 and 'Pendolino' No 390002 encounter engagement problems at Nuneaton on 8 May 2005. *Paul Bigland*

ABOVE The 'Pendolino' speedometer stays steady at 145mph on the successful high-speed test between Rugby and Nuneaton on 31 August 2002. *MP92½*

RIGHT Denize Quest had the daunting task as Communications Director of defending Virgin Trains through six years of chaos and instability. *Chris Green*

Rail, to the huge penalty clauses in the contract, it was not able to re-negotiate its franchise with the DfT until 2006. The PUG2 contract was then closed with a multi-million pound payment given to Virgin. In the meantime, Virgin had to operate on a 'Letter Agreement' (effectively a management contract) in which the DfT kept Virgin on a financial drip-feed for four years during which time there were permanent contract re-negotiations.

Alstom was hit by its own financial problems in this period and was only able to keep train production going by the fact that the French Government bought a temporary 28% share in the company. The instability for Virgin Trains was so great that from that date Chris Green effectively focused on keeping the railway and the projects moving, whilst his deputy, Tony Collins, used his contractual skills to keep the franchise and its shareholders afloat.

Operational instability

But operational instability was to prove every bit as destructive as the financial instability. The wave of speed restrictions which followed the Hatfield derailment severely affected West Coast performance, and the management team spent the year 2000 at the workface, trying to keep the emergency timetables operating. The West Coast was the UK's worst affected route as its upgrade work had just got underway and was causing additional delays of its own. Indeed the planned route-modernisation work was to prove more disruptive to passengers than the unplanned speed restrictions, as the impact of the project work was much less predictable. The West Coast main line was to become the longest building site in Britain.

It was the erratic nature of this early upgrade work which drove customers to fury. A typical example was the renewal of the track at the throat of Euston station. On Saturday mornings the contractors moved onto the site to dig up more track – and most weekends they also dug up signalling cables, air pipes or water mains which brought the entire station to a stand for several hours. It became such a regular occurrence that Chris Green booked himself at Euston on Saturdays to give his team a break. The problems did however trigger the decision to appoint Charles Belcher to a new post of Managing Director West Coast, with a small team dedicated to managing West Coast performance.

The work then moved northwards, where it emerged that the track upgrade was still only 30% complete. The measures to accelerate the work virtually wiped out the lucrative weekend market, and even weekday travel was affected, as several sections of the West Coast were closed for blockade renewals. Passengers suffered long diversions and tedious bus replacement services, although the 'Project Rio' HST service that ran from London St Pancras to Manchester throughout 2003/4 provided an alternative through service, albeit with an increased journey time.

Table 11.4 shows how this intensive period of modernisation triggered a huge decline in passenger

ABOVE The dreaded West Coast Route Modernisation (WCRM) is in full swing at Tring as engineers rebuild track and platforms on 30 August 2003. *MP92½*

BELOW All lines are closed whilst engineers upgrade the overhead catenary. *MP92½*

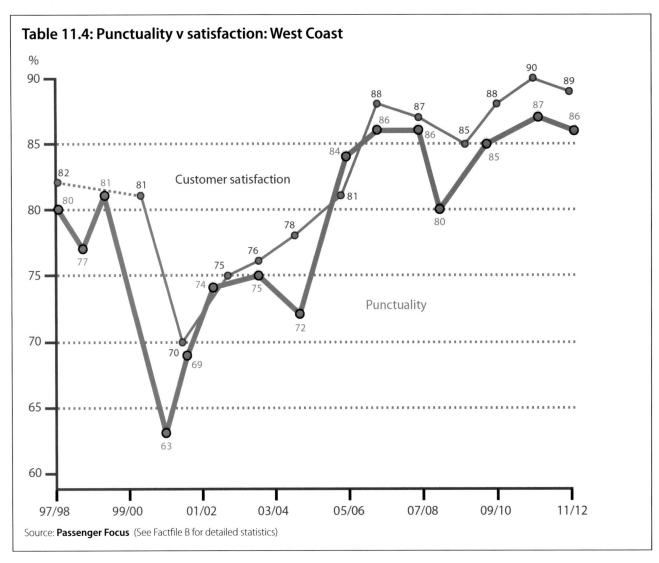

Table 11.4: Punctuality v satisfaction: West Coast

Customer satisfaction

Punctuality

Source: **Passenger Focus** (See Factfile B for detailed statistics)

satisfaction, but whereas East Coast had retained public sympathy after Hatfield, West Coast lost it when the intrusive route upgrading work started and passenger satisfaction plunged to 70% in line with performance.

The Red Revolution

Stability finally returned in 2004 when the new trains started to run on modern infrastructure. Chris Green's final act before handing over to Tony Collins was to mark the end of an era of continuous instability with the introduction of a tilting train timetable. This was a major project in its own right and was code-named 'Red Revolution' to win recognition for the huge step forward that was coming. It had begun in 2002 when Denize Quest and her Communications team had given the world media a dramatic demonstration of the 'Pendolino' undergoing its tilting trials.

The Red Revolution ended with a major ceremony at Euston station in the presence of Prime Minister Tony Blair and Sir Richard Branson on 20 September 2004,

when 36 tilting 'Pendolino' diagrams were introduced on the Birmingham, Manchester and Liverpool routes. Train services increased by 23% and journey times were slashed by 20%. The Red Revolution kick-started a period of super-growth as the headline Manchester – London journey fell from 2hr 41min to just 2hr 6min. Despite the more ambitious timetable, performance returned to 86% and passenger satisfaction hit the 90% target.

Quiet enjoyment at last

Tony Collins, CEO from 2004 to 2013, likes to point to a clause in the original PUG2 contract which promised Virgin a period of quiet enjoyment to double its passengers once the infrastructure upgrade was completed. This period of stability finally began with the launch of the 2008 Virgin High Frequency (VHF) timetable and the ending of the management contract. This completed the West Coast upgrade and brought Glasgow within 4hr 8min of Euston and delivered three

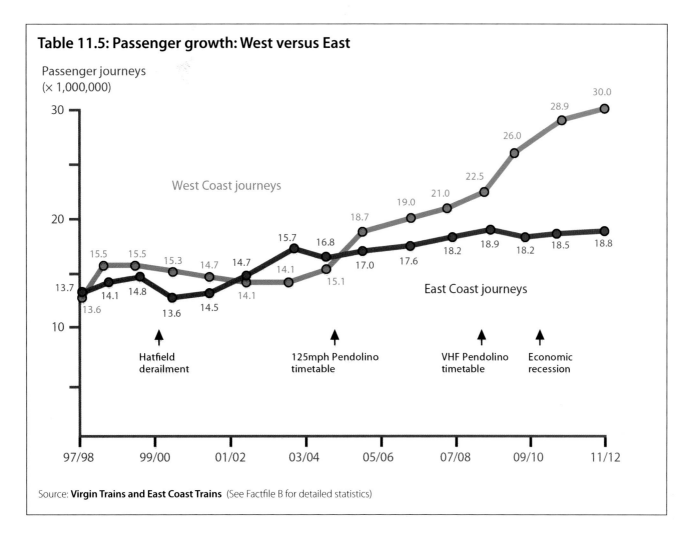

Table 11.5: Passenger growth: West versus East

Passenger journeys
(× 1,000,000)

West Coast journeys

East Coast journeys

Hatfield derailment

125mph Pendolino timetable

VHF Pendolino timetable

Economic recession

Source: **Virgin Trains and East Coast Trains** (See Factfile B for detailed statistics)

ABOVE Virgin Trains CEO Chris Green, Sir Richard Branson and Prime Minister Tony Blair celebrate the launch of the new 'Pendolino' services at Euston on 20 September 2004. *MP92½*

ABOVE Tony Collins, CEO Virgin West Coast 2004-2013. *MP92½*

trains an hour between both London and Birmingham and London and Manchester. A further 21 tilting 'Super Voyager' diesels were transferred from CrossCountry to provide a new hourly service from London Euston to Chester via Crewe, together with a new two-hourly Birmingham–Scotland service. Agreement with the DfT was reached soon afterwards for the further lengthening of 31 'Pendolinos' from nine to eleven cars by the end of the franchise and for the purchase of a further four new 11-car 'Pendolinos'.

The period of quiet – but not complacent – enjoyment finally allowed Virgin to demonstrate that the 10 years of pain were delivering a dividend. No other franchise was able to match the benefits that started to flow after 2004. These included:

a) An almost vertical increase in passenger journeys following the introduction of the 'Pendolino' trains in 2004. Table 11.5 charts the comparative growth of East and West Coast passengers and demonstrates the 'Pendolino' impact after 2004. In 1996 both companies were level-pegging with around 13 million passenger journeys, but by 2012 West Coast had more than doubled to 30 million, whilst East Coast had grown by only 40%, to 19 million.

b) A dramatic increase in journey speeds on West Coast, despite the limiting of top speeds to 125mph.

ABOVE Even the London Evening Standard celebrated the high-speed run on 20 September 2004, when Manchester suddenly became just 1hr 53 min away from Euston. *Chris Green*

Table 11.8 shows that West Coast is the only long-distance company to have significantly increased its speeds since privatisation, with almost half an hour being cut off many journey times from London to the North West and Scotland. This brought West Coast up to East Coast speeds and the Anglo-Scottish services on the two routes now average 105mph on West Coast's hourly non-stop run from London to Warrington – and 94mph on East Coast's hourly non-stop run from London to York.

c) More than doubling service frequencies from 156 train services in 1997 to 331 trains a day in 2008. Table 11.8 shows that both Manchester and Birmingham now have a 20-minute frequency to Euston, seven days a week – a level of service unprecedented in Europe – with the only reduction in service coming on Sunday mornings. InterCity's 15 services from London to Manchester have more than doubled to 39 trains a day and Virgin routinely runs nine inter-city services out of London every off-peak hour compared to East Coast's five.

Whilst domestic airlines still clung onto the London–Scotland market, Table 11.6 shows that rail was remarkably successful in clawing back custom on journeys of between 150 and 300 miles. Liverpool, Blackpool and Durham Tees Valley airports all ceased to operate London flights, while flights between Manchester and Glasgow fell by 67%, and those between Manchester and London by almost a half. In addition, BMI withdrew Heathrow services from Glasgow, Leeds and Teesside, and Ryanair from Glasgow Prestwick to Stansted and from Newcastle to Stansted. A fuller analysis is shown in Factfile B9.

Virgin West Coast's crowning achievement was to win an unprecedented 90% Passenger Satisfaction score in 2010 – the highest any long-distance franchise had achieved. Table 11.4 has shown the long journey from the 2000 'sin bin' of 70% to delivering Britain's most satisfied passengers a decade later. Tony Collins attributes this success to the culmination of three major initiatives: the completion of the West Coast Upgrade: the delivery of the VHF timetable and behaviourally focused 'Vision' programmes which involved every member of Virgin Trains. The final accolade came in 2012 when Virgin won the coveted 'Best Rail Operator of the Year' award at the Travel Globe.

Table 11.6: Domestic air journeys (medium-distance)

Route (000 trips each way)	2000	2011	%
London–Liverpool	201	0	-100%
London–Durham Tees Valley	173	0	-100%
London–Leeds Bradford	228	11	- 95%
Manchester–Glasgow	178	59	- 67%
Manchester–Edinburgh	172	59	- 66%
Leeds Bradford–Edinburgh	31	12	- 61%
London–Manchester	1850	1007	- 46%
Birmingham–Glasgow	284	212	- 25%
London–Newcastle	710	597	- 16%
Birmingham–Edinburgh	287	289	+ 1%

Source: **CAA Airport Statistics**

Re-franchising 2012

However, Virgin's achievements were not enough to win it the second franchise, which was due to start on 9 December 2012. In an increasingly public fiasco, the DfT initially announced that Tim O'Toole's FirstGroup had taken the West Coast franchise only to find itself facing a Judicial Review from a furious Virgin Trains (VT) who could not see how the DfT had reached their conclusions from the published figures.

The DfT then dramatically withdrew its defence the day before the Review was due to start and conceded that its numbers were indeed wrong. An independent investigation by Sam Laidlaw, a non-executive director in the DfT, concluded that the two final bidders had not been treated equally and this had led to different calculations for the huge payments that the winning company would have to make if for any reason it defaulted on the new franchise.

The re-franchising process was suspended and on 6 December 2012, an agreement was announced in which Virgin would have its franchise extended by almost two years to November 2014 and would operate on the basis of the DfT taking the revenue risk and Virgin earning a fee equivalent to 1% of revenue.

The implications and impact of the West Coast re-franchising fiasco were so great that all other re-franchising was suspended until Richard Brown, Chairman of Eurostar, had undertaken an independent report on the lessons to be learned for future franchising.

Summary

Table 11.7 shows that West Coast finally achieved its route modernisation in 2008, almost 20 years after InterCity had first started planning it. The final product was far more extensive than anything InterCity could have dared hope for, despite the failure to deliver 140mph running – a problem that ironically has hit both routes. However, whilst Richard Branson had always predicted 'pain before gain' the protracted and disruptive way in which the route modernisation

ABOVE Congratulatory letter from the Prime Minister, Tony Blair, to Chris Green, CEO Virgin Trains, on the successful launch of the 'Pendolino' timetable. *Chris Green*

was delivered has to be an object lesson for future routes upgrades.

Both East Coast and West Coast demonstrate the need for long franchises in which sustained periods of stability can be used to develop new products, justify long-term investment, motivate staff and deliver high levels of quality. But the increasingly ruthless franchising process ended in tears for both GNER and Virgin as the incumbents were out-bid by bolder rivals.

Table 11.7: West Coast overview

	1997/98	2001/02	2011/12
Punctuality: Annual MAA	80%	69%	86%
Frequency: No trains daily	152	162	331
Average speed: London–Warrington	83mph	85	105mph
Growth: Journeys per annum	14m	14m	30m
Satisfaction: Overall	81%*	70%	89%

*Year 2000

ABOVE Virgin West Coast made considerable investment in additional car-parking provision at its stations, to meet growth. This one at Preston is seen on 11 May 2012. *Chris Dixon*

BELOW Euston station – London's anchor point for the West Coast main line shows strong retail expansion outside its doors. *Network Rail*

Table 11.8: Speed v frequency

Daily services Monday-Thursday 0700-2000hrs

London to:	Frequency (trains run		Average journey time		Average speed (mph)	
	1992	2012	1992	2012	1992	2012
East Coast						
Peterborough[1]	29	41	0hr 46	0hr 45	99	101
Doncaster[2]	28	54	1hr 42	1hr 37	92	95
York[2]	25	37	1hr 56	2hr 00	97	94
Leeds	16	27	2hr 22	2hr 17	79	81
Hull[2]	3	8	2hr 49	2hr 38	73	78
Newcastle upon Tyne	23	27	2hr 57	3hr 03	91	88
Edinburgh	14	19	4hr 22	4hr 33	90	86
West Coast						
Birmingham New Street	26	39	1hr 38	1hr 23	69	81
Manchester Piccadilly	15	39	2hr 35	2hr 08	71	86
Liverpool Lime Street	12	15	2hr 38	2hr 08	73	91
Chester	3	12	2hr 24	2hr 01	75	89
Preston	14	16	2hr 38	2hr 20	79	96
Warrington Bank Quay	10	15	2hr 11	1hr 44	83	105
Glasgow Central	5	12	5hr 17	4hr 32	76	88
Great Western						
Reading[1]	52	90	0hr 24	0hr 26	90	83
Swindon	40	59	0hr 54	0hr 58	86	80
Bristol Parkway	19	24	1hr 17	1hr 24	87	80
Bristol Temple Meads	21	27	1hr.37	1hr 43	73	69
Cardiff Central	18	24	1hr 57	2hr 04	74	70
Exeter St Davids	11	17	2hr 16	2hr 22	77	73
Plymouth	11	13	3hr 26	3hr 21	66	67
Midland Mainline						
Leicester	30	52	1hr 14	1hr 14	80	80
Derby	16	26	1hr 45	1hr 41	73	76
Nottingham	13	26	1hr 41	1hr 53	75	67
Sheffield	14	26	2hr 22	2hr 22	70	70
Anglia						
Norwich	15	29	1hr 44	1hr 54	66	60
CrossCountry						
ex Birmingham						
Reading	14	26	1hr 51	1hr 35	53	62
Bournemouth	8	13	3hr 43	3hr 07	47	56
Bristol Temple Meads	14	26	1hr 33	1hr 27	60	64
Plymouth	9	13	3hr 55	3hr 34	56	62
Manchester Piccadilly	13	26	1hr 38	1hr 35	50	52
Glasgow (West Coast)	6	73	4hr 30	3hr 57	66	74
Newcastle upon Tyne	8	25	3hr 34	3hr 22	59	62
Edinburgh (East Coast)	2	12	5hr 25	5hr 04	61	66
Edinburgh (West Coast)	4	6	4hr 58	4hr 02	59	73
Eurostar						
London–Brussels	5	9	3hr 17	2hr 05	63	112
London–Paris	9	15	3hr 00	2hr 19	102	132

1 Long-distance services only   2 Includes open-access services   3 Operated by Virgin West Coast

Source: **Gordon Pettitt**

Chapter 12
MIDLAND AND CROSSCOUNTRY

ABOVE Later tests were undertaken in France. Here 'Super Voyager' No 221101 *Louis Blériot* demonstrates its six-degree tilt as it runs over the Souillac Lamothe viaduct in the Massif Central on 1 February 2002. *Chris Dixon*

Diversity

Rail privatisation was intended to break up a closed shop and open the industry to a diversity of new ideas and new sources of funding – and InterCity was to become a leader in this move away from 'one size fits all'.

East Coast, West Coast and CrossCountry evolved their own particular ideas on marketing, customer service and investment – but they remained fundamentally long-distance franchises. However, the remaining ex-InterCity companies went through more radical changes, with Gatwick, Anglia, Great Western and Midland Mainline all being merged into regional networks and losing their single-focus inter-city role. Midland Mainline and CrossCountry provide perfect contrasting examples of this new diversity.

Midland Mainline

Franchise freedom

Midland Mainline emerged from a rather constrained period when InterCity could not always give it the attention and investment that it deserved. It did, however, flourish under privatisation. The first impact of that process was to split Midland Mainline and CrossCountry in 1994 into two separate entities for franchising. Richard Brown chose to stay with the new Midland Mainline franchise, first as BR Shadow Director and then as leader of a management buyout. Looking back, he felt that the combined Midland & CrossCountry route had been rather a Cinderella within InterCity and that the separation gave each a new focus and freedom.

National Express won the franchise in 1996 but showed respect for InterCity's achievements and reappointed the ex-InterCity team to run the new franchise. National Express acted as a classic holding company, and Midland Mainline became free to evolve in a way that would have been impossible in BR days. Richard Brown chose to retain the original InterCity Vision, Strategies and Values and adapted them into a Midland Mainline statement which would bind the team together (see Factfile B11). Like Great Western, he sought to maintain the well-established InterCity brand which the public recognised, but he too was rebuffed by OPRAF on the basis that its retention might deter future bidders.

Marketing innovation

The National Express Midland Mainline franchise was characterised by its bold marketing developments. A new interest in rail travel was being raised by the novelty of privatisation and by the creativity that was

ABOVE At Bombardier's works in Derby in 1999 a 'Turbostar' is handed over to Brian Burdsall, MD, Midland Mainline, by Richard Brown, Chief Executive of the new Train Division at National Express. *East Midlands Trains*

blossoming in an improving economy. The team now turned their attention to meeting this demand in a series of developments for the new 1999 timetable which were to transform the route. Their priority was to compete more aggressively with the M1, through better speed, frequency and marketing.

National Express had bid to increase train frequencies from St Pancras to the East Midlands, and this was achieved by a near doubling in daily train services from 59 services at privatisation to 110 by 1999. National Express quickly agreed to the purchase of 17 new 100mph 'Turbostar' diesel multiple-units on the back of an existing order from Chiltern Trains, and they were focused on intermediate stations such as Wellingborough and Kettering which, in turn, allowed the long-distance trains to be accelerated. Richard Brown says that in BR days he never dreamed that he would be ordering his own train fleet – let alone the second new-train order since the early 1990s.

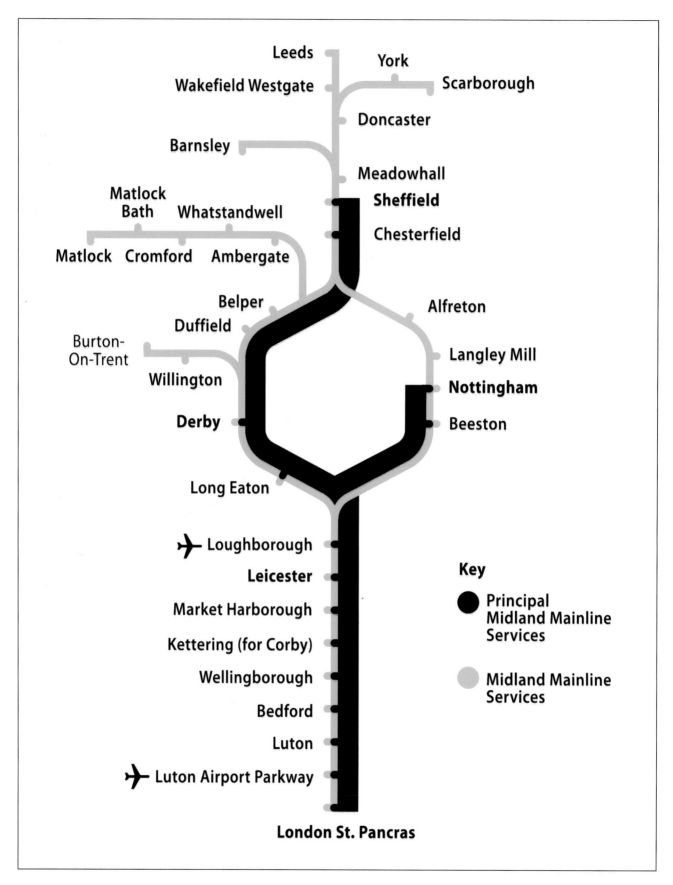

ABOVE Midland Main Line route map, showing the new direct services to Scarborough, Barnsley, Matlock and Burton-on-Trent.
Andrew Smithers

ABOVE 'Turbostar' No 170109 on the new St Pancras–Barnsley service on 4 May 2000. *Gavin Morrison*

RIGHT Midland Mainline launches its teal & tangerine livery together with new uniforms at St Pancras on 10 February 1997. *East Midlands Trains*

The enlarged fleet also provided the opportunity to experiment with direct London services to a range of new destinations such as Burton-on-Trent, Barnsley, Belper – and even Scarborough on summer Saturdays.

Since the InterCity brand was no longer available to the new train operators, the image of the route's HSTs and new 'Turbostars' needed to be brought together under one new Midland Mainline brand. The choice of livery finally came down to two options — a traditional maroon design or a more radical 'tangerine and teal' option. Both were market-tested with customers and staff. A clear majority of passengers preferred the fresh teal and tangerine, and this option was chosen despite the strong reservations of the senior management team. In the event the customers proved to be right!

Richard Brown's stated goal was to double passenger numbers by the end of the franchise. The team was therefore encouraged to use its new freedom to introduce sales campaigns tailored to individual markets. Where InterCity tended to think in terms of generic national advertising, Midland Mainline wanted local offers that would attract motorists away from the adjacent M1. One memorable innovation was '4-Sight', a new fare designed to attract leisure passengers away from their cars by taking up to four people to London for £39 return – the price of a tank of petrol in those days.

Another idea was a 'London Day Out' ticket, which included a full restaurant-car breakfast on Saturdays. The company quickly gained a reputation for innovation and for customer focus after winning Derbyshire Chamber of Commerce's 'Award for New Business' in 1998 and the 'Train Operator of the Year Award' in 1999.

The new train services were expanding into an untapped market so quickly that the three-car 'Turbostars' were unable to cope. An investment case

LEFT An InterCity
Midland Main Line menu.
East Midlands Trains

ABOVE Midland Mainline's marketing campaigns focused on
the local market in contrast to InterCity's generic advertising.
East Midlands Trains

was made for replacing them with a 125mph 'Voyager'-style fleet, but whilst National Express was once again a willing investor, it could not get a return on its investment within the remaining years of the franchise. To solve the impasse, the Strategic Rail Authority agreed a three-year extension to the franchise in return for investment in a new fleet of 'Meridian' units, the order being placed in 2004 for 23 units with train lengths varying from four to nine cars.

Richard Brown was promoted to Chief Executive of the new Train Division of National Express in 1997 and was succeeded by Nick Brown, another member of the original management-buyout team. In due course Nick Brown too was promoted – to lead the Bus Division at National Express – and his role was taken on by former East Coast Managing Director, Brian Burdsall. Both took Midland Mainline's original business plan forward, further strengthening the foundations for sustained growth.

By this time Midland Mainline had developed a productive relationship with Railtrack's Midland Zone, which co-operated in making significant investment in facilitating growth by implementing key projects such as redoubling the layout at Wigston Junction and by building a fourth platform at Bedford to accommodate the 'Turbostars'. It had also initiated a number of important station schemes including the rebuilding of Chesterfield and an award-winning renovation of Sheffield station. They moved on to plan for a new station at East Midlands Parkway, but this was to be delayed for a number of years by objections from 'eon (UK)', the owners of the nearby Ratcliffe-on-Soar power station.

Performance collapse

Unfortunately the early successes of Midland Mainline were marred by a prolonged period of poor performance. This was not just the result of the Hatfield speed restrictions but was also partly triggered by the temporary extension of services to Manchester under the code-name 'Project Rio'. In addition the stable leadership of the early years had also evaporated and, as Table 12.1 shows, no fewer than nine managing directors were to provide leadership over the following 10 years.

Table 12.2 shows the prolonged slump in performance that lasted far beyond the Hatfield era,

ABOVE The 'Meridian' was a later version of the 'Voyager' and went through the same rigorous testing. No 220013 and SNCB locomotive No 1202 pose alongside one another at Kortrijk during test runs in Belgium. *Bob Sweet*

with punctuality dipping to 70% as late as 2003. The situation was only reversed when the Group Director for Rail, David Franks, doubled up as Managing Director Midland Mainline, and appointed Tim Shoveller as Operations Director to help him restore basic operating disciplines. They started with a 'Right Time Departure' campaign which famously included issuing whistles to every member of staff. They then tackled the chronic maintenance problems on the HST fleet, before re-writing a timetable where additional intermediate stops had been introduced to placate local pressure groups to the point where many schedules had become undeliverable. Even the flagship 'Master Cutler' express had been given an impossible two-hour 'headline' journey time which doomed it to a late arrival.

The performance initiatives were hugely successful and David Franks is rightly proud of the fact that only three years later in 2006, Midland Mainline was again awarded 'Best Train Company of the Year' with 92.4% average punctuality for the year. Passenger satisfaction mirrored this achievement, peaking at a record 88% in 2007. Midland Mainline was a classic example of how quickly train performance could collapse – but also how quickly it could be recovered when experienced operators restored basic disciplines.

Table 12.1: Midland Mainline in privatisation

Time frame	
1996	First franchise, 1996-2007 Midland Mainline long-distance franchise Won by National Express Group
2007	Second franchise, 2007-15 East Midland Trains regional franchise Won by Stagecoach plc
Managing Directors	
1996	Richard Brown MD, Midland Mainline (National Express Group)
1997	Nick Brown MD, Midland Mainline (National Express Group)
1999	Brian Burdsall MD, Midland Mainline (National Express Group)
2001	Alan Wilson MD, Midland Mainline (National Express Group)
2003	David Franks MD, Midland Mainline (National Express Group)
2004	Paul Bunting MD, Midland Mainline (National Express Group)
2006	Peter Cotton MD, Midland Mainline (National Express Group)
2007	Garry Raven MD, Midland Mainline (National Express Group)
2007	Tim Shoveller MD, East Midlands Trains (Stagecoach plc)
2012	David Horne MD, East Midlands Trains (Stagecoach plc)

East Midlands Trains

Midland Mainline was to be the last of the ex-InterCity companies to be merged back into its regional network. This was done in a way that maintained a distinct long-distance operation alongside a network of inter-urban trains. The change came in 2007 when the DfT used the second Midland Mainline franchise to re-draw its services. A new East Midlands Trains franchise was created by splitting Central Trains' services and combining its East Midlands operation with Midland Mainline.

The expectation was that National Express would win the franchise after its impressive performance recovery, but it was to be beaten by Stagecoach, which maintained the positive period of performance and development. Tim Shoveller was brought back from West Coast in 2007 and finally gave the franchise stability of leadership for five uninterrupted years.

Tim Shoveller spent some time uniting his two very different franchise teams, as he wanted them to feel that this was a merger and not a takeover. He established a base for the new Central Trains team at Nottingham, whilst symbolically moving Midland Mainline out of its Derby headquarters to a new base at Pride Park in Derby. Both teams were then united by the new Stagecoach uniform and the re-branding of the two fleets in the Stagecoach East Midlands livery.

A further step-change in performance came when Network Rail created a new East Midland Route team, also in 2007, to mirror the train franchise. This led to a close alliance between the two organisations which brought continuous improvements in both train reliability and train planning. The new alliance also created the radical 2008 timetable which accelerated long-distance services. The overcrowding problems were resolved by re-forming the 'Meridian' units into five- and seven-car units, supported by the acquisition of four additional sister Class 222 'Pioneer' units from Hull Trains.

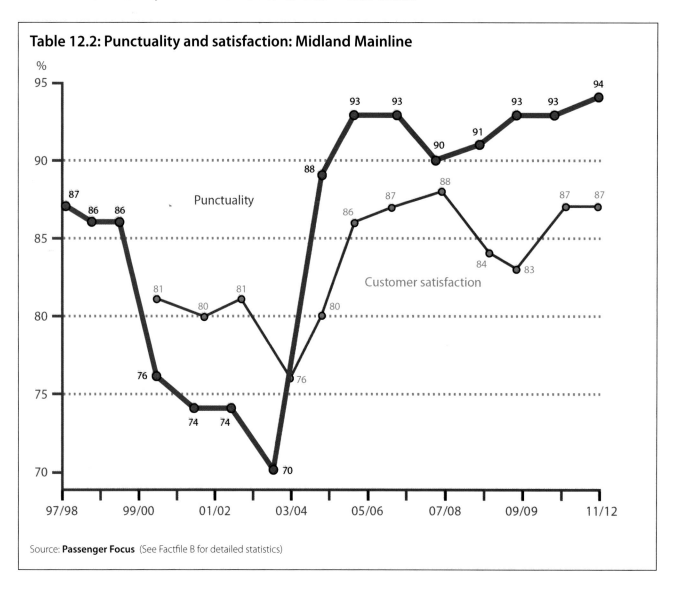

Table 12.2: Punctuality and satisfaction: Midland Mainline

Source: **Passenger Focus** (See Factfile B for detailed statistics)

ABOVE HST power car No 43051 departs Derby station on 14 June 2004 at the head of a St Pancras–Sheffield express. Although this example was clearly in excellent external condition, by this time the Midland Mainline HST fleet was becoming increasingly unreliable. *Gavin Morrison*

The 2008 timetable delivered the original vision of two trains an hour between London and Sheffield but, as Tim Shoveller put it, 'we still had 125mph train fleets running over 110mph track'. Network Rail agreed a £70 million investment package in 2011 which will finally deliver 10 minutes' acceleration to bring Sheffield below the magic two-hour threshold in 2013/14. This project will finally raise Midland Mainline's line speed from 110 to 125mph at the southern end of the route, thus delivering another InterCity aspiration.

The 2008 timetable improvements were also supported by the delivery of the £93 million investment commitments in Stagecoach's winning bid. These led to the opening of the £8 million new East Midland Parkway station in 2009 to provide 850-car parking spaces close to both the M1 and the regional airport.

ABOVE 'Project Rio' put further stress on HST reliability as it attempted to provide an alternative London–Manchester service for West Coast passengers in 2003/4. *East Midlands Trains*

A new £10 million station was opened at Corby in the same year and the 'Pioneer' trains were used to operate a new fifth path out of London every hour to give Corby a direct service to London, whilst also strengthening the service to the intermediate stations. Investment was also made in improving maintenance facilities at both Derby Etches Park and London Cricklewood.

Stagecoach was unlucky to have launched its imaginative timetable improvements in the teeth of the 2008 economic recession. In the space of less than a year, the Master Cutler went from being overcrowded to half-empty. Despite this, Stagecoach honoured all its investment commitments through the recession, although it made savings by withdrawing most restaurant-car services and providing a First Class Trolley service instead.

Summary
Midland Mainline undoubtedly benefited from the sharper focus and greater independence that came with

ABOVE HST power car No 43083 shows off its new Stagecoach livery as leads the 0734 Leeds–St Pancras across the River Don at Attercliffe, Sheffield, on 11 July 2009. *Gavin Morrison*

privatisation. The new Midland Mainline franchise took full advantage of the freedom that its new owners were offered to accelerate the timetable, double service frequency and market new business. Despite its period of poor performance, Midland Mainline produced almost uninterrupted passenger growth, with the result that it delivered Richard Brown's original challenge to double its passenger numbers.

Table 12.3 shows that Midland Mainline more than tripled its train frequencies after privatisation, raised its punctuality to a record 94% and lifted its passenger satisfaction to 87%, despite the distraction of being merged into a regional franchise. Its recently-authorised upgrading and electrification programme should help the route achieve even greater success.

Table 12.3: Midland Mainline overview

	1997/98	2001/02	2011/12
Punctuality: Annual MAA	87%	74%	94%
Trains run: Daily weekdays	59	123	195
Avearage speed: London–Sheffield	70mph	70mph	70mph
Growth: Journeys per annum	6m	9m	13m
Satisfaction: Overall	81%*	80%	87%

* 2000/01

(See Factfile B for detailed statistics)

ABOVE Class 222 'Meridian' unit No 222007 provides welcome new capacity in the form of a nine-car set as it passes Harrowden Junction, Wellingborough, on the 1630 Nottingham–St Pancras. *Gavin Morrison*

BELOW A shorter (five-car) Class 222 unit in Stagecoach livery threads its way along the scenic Hope Valley. *East Midlands Trains*

ABOVE A contrast in liveries provided by HST power cars Nos 43007 and 43301 at Brush Traction on 16 July 2008. *Paul Bigland*

BELOW One of the few InterCity Parkway stations to be built since privatisation, East Midlands Parkway has been successful in abstracting traffic from the nearby M1. Here an HST glides into the station on 6 March 2012. *East Midlands Trains*

ABOVE David Horne, Managing Director, East Midlands Trains. *East Midlands Trains*

ABOVE Franchise tenders have brought a significant improvement in station information and ticket systems. Here customers are guided on their way at Sheffield on 9 May 2010. *Paul Bigland*

BELOW East Midlands Trains-liveried 43058 trails a Sheffield-bound service at Chesterfield as a southbound 'Voyager' also awaits departure. *Antony Christie*

CrossCountry

A difficult birth

CrossCountry assumed a new significance with the closure of InterCity in 1994, when it became Britain's only national passenger rail operator. This was a far cry from its early days in 1985, when a rag-bag of non-London 'cross-country' services was given to the new InterCity sector. A new CrossCountry sub-sector was formed, led by Brian Johnson, who fathered the development of CrossCountry over the following 20 years. He recollects that CrossCountry nearly did not make it into the InterCity family, when serious talk arose of transferring it into the Provincial Sector and equipping it with Class 158 'Express' units. But it was finally established as an InterCity sub-sector, and Brian Johnson is proud of the way his team rationalised an assortment of eclectic services into a more saleable hub-and-spoke network based on Birmingham.

But their work was hardly finished before CrossCountry was absorbed into a bigger Midland & CrossCountry operation under the InterCity 'OforQ'[1] proposals in 1992. Richard Brown was the new Route Director, and he was supported at CrossCountry by Chris Tibbits and Brian Johnson. This was a period of frustration in which CrossCountry was unable to

ABOVE Brian Johnson, long-term champion of the Cross-Country operation. *Brian Johnson collection*

Table 12.4: CrossCountry in Privatisation

Timeline	
1997	First franchise, 1997-2012 Virgin Group wins tender
2002	Virgin negotiates management contract
2002	'Operation Princess' launched
2004	SRA decides franchise to be re-tendered
2007	Second franchise, 2007-16 Arriva Trains wins franchise

Managing Directors	
1994	Chris Tibbits, Director BR Shadow Train Unit
1997	Brian Barrett, Virgin Trains (CEO)
1999	Chris Green, CEO Virgin Trains*
2004	Tony Collins, CEO Virgin Trains*
2007	Andy Cooper, MD (Arriva Trains Wales)

* Chris Gibb MD CrossCountry 2003-6

get either its planned cascade of Mk3 fleet coaches from the West Coast or the proposed new Class 48 locomotives to haul them. In 1994 Chris Tibbits – with his extensive knowledge of planning complex railways – was instrumental in preparing the route for franchising as a self-contained business.

Virgin won the 15-year franchise with an innovative bid which replaced every CrossCountry train with 352 new 'Voyager' coaches. CrossCountry was to be transformed from the lower rung of the rolling-stock cascade to the top with high-performance 125mph trains. This was a jaw-dropping proposition for the rail industry and was the key step in turning CrossCountry into a major train company with a turnover of some £640 million. Virgin went further and committed to transforming CrossCountry's subsidy into its first-ever profit by the end of the franchise.

But CrossCountry's new independence was to be short-lived. Just two months later Virgin won a matching 15-year bid for the West Coast franchise, and this raised the issue of how the two franchises were to be managed. The industry expectation was that they would be run as two separate franchises, but Virgin chose to merge them into a single Virgin Trains' unit and the bid leader, Brian Barrett, was appointed as CEO. CrossCountry was once again the junior partner in a much bigger operation and inevitably lost some focus and independence.

---

[1] Organising for Quality organisation (see Chapter 9)

ABOVE On 3 February 1997 HST power car No 43063 awaits departure with the first Virgin-liveried train from Bournemouth. *Bob Sweet*

BELOW The venerable Class 47 fleet was becoming increasingly unreliable by 24 February 2000, when Class 47/7 No 47712 was caught hurrying through Besford. *Bob Sweet*

CrossCountry routes

Change at one of
these stations
to avoid changing
at Birmingham
New Street.

CrossCountry routes ——— Summer weekend services – – – Connecting services ———

Please note: not all stations are shown

ABOVE Arriva CrossCountry route map *Arriva CrossCountry*

Cinderella to Princess

In 1999 Chris Green took over as Chief Executive of Virgin Trains with a remit to manage the transition period until the new train fleets and timetables were introduced. He coined the name 'Cinderella into Princess' for the CrossCountry mission, as he felt that this captured the dramatic overnight transformation of services that was planned. As CrossCountry struggled through the low point of 2000/01 with half the fleet out of service from flood damage and the remainder crawling through the speed restrictions, Sir Alastair Moreton wrote a supportive letter in March 2001 in which he summed up the significance of 'Cinderella into Princess', stating that '… it would be a tremendous morale-booster for the entire rail system if CrossCountry Trains became a showpiece instead of a tail-end Charlie'.

CrossCountry's big moment came when Virgin signed a £390 million contract for a complete fleet renewal. The company ordered a fleet of 78 new 'Voyager' trains, supported by a further £670 million contract with Bombardier to maintain the trains to the end of the franchise, together with a major new £30 million depot at Central Rivers, near Burton-on-Trent. The 'Voyagers' would not only promote CrossCountry

ABOVE Virgin CrossCountry was launched on Monday 6 January 1997, when the first refurbished and re-liveried HST was used on the Edinburgh-Penzance service – the 'Cornish Scot'. Here the set is being prepared at Neville Hill depot, Leeds, on 3 January 1997. *Chris Dixon*

ABOVE On Monday 3 February 1997 Virgin CrossCountry launched itself in the North West by naming an HST power car *Lady in Red* prior to its departure on the 0817 'Pines Express' from Manchester to Bournemouth. In true Virgin style, a cake was made especially for the occasion. *Bob Sweet*

ABOVE The new £30m Central Rivers depot provided a single 'mother ship' for the entire CrossCountry fleet. Here specialist jacks lift an entire train off the depot floor to a comfortable working height. *Arriva CrossCountry*

BELOW Two pre-formed front ends await their turn of duty at Central Rivers. *Arriva CrossCountry*

ABOVE Arriva CrossCountry 'Voyagers' undergo maintenance at Central Rivers depot, situated alongside the Birmingham–Derby line. *Matthew Wilson*

into the 125mph league but would also take it into the tilting league with Class 221 'Super Voyagers'.

The decision to introduce 'Voyagers' was controversial, as it meant replacing seven-coach trains on broadly hourly frequencies with four or five-coach trains at double the frequency. Virgin had agonised over making all the trains five- or even six-car, but it could not justify the extra investment at over £1 million a coach. The second controversial decision was to order tilting 'Super Voyagers' for use on the West Coast Upgrade north of Stafford, as the 6° tilt had the side effect of reducing the bodyshell width for both fleets, whilst the narrower tilt profile restricted the size of the overhead luggage racks and the width of the aisles and seats.

Virgin had not just committed to a new train fleet; it had also promised a radical new timetable which would cut journey times by 20%. Table 12.5 shows the revolutionary nature of the journey accelerations that were proposed, but delivering these aspirations on

Table 12.5: 2002 timetable aspirations

Birmingham to	1999	2002	Acceleration
Bristol	1hr 30	1hr 10	20%
Edinburgh	5hr 11	4hr 33	12%
Manchester	1hr 44	1hr 23	20%
Newcastle	3hr 16	2hr 48	14%
Reading	1hr 50	1hr 27	21%

Source: Virgin CrossCountry

an increasingly congested network was to be another matter. The national nature of the CrossCountry timetable meant that all seven Railtrack Zones had to be involved in every decision as a completely new interval timetable was carved across Britain. Chris Green remembers supporting the project team through endless timetabling sessions between 2000 and 2002, which then escalated into 'Town Hall'-size meetings where 13 train companies, five PTEs, and 120 local authorities had to be consulted.

The core timetabling principle was the establishment of an hourly-interval pattern through Birmingham. CrossCountry was planning to run an awesome 424 trains arrivals and departures a day through the most congested station outside London. This meant identifying 10 arrival and 10 departing slots every hour. It was agreed that every operator would adapt its services to the new hourly interval at the Birmingham hub and that the ripple effects would be managed across the network.

At one point CrossCountry came close to introducing a new five-car HST 'Challenger' fleet with power cars named as 'Western Challenger' etc. This would have meant sets running every two hours between Paddington, Swindon, Cheltenham, Birmingham and Manchester. However, as the complications multiplied and the difficulties increased, the idea was dropped.

ABOVE The initial 'Voyager' trains were built at Bruges, Belgium, and had their test runs on Belgian metals. Here No 220001 and SNCB EMU No 714 provide an interesting contrast while stabled at Ostend on 28 November 2000. *Bob Sweet*

BELOW On 8 October 2002 there was a major failure of a 'Voyager' alongside the Dawlish sea wall, where saltwater spray left the set stranded without power. A solution was quickly found, and, on a much calmer day, another 'Voyager' is seen running unhesitatingly past the sea wall at Teignmouth. *Bob Sweet*

ABOVE Heading south on the West Coast main line, a 'Super Voyager' leans gracefully into the curve at Wreay on 26 October 2004. *MP92½*

The new timetable depended on line-speed improvements which would raise more than half the CrossCountry's extensive network to 100mph or more. Despite its growing financial problems Railtrack bravely signed a £200 million package with Virgin in March 2001. This was used to improve junction capacity at Reading, Didcot and Bristol as well as raising line speeds over 300 miles of track. Virgin contributed a further £80 million to enhance track speeds to 100-125mph where appropriate. The project was to involve over 500 track possessions on the core network, which further worsened performance in the short term and which was not completed until a year after the new timetable took effect.

The timetable specification ultimately went through 80 consultation iterations before it was finalised – and only then could it be given to the six Railtrack Zones to be turned into robust slots for the 2002 timetable. By this time, huge management effort was also being diverted into keeping the ageing CrossCountry fleets operational and both performance and passenger satisfaction were in freefall. Chris Green feels that it was quite remarkable that the timetable deadline was ever achieved, bearing in mind that the work was being done in the midst of the industry's nervous breakdown; the impact of national flooding and the collapse of Railtrack.

Launch and collapse

The initial launch of 'Operation Princess' in September 2003 was a great success. The marketing campaign included a national TV advert supported by an extensive regional marketing campaign. Richard Branson led a major launch event in Birmingham with civic and media representatives from all the destinations to be served. The new timetable met with a phenomenal response and released repressed demand for better cross-country services. Within just six months, CrossCountry was carrying 40% more passengers, thanks to the huge increase in frequencies which had almost doubled services from Birmingham to Reading and Bristol and had actually tripled the frequency to Newcastle as shown in Table 12.8.

Alas, it was to be a false start. Poor performance was once again to dog a franchise's success. Table 12.6 shows the drop in train performance that followed the launch of the new timetable. The Railtrack zones had done their best to find paths across the network but they were not robust paths. The network had become far more congested in the five years since the bid was accepted, and the CrossCountry slots had not been protected whilst the new trains were being built. CrossCountry

ABOVE Arriva Trains increased CrossCountry capacity by bringing back five refurbished HSTs, one of which is seen approaching Berwick-upon-Tweed on an Anglo-Scottish service. *Matthew Wilson*

ABOVE 'Voyagers' were identified by red nameplates and 'Super Voyagers' by blue. Here 78 princesses make the point at the launch of 'Operation Princess' on 30 September 2003. *MP92½*

LEFT Richard Branson and Julie Beck-Richards of Virgin Trains pose with a 'Princess' and a 'Cinderella' at the Birmingham launch. *Colin J. Marsden*

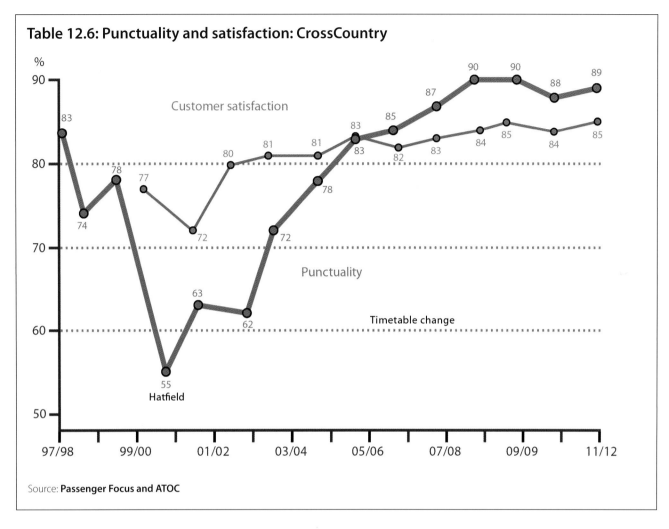

Table 12.6: Punctuality and satisfaction: CrossCountry

Source: **Passenger Focus and ATOC**

had become a victim of fragmented railway planning in a period of rapid growth and increasing congestion. The only solution was to sit down with Railtrack, now in railway administration, and pragmatically evolve the new timetable into something that the operators could reliably deliver. The choice lay between leasing more trains to match the slower schedules – or shrinking the network to match the 78 trains available.

Virgin again tried to make an investment case for lengthening all 'Voyagers' to five cars, but this still proved resolutely uneconomic. It then asked the SRA to fund the retention of the remaining five HSTs to restore seven-car trains on the busy Plymouth–Newcastle route but this too was rejected on financial grounds. All that could realistically be done was to shrink the destinations served and divert the trains saved to relieve the overcrowded central core.

This led to the withdrawal of the new interval services to Liverpool, Cardiff, Portsmouth and Brighton. Chris Green remembers this as a time when the industry came together and the SRA, ORR and Railtrack all supported Virgin Trains in finding swift

compromises. An entire timetable involving the whole national network was re-written in just six months – in stark contrast to the two years that would normally be needed for the process. The result of this teamwork was a resounding success and Table 12.6 also shows the dramatic improvements in punctuality that followed from May 2003.

The 2003 timetable triggered a period of continuous improvement on CrossCountry in both performance and passenger satisfaction which was to be maintained for the remaining decade. It was finally recognised that the operation of West Coast and CrossCountry had to be separated and Chris Gibb was appointed to the new post of Managing Director CrossCountry in 2003. Punctuality rose to an unprecedented 90% for two successive years and passenger satisfaction reached an equally unprecedented 85%. Both business and leisure travel continued to rise, and by 2005 passenger journeys reached 20 million – a doubling of travel since 1994 despite all the problems. Table 12.7 charts the remarkable impact that the new train fleet and timetable had on customer satisfaction.

An independent franchise

But even as CrossCountry was turning into a Princess, Virgin Trains was facing financial problems on its West Coast PUG2 contract which were to put both franchises into a temporary management contract. This led to an abrupt decision by the SRA in 2004 to re-tender the CrossCountry franchise, but to leave Virgin running it under a management contract until 2006.

Arriva Trains won the re-tender in 2007, delivering a sad blow to Virgin which had put so much into giving CrossCountry a complete makeover. But at least CrossCountry had finally become an independent franchise from 2007, and, as Brian Johnson likes to say, 'CrossCountry was always at its best when run as a stand-alone company.' Arriva Trains then appointed Andy Cooper as Managing Director, with a mission to turn CrossCountry into a premium-paying business.

The new franchise required Arriva CrossCountry to take on the Cardiff–Nottingham–Stansted Airport services together with their Class 170 fleet. The 2008 VHF West Coast timetable also triggered big changes at CrossCountry as it ceased operating to Scotland via the West Coast and had to transfer 21 'Super Voyagers' to Virgin West Coast. Arriva considered increasing the 'Voyagers' to five cars but instead did what Virgin had sought to do in 2003 and leased five HST sets, following a £5 million refurbishment to increase their seating, to provide extra capacity on the core Newcastle–Plymouth route.

Having established a reliable product, Andy Cooper moved on to create his own revolution through information technology. His vision was to make electronic ticketing the norm – whether through E-ticketing, with tickets collected at station machines, or M-ticketing, whereby a barcode on a mobile phone actually becomes the ticket. Arriva was also starting to allow passengers to make a seat reservation whilst the train was on the move, using the 'Voyagers' electronic seat-reservation system. Passengers could also use the real-time information to check train performance, to buy their tickets, to make

Table 12.7: CrossCountry satisfaction

% Satisfaction	2001 Old fleet	2004 New fleet
Punctuality	46%	77%
Frequency of trains	58	78
Comfort of seats	71	79
Staff helpfulness	82	88
Cleanliness of trains	72	90
Overall journey	65	85

Source: National Passenger Survey

real-time reservations – and to communicate with Arriva through sites such as Twitter.

An increasingly sophisticated yield management model was allowing CrossCountry to vary seat prices daily to fill every possible seat. Costs were being cut on catering services, and Arriva created extra seats by eliminating the shop and replacing it with a trolley service. Despite being badly affected by the 2008 economic recession, all of these measures finally enabled CrossCountry to turn the financial corner, and in 2010/11 CrossCountry paid a premium to Government for the first time – ironically exactly as the original Virgin franchise had planned.

Summary

Virgin Trains gave CrossCountry a modern 125mph train fleet and almost tripled its train services. Arriva Trains brought extra capacity and a software revolution which has continued to fill the seats. Between them they honoured Virgin's original commitment to double CrossCountry's passengers and eliminate its subsidy. In doing so, they created a £640 million turnover national train company which is, at the time of writing, amongst the most punctual of the long-distance companies and enjoys an 84% customer satisfaction.

Table 12.8: CrossCountry overview

	1997/98	2001/02	2011/12
Punctuality: Annual MAA	83%	63%	89%
Trains run: Daily (weekdays)	94	123	281
Average speed: Birmingham–Newcastle	59mph*	59mph	62mph
Growth: Journeys per annum	10m	15m	27m
Satisfaction: Overall	77%**	72%	84%

* 1992 / ** 2000/01

ABOVE CrossCountry supplements its electronic information systems with the human touch. Here a Customer Sales Assistant 'makes the difference' at Birmingham New Street station. *Arriva CrossCountry*

ABOVE Andy Cooper, Managing Director of Arriva CrossCountry Trains, prepares to catch one of his own sets north from Bristol Temple Meads. *Arriva CrossCountry*

LEFT Birmingham New Street has been the hub of CrossCountry operations since 1986. Network Rail's major station reconstruction will provide a more prestigious marketing hub from 2015. *Network Rail*

RIGHT A microcosm of today's privatised and quasi-competitive railway: an Arriva CrossCountry 'Voyager', an East Midlands Trains 'Meridian' and a Grand Central HST (headed by power car No 43423 Valenta) line up for business at Network Rail's refurbished station at Derby. *Antony Christie*

Chapter 13
GATWICK, ANGLIA AND WESTERN

ABOVE The Gatwick Express franchise inherited an ageing Class 73 push-pull fleet that was in urgent need of replacement. Here No 73208, with blinds already turned to red, gets ready to propel an early-evening service from Gatwick to London Victoria on 12 March 2005. *Antony Christie*

Gatwick Express

If evidence were needed that the railway had been over-fragmented at privatisation, the key case in point was to be Gatwick Express. It had originally been transferred to InterCity in 1985 as a cash-cow dowry, and InterCity duly applied its quality standards to transform it into a prestige airport shuttle service. The potential marketing conflict with the other, much bigger train operator – Network SouthEast – was avoided because BR managed the interface and discouraged predatory behaviour. This was all to change with privatisation.

In preparation for franchising, Gatwick Express was separated from the joint Anglia & Gatwick route in 1994 and Rob Mason took the lead as BR's Shadow Director. Gatwick Express was franchised as a small 'niche' franchise in 1996 and became one of the first franchises to be let – and the only ex-InterCity franchise which did not need an initial subsidy under the new track-access regime. The tender was won by National Express, and two experienced BR managers were put in charge, with Mac McIntosh as Managing Director and Jackie Townsend as Service Delivery Director.

The new niche franchise demonstrated all the entrepreneurial diversity that could have been expected of it. The private owners funded a new train fleet which was purpose-built for the route with extra luggage space

and a luxurious First Class accommodation. Just eight new Class 460 'Juniper' trains were provided to replace the 14 ageing Class 73 locomotives and their Mk2 coaches, which had not even made it onto InterCity's investment list.

Gatwick Express was able to negotiate cutting-edge manning agreements with the same unions that had tried to deny BR more flexible rostering. The drivers rotated with the senior conductors to mitigate the boredom of a short shuttle route: the customer service teams were paid more for multi-lingual skills – and the passengers were allowed to pay on board without penalty.

Jackie Townsend recalls that: 'we were only a small team of 328 people and it is hard to exaggerate the motivating effect that this operating flexibility had on our morale'. Gatwick Express raised its prices above those of the local operator – Connex Trains and later Southern – to reflect a quality service that ran round the clock, including Christmas Day, and which delivered 93% punctuality and 95% customer satisfaction.

But Gatwick Express was generating head-to-head competition with its aggressive marketing approach, and

BELOW Gatwick Express ordered a brand-new fleet of purpose-built Class 460 units for the airport shuttle. Here No 460001 passes through Clapham Junction on 29 April 2003. *Bob Sweet*

Table 13.1: Gatwick Express in privatisation

Timeline	
1996	Gatwick Express franchise Won by National Express Group
2008	Absorbed into South Central for one year
2009	Greater Southern franchise Won by Go-Ahead (Southern)
Managing Directors	
1994	Rob Mason MD, BR Shadow Train Unit
1996	Mac McIntosh MD, Gatwick Express (National Express)
2000	Peter Cotton MD, Gatwick Express (National Express)
2002	David Stretch MD, Gatwick Express (National Express)
2009	Chris Burchell MD, Southern (Go-Ahead)

the rival operators could not afford to turn a blind eye. By 2003 Go-Ahead's Southern Railway was undercutting Gatwick Express's £13.50 fare with a £7.50 ticket that was heavily promoted at both Victoria and Gatwick Airport, but which was only available on Southern trains.

The resulting loss of income to Gatwick Express was compounded by the impact of the 9/11 terrorist attacks in the USA, which had a sobering effect on Gatwick Airport passenger numbers as many of the high-value airlines returned to Heathrow Airport. The half-empty shuttle trains then became vulnerable to the argument that they were wasting valuable peak capacity, and the DfT duly merged the two franchises into a 2008 Greater Southern tender, despite protests from Gatwick Airport and its airlines.

It had proved impossible for a small niche franchise to offer head-to-head competition within a much larger franchise. David may have been swifter of foot, but – without BR regulation – Goliath had the resources to win the pricing and marketing war. Gatwick Express ceased to be a bespoke inter-city franchise from 2008. GoAhead won the new Greater Southern franchise after committing to retain a distinctive 'Express' service within its portfolio, which would be extended to Brighton in the peak periods. It also replaced the purpose-built Gatwick Express trains with older Class 442 'Wessex' units. Gatwick Express returned to its roots inside the larger Southern franchise with its original GatEx sets planned for conversion back to standard 'Juniper' units for South Western Trains.

Anglia Railways

Anglia Railways was destined to mirror Gatwick's fate under privatisation after it was set up as a small niche operation, within the Great Eastern network. The London–Norwich route had joined InterCity in 1985, when Andy Cooper was appointed to run the combined Anglia & Gatwick operation. He chose to stay with Anglia when the route was split for privatisation in 1994 – and when GB Railways won the franchise two years later it retained both the Anglia Railways name and Andy Cooper as Managing Director.

Like Gatwick Express, Anglia Railways epitomised the entrepreneurial spirit that the more centralised InterCity did not always encourage. The new franchise was owned by a creative consortium that was ready to take financial risk. It was one of the first franchises to commit to doubling the frequency of its ex-InterCity services to half-hourly in 1999. Andy Cooper remembers this as a 'leap of faith for a small company' – and certainly not a leap that he would have considered when he was at InterCity.

The new franchise included some rather unloved local services in the Norwich area, and the new owners ordered a fleet of eight Class 170 'Turbostar' diesel units to exploit the potential of these routes and to provide new direct links to London from Yarmouth, Sheringham and Lowestoft. Andy Cooper contrasts the speed of decision-making for this new investment with the tortuous process that BR would have had to

follow. GB Railways then stretched its 'Turbostar' fleet to launch an innovative 'London CrossLink' service in 2000 which ran six services a day from Ipswich to Basingstoke with a call at Highbury & Islington on the North London Line.

However, this was to prove to be the high-water mark of entrepreneurialism on the franchise. Like Gatwick Express, Anglia Railways was to prove too small a franchise to hold its own against aggressive competition and an adverse economy. Anglia had chosen head-to-head competition because it needed to fill the extra seats on its new half-hourly Norwich service by calling at lucrative commuter stations such as Chelmsford, Manningtree and Ingatestone. But Chelmsford was a key station in the rival Great Eastern franchise and it provoked FirstGroup to extend its own services to Ipswich – previously an Anglia monopoly. This created a rival half-hourly service from Ipswich to London at much cheaper walk-up fares and without the need for Anglia's advanced seat reservations.

Bob Breakwell, Managing Director of the Great Eastern franchise, reflected that the competition for stops and paths was de-stabilising for both franchises, but the company had to respond to protect its own core

BELOW Anglia ordered 'Turbostar' diesel units to provide a new Ipswich-Basingstoke service. Here No 170208 passes Riventall, near Witham, on the 1012 Ipswich–Basingstoke on 23 December 2001. *Antony Guppy*

ABOVE Full English breakfast, Anglia-style. The catering crew offer a warm welcome to customers on 2 February 2000. *Anglia Railways*

income. The reality was that, without BR's internal regulation, the bigger fish in the pond had greater firepower and deeper pockets. Anglia Railway suffered seriously at Ipswich, and just months later were faced with the further drop in traffic that followed the post-Hatfield speed restrictions. GB Railways had to apply to the SRA in December 2000 for its franchise to be converted into a management contract in which it received cash support.

GB Railways was forced to withdraw its new London CrossLink service in September 2002 due to lack of demand, but it used the displaced 'Turbostars' to launch a new direct Norwich–Cambridge express service in September 2002 which was to double travel on the route in the following 10 years.

But despite this success, Anglia Railways sold out to its FirstGroup rivals in 2003. In its short six-year history it had increased passenger travel by 75% and revenue by 84%. It had also won the prestigious Charter Mark for quality of service on three separate occasions, supported by its popular train catering, its extensive advance purchase tickets and its modern information systems. Above all, it had united the quality standards of InterCity with the entrepreneurial flair of GB Railways. It had been a potent mix.

The Anglia experience helped to convince the newly formed SRA that parts of the railway had been over-fragmented at privatisation, and in 2004 it announced that Anglia Railways, Great Eastern and West Anglia were to be re-tendered in 2004 as a single Greater Anglia franchise. It made good sense to have a single franchise operator on the complex and overcrowded

routes out of London's Liverpool Street station, and competition in Anglia would in future be restricted to the winning of the franchise.

National Express won the Greater Anglia franchise in 2004 and appointed Tim Clarke from Anglia Railways to be the first Managing Director. The franchise specification saw more paths on the main line allocated to container trains to Felixstowe Port, and this required the withdrawal of duplicate Great Eastern services to Ipswich. This in turn led to the deceleration of the Norwich expresses by the inclusion of additional intermediate stops, although this was balanced by the upgrading of the Norwich services with Class 90 locomotives and Mk3 coaches cascaded from the West Coast.

National Express under Dominic Booth and Andrew Chivers went on to restore performance to a respectable 86%, but mounting financial problems forced them to withdraw the popular restaurant-car service in 2009. Despite further service upgrades, on-board wi-fi and investment in longer trains, National Express lost the franchise to Abellio in 2012.

Abellio adopted the Greater Anglia brand name and recognised that passengers on its flagship London–Ipswich–Norwich route expected InterCity standards to be retained and improved. They responded with the introduction of free tea and coffee in First Class for the first time – and also began exploring further on-board improvements. They also worked with other operators in finding ways of accelerating the flagship services on the congested Great Eastern main line. The record 1hr 21min run from London to Norwich in 2004 shows the potential for significant acceleration on a journey that normally takes 1 hour 54 minutes.

ABOVE Greater Anglia Managing Director Ruud Haket's rail career began when he joined NedTrain, the maintenance arm of Netherlands Railways, in 1996. Abellio took over a short franchise in February 2012, lasting just over two years. *Greater Anglia*

ABOVE Class 90 No 90009 *Diamond Jubilee* propels the 1733 Shenfield–Norwich towards Marks Tey on 7 May 2012. *Antony Guppy*

Western

Unlike Anglia and Gatwick, Great Western was a big fish in a big pond and had the critical mass needed to face the crises ahead. Despite this, it was still destined to follow the roller-coaster ride that seemed to dog every franchise at some point.

An innovative start

Great Western had always been a proud member of the InterCity family and was also the home of the world-class HST diesel train. Brian Scott was able to provide the perfect transition from his early role as Route Director to BR Shadow Director in 1994 and then to winning a management buyout in 1996 for GW Holdings Ltd. He vividly remembers that they nearly didn't win the franchise, as the tender was initially awarded to Renaissance Railways, which failed to raise the funding within the deadline. GW Holdings was then awarded a franchise that was extended by OPRAF from seven to 10 years at a second ceremony. The MBO partners in GW Holdings Ltd included Badgerline Holdings (24.5%) and 3i Investors (24.5%)

Table 13.2: Anglia in privatisation

Timeline	
1997	First franchise, 1997-2004 GB Railways wins tender
2000	GB Railways onto management contract
2003	FirstGroup buys GB Railways
2004	Second franchise, 2004-2012 National Express Group wins tender
2012	Third franchise, 2012-2016 Abellio win short franchise

Managing Directors		
1994	Andy Cooper	Director BR Shadow Train Co
1997	Andy Cooper	MD, Anglia Railways (GB Rail)
1998	Tim Clarke	MD, Anglia Railways (GB Rail)
2004	Tim Clarke	MD, ONE Railway (National Express)
2006	Dominic Booth	MD, ONE Railway (National Express)
2007	Andrew Chivers	MD, East Anglia (National Express)
2012	Ruud Haket	MD, Greater Anglia (Abellio)

ABOVE A further change of livery is shown by HST power car No 43012 at Westbury on 13 September 2003. *Bob Sweet*

– but this partnership did not remain in place for long. FirstGroup bought Badgerline in 1997 and then went on to buy out both GW Holdings and 3i's share to create First Great Western. It faced an undemanding commitment to reduce a subsidy of £61 million to £27 million by the end of the franchise. The continuity from BR InterCity to Great Western franchise was almost seamless, with the whole team surviving the transition and hitting the ground running as they exploited their new freedom to invest and innovate.

Richard George became Deputy MD and sought to keep the best of InterCity. He ensured that the early marketing material used phrases such as: 'Great Western – providing InterCity services to Bristol', but when he asked OPRAF whether all long-distance franchises would be required to adopt the InterCity brand he was told that this would not be possible. From that point onwards, the InterCity brand was dead and GW Holdings developed its own green train livery – which included a 'Merlin' bird symbol that bore a striking resemblance to the InterCity swallow.

This was a period of marketing innovation in which Great Western pioneered free trolley services in First Class, the abolition of smoking, the first Quiet Coaches,

pilot Family Coaches at weekends and an experimental return of Motorail to the West of England. GW Holdings' big marketing initiative was the doubling of frequencies on both the Bristol and Cardiff routes to half-hourly.

Where InterCity had a two-dimensional focus on speed and quality, Great Western went three-dimensional and introduced frequency into the formula. Long-distance services were to rise steadily from 134 trains a day at privatisation to 195 fifteen years later – an increase of almost 50% on an already well-developed railway.

The extra resources for the half-hourly Bristol services in 1998 were found by experienced insiders who knew how to tighten the existing train diagrams and crew rosters. But the additional Cardiff services in 2002 required investment in a fleet of 14 new 'Adelante' Class 180 diesel units – which ended the search for an affordable five-car HST. This new 125mph fleet offered modern passenger comfort together with a high level of acceleration for the intermediate stops that were being added. HST-fleet productivity was also improved at this time through a new single-manning agreement for 125mph running.

Unlike Anglia and Gatwick in its early days, Great Western was also willing to enter into partnerships with its rivals on the route. Despite their competition

ABOVE Great Western sought to maintain the InterCity link by developing a 'Merlin' brand which echoed the InterCity swallow. Here HST power cars 43183 and 43185 leave Bristol Temple Meads for St Philip's Marsh depot following the brand launch in 1996. *Bob Sweet*

BELOW The last Motorail service was provided by the 'Night Riviera' sleeper to Paddington, on 16/17 September 2005. Motive power was provided by Class 47/4 No 47840, seen in the background. *Antony Christie*

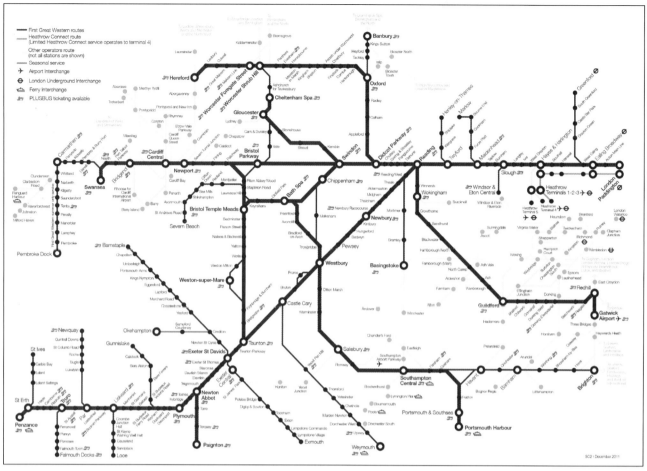

ABOVE Greater Western route map 2012. *FirstGroup*

over stopping patterns in the lucrative Thames Valley area, Great Western and Thames Trains created a new Bristol–Swindon–Oxford joint service by pooling their track-access rights. However, this innovation was destined to be short-lived, becoming one of the many victims of the post-Hatfield speed restrictions.

Performance collapse

Great Western's honeymoon was only to last a year before being overshadowed by an endemic instability which arose from a string of serious train accidents, followed by constant changes of management. Table 13.3 charts the collapse in train performance that was to take nine years to restore and shows the impact that this had on passenger satisfaction scores.

The accidents started in 1997 when a Great Western HST passed a signal at red before hitting a freight train in a high-speed collision at Southall, leaving seven people dead. The second accident came in 1999 just outside Paddington at Ladbroke Grove, where a Thames Train passed a signal at red and collided head-on with another Great Western HST, leaving 31 people dead and no fewer than 520 injured. Yet another Great

Western HST came to grief in 2004 in a level-crossing collision at Ufton Nervet, where a further seven people died and around 100 were injured.

It is small wonder that these headline accidents created a crisis of confidence – or that they sapped public support for the newly-privatised rail industry. The effect on Great Western was especially traumatic and the company was fined £1.5 million for its failure to have an operational train protection system at Southall.

Moir Lockhead, Chief Executive of FirstGroup, went on to become a leading crusader for rail safety thereafter and supported the radical improvement in train safety systems that followed across the industry. But the safety crises helped to take managerial eyes off the performance ball, and Great Western went into melt-down after 2000 as the HSTs struggled though endless speed restrictions in the wake of GNER's Hatfield derailment. Table 13.3 shows that it was to take eight years before its performance returned to a stable 85%.

Franchise instability

Performance recovery on the Great Western was further

Table 13.3: Punctuality and satisfaction: Gatwick, Anglia and Western

%

Punctuality

Customer Satisfaction

97/98 · 99/00 · 01/02 · 03/04 · 05/06 · 07/08 · 09/10 · 11/12

Source: **Passenger Focus** (See Factfile B for detailed statistics)

delayed by organisational instabilities. FirstGroup won a bid to operate Thames Trains in 2004, albeit that it had to operate it as a parallel franchise called Great Western Link. Then in 2006 the Department of Transport went further and combined Great Western, Great Western Link and Wessex Trains into a new regional franchise called Greater Western. FirstGroup won this bid too, together with the task of bringing three very different railways together – and committing to a premium of more than £1 billion to the DfT over the life of the 10-year franchise.

The new franchise got off to a bad start with a three-year collapse in performance that followed the instability of integrating three companies. The situation was compounded by a continuation of the leadership changes that had bedeviled the Great Western franchise from the beginning. Table 13.4 shows that Great Western had no less than nine Managing Directors in the first 12 years of privatisation, whilst the parallel Network Rail route suffered a similar handicap. A further problem lay in the dysfunctional contracts that the players were trying to deliver. The new franchisee was required to reduce the train fleet in a period of growth and Great Western and

DfT were soon in disagreement over how much rolling stock could be saved through the Greater Western mergers.

This resulted in a period of overcrowding of local trains in the Bristol and Thames Valley areas at a time of strong growth. The issue reached national television news when it was revealed that many of the West Country branches were being run by emergency bus services, whilst 17% of Great Western passengers were having to stand in the peak – the worst on any route. Whatever the rights and wrongs, the Bristol area problems were not solved until 147 vehicles were eventually provided in place of the 102 that were originally written into the franchise. The Thames Valley overcrowding was further improved by requiring some long-distance services to make extra peak-hour stops at Thames Valley commuter stations such as Slough and Maidenhead.

Meanwhile Great Western and its Network Rail route entered a prolonged public disagreement over who was responsible for the worsening punctuality and cancellations. The reality was that the problems lay with both teams, and ranged from HST train failures

ABOVE Moir Lockhead, Chief Executive (FirstGroup), and Alison Forster, Managing Director (First Great Western, reflect upon the nameplate commemorating the death of Stan Martin, the driver killed in the Ufton Nervet accident. Taken at the renaming of HST power car No 43009 as *First – Transforming Travel*, this picture shows the power car at the other end of that train. *Bob Sweet*

BELOW In 2006 Great Western and Thames Trains were combined to form a new Greater Western franchise. Here power cars 43124 and 43187 pass a 'Turbo' at Old Oak Common, on the approach to Paddington, on 2 April 2012. *Antony Christie*

ABOVE The Ladbroke Grove memorial, pictured in 2012. *Bob Sweet*

ABOVE Performance on First Great Western collapsed between 2000 and 2006. Here an HST stands at a red signal at Wallingford on 4 May 2006. *Paul Bigland*

and over-tight staff diagramming to chronic track conditions with mushrooming speed restrictions. The problems finally reached a stage where the DfT pressed the nuclear button and issued a formal Breach Notice on Great Western for the high levels of cancellations and passenger dissatisfaction in 2008. Only then did all players start to work in a more co-operative spirit that was brokered by the senior industry players.

The arrival of Andrew Haines as Managing Director in 2007 brought a new relationship with Network Rail in which contractual warfare was replaced with pragmatic teamwork and the new partners agreed to a fresh start with problems being shared rather than hidden. The new managing director wisely recommended that the franchise's DfT Breach Notice fine should be paid as extra investment in operational robustness – including more staff and trains, together with an agreement to double much of the North Cotswold line to improve GW reliability. Mark Hopwood was also brought into

the company as an experienced Operations Director from the award-winning C2C franchise.

Mark Hopwood became Managing Director in 2008 and was to provide welcome stability to the end of the franchise. He also demonstrated how quickly performance could be restored in a period of stability when a very respectable 88% was achieved by 2009. First Great Western was transformed from the worst-performing long-distance passenger train company in 2007 to the highest performer in 2009 by investing in realistic train and track maintenance schedules. This was achieved by focusing on the issues rather than on where to lay the blame.

Train innovations

Sadly the overriding public dissatisfaction after 2006 distracted attention from one of the great achievements of the re-franchising – the award-winning refurbishment of the 30 year-old HST fleet to the point where many

Table 13.4: Great Western into privatisation

Timeline	
1996	First franchise, 1996-2006 Won by Great Western Holdings
1997 1997	FirstGroup acquires Badgerline FirstGroup buys out GW Holdings
2004	First Great Western acquires Thames Trains
2006	Second franchise, 2006-16 Greater Western won by FirstGroup; combines First Great Western/Great Western Link, Wessex Trains
2008	DfT issues Breach Notice
2013	Third franchise, 2016
Managing Directors	
1994	Brian Scott Director, Shadow Train Unit
1996	Brian Scott MD (Great Western Holdings)
1997	Richard George MD (Great Western Holdings)
1999	Dr Mike Mitchell MD (Great Western Holdings/ FirstGroup)
2000	Andy Cooper MD (FirstGroup)
2002	Mike Carroll MD (FirstGroup)
2002	Chris Kinchen-Smith MD (FirstGroup)
2004	Alison Forster MD (FirstGroup)
2007	Andrew Haines MD (FirstGroup)
2008	Mark Hopwood MD (FirstGroup)

TOP The electrification of the Great Western was announced in 2009. Prime Minister Gordon Brown and the Secretary of State for Transport, Lord Adonis, talk with a member of First Great Western staff after the announcement on 23 July 2009. *Paul Bigland*

BOTTOM Mark Hopwood, Managing Director of First Great Western, seems deep in conversation with Lord Adonis after the electrification announcement. *Paul Bigland*

passengers believed that they were travelling in new trains. Initiated by the then Managing Director, Alison Forster, this was a major investment in a fleet of more than 400 vehicles, which included a full refurbishment ranging from the re-engining of the power cars with the highly reliable MTU engines to the impressive First Class interiors with their leather seats. There was also a 10% increase in Standard Class seating provision.

Great Western also found time to reorganise its catering. The original plan was for about half of the sets to operate with a trolley service in place of a buffet car. This was then modified so that all sets retained a buffet car, even though this required adding a small buffet area into a number of Standard Class coaches. Twenty services a day continued to provide the innovative 'Travelling Chef' service, which offered a flexible cooked meal service on the most popular trains. Great Western is also proud to be operating Britain's only surviving restaurant-car services between London and Plymouth.

Once operating stability had been restored, a further memorable achievement was the 2011 timetable, which delivered an extra 4,500 seats in the London peak, supported by the return of five 'Adelante' sets from East Coast in 2012 to operate over the newly doubled Cotswold line.

Route upgrade

The great benefit to emerge from the years of pain was a collective understanding that the Great Western was overdue for a major route upgrade. The DfT and Network Rail responded with a radical £6 billion upgrade project to remove the Reading bottleneck, electrify the routes from London to Bristol/Cardiff and

---

[1] InterCity Express Programme (see Chapter 14)

ABOVE Train liveries proved a good way for train companies to differentiate their brands. Here HST power car No 43004, in pre-production colours, pauses at Newton Abbot station while on its London–Penzance press run on 3 April 2006. This was the only train ever to operate in this particular livery. *Colin J. Marsden*

BELOW First Great Western put considerable effort into the interior refurbishment of its HST fleet in 2006. The Standard Class refurbishment brought additional seats as well as smarter interiors. *Colin J. Marsden*

ABOVE A challenge for the electrification engineers. Sydney Gardens in Bath will require sensitive environmental solutions to protect this beautiful Georgian setting. *Bob Sweet*

BELOW The £900 million Reading station project will remove the worst bottleneck on the Great Western route by 2015. Rapid progress had been made on the station's new northern entrance by June 2012. *Network Rail*

ABOVE Network Rail's beautifully restored entrance to Paddington enhances the rail-travel experience. *Network Rail*

ABOVE There is little spare capacity at Paddington at 0828hr 52sec on 7 March 2007. *Paul Bigland*

finances and reputation. This was also one of the last franchises which could exercise a right to end its franchise period early – and the operational risks were now adding to very high premium payments written into the final three years of the franchise. FirstGroup therefore announced in 2011 that it would be handing back the franchise in 2013 and not exercising its option to continue to 2016, when the high-premium payments were due. This would allow a clean start to be made with a new 15-year franchise in 2013, for which it would bid against others and reflect the transitional risks and the new opportunities in its tender.

The Great Western in 2013 is unfinished business. It has yet to achieve its full potential as a private company and this will not happen until the route modernisation is completed in 2018 and it gets its own period of 'quiet enjoyment' to show its true potential. Table 13.5 does however demonstrate that Great Western has recovered its ability to deliver robust performances on a crowded route. Mark Hopwood summarised it well when he said, 'I only restored basic operating principles and improved the quality of customer service. I could not have improved performance without a close partnership with my Network Rail Route Director'.

replace the HSTs on these routes with modern electric IEP trains[1]. There would also be a complete renewal of infrastructure, signalling and stations on the route. The professional planning of the project demonstrated that the lessons of the chaotic early stages of the West Coast Upgrade had been well and truly learned.

However, with the threat of five years' disruption, the complex route upgrade was seen by FirstGroup as one risk too far for the company's performance,

Table 13.5: Great Western overview

	1997/98	2001/02	2011/12
Punctuality: Annual moving average (%)	77	72	85
Trains run: Weekday trains	134	175	195
Average speed (mph): London–Bristol Parkway	87*	87	80
Growth: Journeys per annum	n/a	19m	35m
Satisfaction: Overall %	80**	73	82

* 1992 ** 2000/01

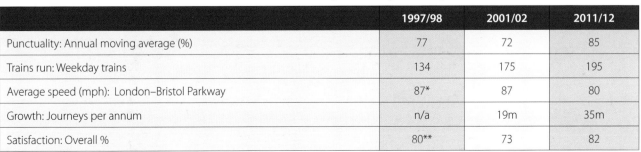

Chapter 14
MOVING TO
MATURITY

ABOVE Four tracks deliver the goods on 4 October 2010 as a 'Pendolino' and a Freightliner train pass on the WCML's fast lines. *Bob Sweet*

The roller-coaster ride

Table 14.1 illustrates the difficult journey that the long-distance companies have undertaken since 1994 – a trip that has been memorably described by Christopher Garnett as 'the worst kind of roller-coaster ride imaginable'. InterCity's managers helped to smooth the route into privatisation, and to provide an initial honeymoon period as they joined the new franchise companies. However, when the Hatfield disaster occurred there was nothing to save the new companies from Railtrack's sudden collapse and the crippling speed restrictions that followed on every main line.

The long recovery started only when the industry learned to work together again to restore the basic disciplines needed to run the complex railway production line. This chapter will consider how far the lessons have been learned and whether a new age of maturity is finally delivering inter-city services that are both better and stronger than the original model.

Things that are worse

Industry costs

There is general agreement that rail costs spiralled out of control once BR's iron grip was released. It is quite extraordinary that an industry that only needed a £1 billion subsidy in 1992 should need £4 billion two decades later. Andy Cooper remembers InterCity as being 'good at giving value for money' and the BR OforQ organisation was the culmination of a decade of work in breaking down rail costs and income to provide a high level of transparency. It was, however, achieved only by minimising investment to a level unsustainable in the following decade.

InterCity knew the cost of its routes, and even its individual trains, to the point where each train was a profit centre and where the 1993 timetable could be built around eliminating individual loss-making services. Its costs were transparent to both the BRB and the Government and were amongst the lowest in

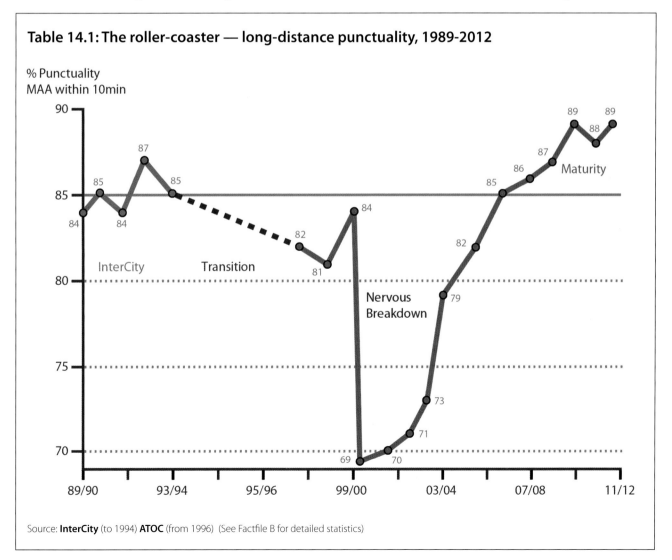

Table 14.1: The roller-coaster — long-distance punctuality, 1989-2012

Source: **InterCity** (to 1994) **ATOC** (from 1996) (See Factfile B for detailed statistics)

Table 14.2: The Cost challenge

McNulty Report: Target: £1.0bn; Command Paper Target: £1.7bn

£bn 2008/09 prices	Low estimate	High Estimate
Network Rail gap	1.8	2.3
TOC gap (incl ROSCOS)	0.7	1.2
Total Efficiency Gap	2.5	3.5
Less known NR savings	-1.8	-1.8
Net Efficiency Gap	0.7	1.7

Source: Rail Value for Money study 2011: DfT Command Paper 2012

Europe: but this unsung BR legacy was largely thrown away at privatisation. The new contractual frameworks raised track-access costs to the point where virtually every ex-InterCity company needed subsidy to run the same services. The Hatfield crisis led to a further step-change in infrastructure costs – but there was no longer a BR 'directing mind' to drive the costs back down again.

The causes of the cost increases are complex and diverse. Justifiable increases include a catch-up on BR under-investment; the costs associated with a growing railway; better disabled access; and expenditure on developing higher safety standards. Unjustifiable costs include inflated project costs – often caused by applying standards inflexibly, or factoring in every conceivable risk – inflated rolling stock costs and excessive compensation for disruption amongst other things.

[1] Sir Roy McNulty 'Realising the Potential of GB Rail'

However, it was to be another 15 years before the McNulty Report[1] was commissioned by the DfT in 2010 to regain control of rail costs and subsidy. The report concluded that the industry was costing at least 30% more than the best European railways to deliver the same activities – and that this had in turn caused passenger fares and taxpayer subsidies to become much higher than necessary. It concluded that inter-city services should be operating without subsidy and pointed out that whilst Britain now has the most frequent services in Europe it also has some of the lowest load factors.

Table 14.2 shows how McNulty identified a 'low' efficiency gap of £0.7 billion and a 'high' gap of £1.7 billion, before calling for the removal of £1 billion of costs by 2018/19. But the Government went further in its Command Paper in 2012 requiring that the 'high' gap of £1.7 billion should be closed in the same period. A more mature rail industry has responded by creating a new Rail Delivery Group to take collective action on making the tough decisions. If the rail industry can bring costs back by 2018, it will have removed the major downside of privatisation and, in the words of McNulty, 'will have earned the right to grow.'

The impact of the cost savings on subsidy levels is critically important. The Command Paper is clear that Government wants to return to the original InterCity position where long-distance routes operated without subsidy. The current funding position is opaque, because 'profitable' train companies can still be getting a hidden subsidy for their track-access charges in payments that the DfT make direct to Network Rail. Long-distance train companies generally went into loss around 2002, as the track problems triggered by the Hatfield accident saw costs rise and income fall.

Table 14.3: The subsidy challenge

	TOC subsidy per passenger mile (pence)	Network grant per passenger mile (pence)	Overall subsidy per passenger mile (pence)
	2010/2011	2010/2011	2010/2011
Cross Country	-2.9	19.8	16.9
East Coast	-5.8	6.5	0.7
East Midlands Trains	-1.7	14.2	12.5
First Great Western	-3.0	9.2	6.2
Virgin West Coast	-4.7	8.4	3.7

Note: A negative figure denotes a premium to DfT

Source: **DfT** and **ORR: Dr Nigel G. Harris**

However, Table 14.3 shows that by 2011 all ex-InterCity companies were once again covering their train costs but were still effectively receiving a Network Grant for some of their track costs. The result was a net subsidy ranging from 0.7 to 16.9 pence per passenger mile. The future is going to be about eliminating this remaining long-distance subsidy. Factfile J provides more detail on unit costs since privatisation.

The Franchising Process

The franchising process worked remarkably well in the early days, when an independent OPRAF was able to complete all 26 franchise competitions in the two years before the 1997 election. The process was relatively straight forward and a typical bid cost the owners about £0.5 million.

However, fifteen years later, the competition for franchises has become immeasurably more complex with box loads of documents and bidding costs reaching £10 million or more. With the closure of the SRA in 2004, civil servants in the DfT became responsible for managing an extended franchising process that culminated in the fiasco that led to the second West Coast franchise competition being suspended in 2012.

The crisis did however trigger a fundamental review of how things could be improved, and Richard Brown, Chairman of Eurostar, was commissioned to report on the options. His report[2] was published in January 2013 and his prime conclusion was that the franchising system needed repairing rather than replacing. The report pointed out that the system had served the industry well since 1994 and had enabled the railway to achieve unparalleled successes in passenger growth, frequency of services and investment and he stated that 'it is highly unlikely that these successes could have been delivered if franchising was fundamentally flawed'. He also pointed out that only three franchises had failed in this period and in every case the train services continued to operate without interruption.

He did however identify fundamental repairs that needed to be made to the franchising process before it was restarted, to make it simpler and more transparent. He recommended that if the DfT was to continue managing the franchising process, then it should be re-structured to bring all franchising matters under a single Franchise Director, rather than spreading it across a number of departments. It would also need to strengthen its team with professionals from both the rail and procurement disciplines. It should also allow 24

[2] The Brown Review of the Rail Franchising Programme January 2013

Table 14.4: Organisational instability, 1996-2013

Train company	Franchises (number)	MDs* (number)
East Coast*	6	5
Great Western	3	9
Midland Mainline	2	10
West Coast	2	3
CrossCountry	2	4
Anglia	3	57
Total	18	36

* including Directly Operated Railways

Source: **Modern Railways Directories**

months for a franchise tender and should not attempt to let more than four franchises a year.

Another key recommendation was that franchisees should not be expected to take external risk on things they cannot control, such as major changes within the national economy and that there should be adjustment mechanisms for issues such as changes in GDP or Central London employment. Franchise length should start at 7 – 10 years, with the ability to extend to a maximum of 15 years if the agreed criteria are being met. The government should not try to insure fully against the relatively rare risk of a franchise defaulting, as this simply inflates franchising costs still further.

The Brown Report was accepted by Government and allowed the franchising process to be relaunched in February 2013, when East Coast became one of the first franchise tenders. Hopefully, the boil has been lanced and future inter-city franchise bids will take place in a calmer and more creative atmosphere.

West Coast is living evidence that a 15-year franchise can attract major investment whilst encouraging franchisees to develop long-term customer service and marketing strategies. It is encouraging to find the 2012 Command Paper proposing longer franchises to attract investment and stabilise behaviour. This seems to be the best way of encouraging long-term thinking whilst still occasionally market-testing franchise value and innovation. If these longer franchises can be aligned with closer management partnerships with Network Rail and provide stability of tenure for managing directors and senior teams, there is every chance that a more stable structure will emerge in future years.

Neither better nor worse

Some areas of rail performance are neither better nor worse than before privatisation, but there are three aspects where the InterCity legacy took a real downturn on the roller-coaster before the industry got its act together once more.

Safety and performance

Soon after privatisation the industry suffered from a number of serious accidents which shook public confidence and which served as an urgent wake-up call for everyone involved. Lessons were learned, attitudes changed and a better industry has subsequently emerged from the wreckage.

The safety crisis involved two high-speed accidents on the Great Western at Southall and Ladbroke Grove – and a further two on the East Coast at Hatfield and Great Heck in the early years of privatisation. These had a traumatic effect across the rail industry and an even greater effect on its passengers and staff.

The accidents forced a newly fragmented industry to re-discover the power of co-operation. The Deputy Prime Minister, John Prescott, chaired a number of Safety Summits before the industry started to put its own house in order. The big breakthrough was the installation of the new TPWS[3] safety system in every train cab and on the approach to every high risk signal. This dramatically reduced the number of signals passed at danger (SPAD) by 90%. From that moment, the industry started to improve matters through its newly created RSSB[4] to the point where Table 14.5 shows how the high profile derailments of the first five years of privatisation have been transformed into a period of unprecedented high safety performance in which the railway did not cause a single death or injury in the last three years of the graph.

But the high-speed accidents of the early privatisation years impacted on train performance and triggered an unprecedented collapse in punctuality in 2000 in the shape of a thousand speed restrictions across the national network which reduced long-distance journeys to constant 20mph crawls. Table 14.1 has already shown how inter-city performance dropped from 84% to just 69% within weeks of the Hatfield derailment. Once again, a crisis forced an immature industry into co-operation and a National Performance Task Force was formed between Network Rail and ATOC which brought together all the railway's senior figures.

[3] Train Protection & Warning System

[4] Rail Safety & Standards Board (created in 2003)

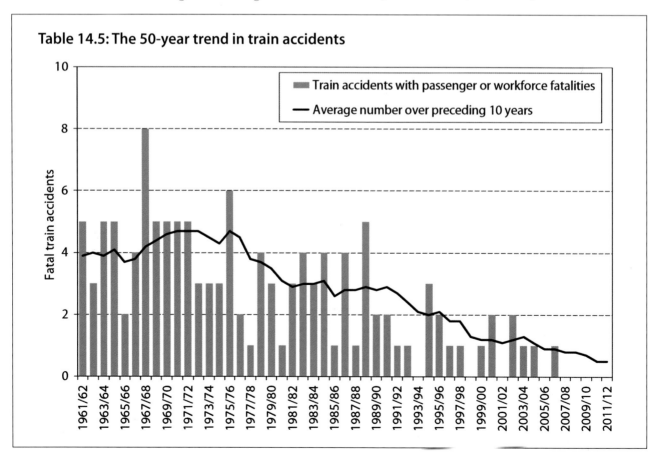

Table 14.5: The 50-year trend in train accidents

Train accidents with passenger or workforce fatalities

Average number over preceding 10 years

Despite this, it took an agonising five years to restore national performance to InterCity's 85% level. The silver lining was that the new industry then kept on improving and delivered a record punctuality of 88-89% in the following three years – well in excess of anything InterCity had delivered. Long-distance operators do, however, face a growing performance problem on a mixed railway that is getting ever more congested, and they no longer have the absolute regulatory priority that InterCity trains used to enjoy.

After a dreadful start, both safety and performance have become exemplars of a more mature leadership working together to produce results which now equal and better InterCity delivery. The first five years of privatisation produced a succession of high profile derailments which damaged the industry and impacted on performance. But the lessons have been learned, and Factfile B shows that Britain has gone on to win its place as the safest of the EU rail operators other than that of the Grand Duchy of Luxembourg.

Fares

Long-distance fares are a good example of being both better and worse since privatisation. On the one hand the cost of walk-up tickets has risen faster than inflation to create some of the most expensive fares

ABOVE Track safety (1): attention to detail. A rail worker tightens fishplates at Didcot on 26 March 2008. *Paul Bigland*

BELOW Track safety (2): watching other people's backs. A lookout on duty at Crewe. *Paul Bigland*

ABOVE Fast ticket machines have allowed tickets to be purchased on the internet and then collected in seconds at any station. Virgin Trains offers a generous supply of machines at Euston. *Colin J. Marsden*

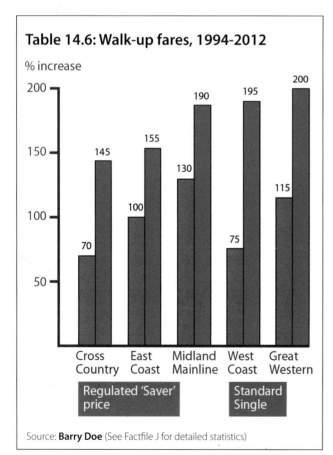

Table 14.6: Walk-up fares, 1994-2012

% increase

Cross Country — Regulated 'Saver' price 70, Standard Single 145
East Coast — 100, 155
Midland Mainline — 130, 190
West Coast — 75, 195
Great Western — 115, 200

Regulated 'Saver' price

Standard Single

Source: **Barry Doe** (See Factfile J for detailed statistics)

in Europe. But on the other hand, advance-purchase tickets now account for around half of all long-distance travel and offer some of the cheapest fares in Europe. Long-distance passengers are faced with an increasingly polarised pricing system which can offer tickets for £20 or £150 on the same train to the same destination.

On the bargain front, InterCity's original Apex Advance has evolved into a low cost airline model that is now used by over 50% of long-distance passengers. A new generation of travellers are willing and able to use their laptops to trade journey flexibility against cheap fares. The result has been a bonanza of bargain fares for those who are willing to book early, with West Coast alone offering over a million Advance Purchase fares a week. This has proved a neat way of raising load factors on quiet trains, whilst reducing overcrowding on the busier services. But more flexibility is needed when a passenger misses a train, or arrives in time for the previous service, and Britain could usefully adopt the French TGV model, where passengers can change their tickets for an earlier or later train at an automatic machine on the station concourse.

On the walk-up front, passengers seeking flexibility in their journey plans can choose between Open and Saver tickets, but Table 14.6 shows how expensive and complex some of these tickets have become. Where inflation rose by 60% from 1994 to 2012, unregulated Standard Single tickets have risen by 200%.

Even the 'regulated' Saver tickets have risen well beyond inflation on the RPI+1 formula. These anomalies have happened because the walk-up fares have become one of the few areas where companies can raise prices in a culture where governments expect rising rail costs to be borne by the train traveller rather than the taxpayer. This has skewed fare increases onto the unregulated Open tickets and forced companies to restrict the under-priced Off Peak Savers to the minimum possible time zones in lieu of fare increases.

There is clearly unfinished business in rationalising long-distance pricing into a more customer-friendly

ABOVE Hull Trains prepares a traditional hot meal for First Class customers on 12 October 2006. *Paul Bigland*

RIGHT CrossCountry offers a snack from the trolley on the 0844 Derby–Edinburgh train on 1 December 2011. *Arriva CrossCountry*

product. Britain may boast the most frequent long-distance services in the world, but it negates this unique selling point by forcing Advance Purchase passengers to commit to a fixed train in each direction. Britain has also created some of the most expensive walk-up fares in the world because well-intentioned legislation has skewed fare increases and led to over-priced Open tickets and over-restricted Saver tickets. More details are shown in Factfile J.

Train catering

Train catering is alive and well in Britain today and 97% of long-distance trains still match the InterCity promise of a buffet car or trolley on every service. However the new owners have had to adapt to some radical changes in the traditional restaurant-car market – a once common feature of InterCity's trains. Today's passengers increasingly prefer to keep working whilst they are served a hot dish or a drink at their seat, whilst health-conscious travellers are less willing to consume the 'Great British Breakfast' and often skip lunch or dinner. Train operators

Table 14.7: Train catering: Number of trains serving hot meals

Year	Anglia	Cross Country	East Coast	Great Western	Midland Mainline	West Coast	Total inter-city
1993/94 Restaurant cars	22	0	60	28	13	117	249
2011/12 At-seat First Class*	0	92	142	29	125	151	539

* Excludes Hull Trains 14 daily and Eurostar 48 daily
Source: Barry Doe

have also found it increasingly impossible to justify the cost and space of providing passengers with a second seat in the restaurant car on trains that are increasingly crowded.

By 2012 only 12 trains continued to offer a classic restaurant-car meal, compared with the 249 services provided by InterCity. However, Table 14.7 shows that the number of trains serving hot meals to First Class passengers at their seat had more than doubled, to 539 services. The original restaurant cars were generally loss-leaders, retained to protect the high-value First Class income. But the market has moved on and so have the restaurant cars: train catering is neither better nor worse than in 1994 – it is just very different.

Things that have improved

And finally … a whole range of areas have emerged where long-distance travel has visibly improved since 1993. In some cases these have been achieved by building on the inherited InterCity legacy, but in many others it has been the result of new thinking, new technology and new sources of investment.

Record growth

Table 14.8 records the new railway's success in stimulating a huge and unexpected growth in long-distance passenger travel. The 100% growth in the last 15 years is in sharp contrast to the seven years of decline

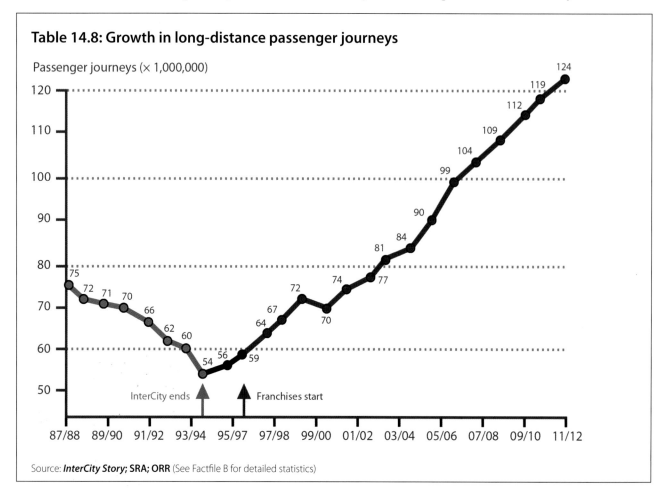

Table 14.8: Growth in long-distance passenger journeys

Source: *InterCity Story*; **SRA; ORR** (See Factfile B for detailed statistics)

that InterCity suffered as it struggled to remain in profit in a deep recession and whilst facing privatisation. This welcome growth did not only happen because the economy picked up; but because the new owners were encouraged to harvest the maximum possible growth through investment in new trains and extra services. InterCity would undoubtedly have been forced to 'price off' some of the growth to minimise the extra investment.

The owners' new interest in growing income led to a welcome period of growth in long-distance passengers that began around 1996 and which was still delivering a 6% growth rate in the depths of the 2012 recession. Every one of the new long-distance companies committed to increasing train frequencies, and they supported this with new rolling-stock orders, more staff and low budget fares which generated more demand. Where they invested over the odds, they were rewarded with even stronger growth – and Virgin Trains is an example where high investment levels have actually increased travel by 100% since privatisation on both its West Coast and erstwhile CrossCountry franchises.

Private owners were fortunate to be helped by a growing economy from 1996, but they deserve credit for their bullish growth policies which have pushed long-

ABOVE Releasing suppressed demand: passengers queue to board a Virgin CrossCountry train at Manchester Piccadilly on 8 August 2005. *MP92½*

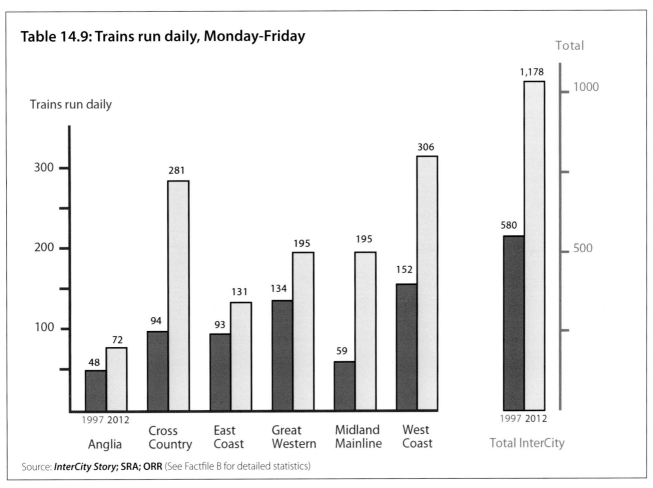

Table 14.9: Trains run daily, Monday-Friday

Source: *InterCity Story*; **SRA; ORR** (See Factfile B for detailed statistics)

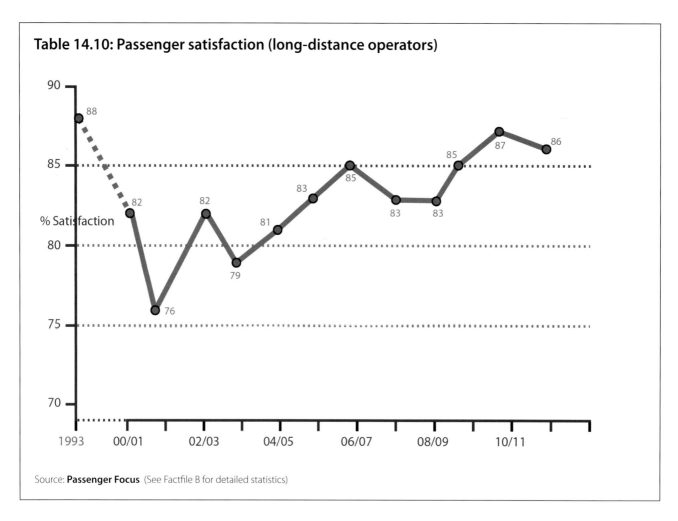

Table 14.10: Passenger satisfaction (long-distance operators)

% Satisfaction

Source: **Passenger Focus** (See Factfile B for detailed statistics)

distance rail into an unprecedented period of sustained growth. Faced with a largely fixed cost structure, the new owners focused on maximising passenger travel.

Doubling of train frequencies

The most immediate impact of privatisation was a dramatic increase in train frequency on almost all routes, and Table 14.9 shows that the number of inter-city services run by the new companies has actually doubled since privatisation. This remarkable achievement is a far cry from InterCity's narrower remit to minimise costs and investment.

Factfile B6 shows that the private owners have focused on improving frequencies rather than journey speeds, with the exception of the West Coast upgrade. It shows speeds remaining largely static on other routes, partly because InterCity had already reached line speed limit on many routes and partly because it became much harder to accelerate trains through an increasingly congested network as the number of services expanded.

The frequency improvements touched every major city in Britain, with Reading seeing fast services to

Table 14.11: Passenger satisfaction

Activity Customer importance	Satisfaction 1992 mean score	Satisfaction 2011 satisfied/ good
1. Punctuality	75%	83%
2. Information stations	68	86
3. Ease of finding seat	76	79
4. Frequency of trains	70	84
5. Journey time	71	88
6. Direct trains	70	79
7. Train cleanliness	68	82
8. Train-toilet cleaning	53	52
9. Helpful station staff	68	87
10 Train-seat comfort	67	70
Overall satisfaction	71	86

Sources: **Millward Brown International** (1992 figures),
Passenger Focus, Autumn 2011 (2011 figures)

London increase from 52 to 90, Doncaster from 28 to 54 and Manchester from 15 to 39. The doubling of inter-city services was a major achievement for the privatised railway and has been a major driver in generating the increase in passenger journeys and in attracting new business from motorways and airlines.

Better services

The new owners have generally built on a strong InterCity customer-service legacy to develop standards further in a market where expectations continue to rise. InterCity's mission was focused on creating a civilised journey experience and it put considerable effort into raising its customer service standards. Table 14.10 graphs the continuous improvement in customer satisfaction since 2001 against a backdrop of rising expectations whilst Factfile B11 shows how closely the four main companies have kept to the original Vision, Strategy and Values.

This continuous improvement in customer satisfaction is analysed in more detail in Table 14.11 which also shows the sharp improvement in station information scores following investment in areas such as train frequencies, on-train cleaners and modern information systems. General perceptions have been helped by the provision of more modern trains and modernised stations. The results speak for themselves and show that customer service standards have in general been steadily improving since the low point of 2001/02.

More train investment

Privatisation has also brought a far more intensive investment in fleet refurbishment. Since 1996, private owners have refurbished more than 800 coaches, including the HST fleet on the East Coast, Great Western, Midland Mainline, CrossCountry and Grand Central. In the previous decade, BR InterCity only

[5] *Modern Railways* July 1999

ABOVE The format of the electronic train indicator shown at Newton Abbot is rapidly becoming the model for national customer information, both for the next three trains due and for their expected arrival times. *Antony Christie*

managed to upgrade the First Class coaches on its West Coast Mk3 fleet – it could not even afford to continue the upgrade to Standard Class.

The HST fleet is also more productive than ever, with higher service frequencies being covered with 85 sets instead of the original 90. Further productivity has been achieved by a 9% increase in total seats despite the loss of the five sets – thanks to train lengthening, conversion of buffet cars and increasing seating densities. The only missed opportunity had been the failure to introduce powered external doors and controlled-emission toilets on MkIII coaches during refurbishments – an omission that the inspired Chiltern Mk3 refurbishment has recently put right.

Roger Ford wrote in 1999[5] that: 'privatisation meant an end to poor relations accepting hand-me-down kit',

Table 14.12: Rolling-stock investment

Route	New stock		Refurbished stock	
	1984-1994	**1996-2012**	**1984-1994**	**1996-2012**
Anglia	0	42 Class 170	0	120 Mk3
CrossCountry	0	251 Class 220/1	0	50 HST
East Coast	282	0	0	438 Mk4/HST
Gatwick Express	0	64 Class 460	0	0
Great Western	0	25 Class 180	0	548 HST
Midland Mainline	0	142 Class 222	0	100 HST
West Coast	0	684 Class 390	150	0
TOTAL	**282**	**1,265**	**150**	**1,256**

Sources: **InterCity** (1984), **Train Operating Companies** (1994-2012)

Table 14.13: Network Rail major station investment

Station	Years	£m	Customer benefit
London St Pancras International*	2006-09	850	Station reconstruction
London King's Cross	2010-13	480	Station reconstruction
London Paddington	2002-12	120	Shopping Mall, Span 4 and new taxi area
Birmingham New Street	2011-14	600	Imaginative station redevelopment
Manchester Piccadilly	2000-02	50	Major upgrade of concourse and interchanges
Liverpool Lime Street	2009-11	10	Restoration of external façade and interior
Leeds City	2002-04	50	Major station upgrade
Edinburgh Waverley	2011-13	140	Major upgrading of roof and facilities
Glasgow Central	2006-10	200	More platforms and capacity
		£2.5bn	

* CTRL station operated by Network Rail Source: **Network Rail**

ABOVE Durham demonstrates how good Britain can be at stylish station refurbishment. This photograph was taken on 22 May 2011. *East Coast Main Line Co Ltd*

ABOVE King's Cross station in LNER days, with attendant jumble of buildings in front of William Cubitt's original façade. *East Coast Main Line Co Ltd*

and he was to be proved right as fresh sources of funding quadrupled the number of new and refurbished long-distance coaches. Table 14.12 demonstrates that more than 1,300 new coaches have been delivered since 1996, compared to the 300 purchased by InterCity in the previous decade.

Even more investment has gone into upgrading the maintenance depots that keep the fleets reliable. InterCity's biggest success was getting a new Mk4 fleet for the East Coast electrification, but the privatised railway has gone much further and renewed entire fleets on West Coast, CrossCountry, Gatwick Express and Hull Trains, whilst also increasing fleet sizes on Midland Mainline, Great Western and Grand Central. Still further investment will come when IEP trains brings a tranche of new coaches to the Great Western in 2017. Private funding has brought levels of train investment

ABOVE The upgrade of the western concourse at King's Cross in 2012. *Network Rail*

BELOW King's Cross today, with its open public square moving out into the Euston Road. *East Coast Main Line Co Ltd*

Table 14.14: Route Capacity Investment 2000-16

Capacity project	Year(s)	Capacity benefit
West Coast: £9bn		
PUG2 upgrade	2000-08	Route upgrade to 125mph
Nuneaton flyover	2011-12	Reduces freight conflicts at Nuneaton
Norton Bridge flyover	2016	Reduces conflicts at Norton Bridge
East Coast: £ 580m		
King's Cross approaches	2011	Platform Zero and sixth track Finsbury–Alexandra Palace
Hitchin Flyover	2013	Flyover to reduce conflicts on flat junction
Peterborough	2014	Provision of three extra platforms
GN/GE Joint Line	2014	Diversion of freight to release capacity Peterborough–Doncaster
North Doncaster Chord	2014	Shaftholme Junction flyover releases capacity on main line
York Holgate Jct	2011	Increased capacity on approach to York
ECML power supply	2013	Enables more and longer trains to run on East Coast
Great Western: £6.9bn		
Great Western Reading	2010-15	Provision of flyovers and five new platforms
GW Route Upgrade	2010-17	Electrification, signalling, line speed improvements and extra capacity
Midland Mainline: £80m		
MML line speeds	2013	Journey-time improvements (includes 125mph)
Nottingham re-signalling	2013	Re-signalling with capacity improvements
CrossCountry: £1.3bn		
Cross Country upgrade	2002-03	Double junctions Didcot and Filton Abbey Wood
Cross Country speeds	2002-06	Line-speed improvements to reduce journey times
TOTAL: £18bn		

Source: **Network Rail**

that InterCity could only dream about and this has given rail travel a more modern image, helping to attract new business from domestic airlines and motorways.

More station investment

Table 14.13 shows that Network Rail alone has invested around £2.5 billion in upgrading its Major Station portfolio. InterCity was only able to fund station improvements where there was an immediate payback and this tended to limit investment to areas such as retail trading and travel centres. It was left to Railtrack to invest serious capital sums in the core fabric of the stations, including the great Victorian roofs at stations such as Liverpool Lime Street, Glasgow Central, Newcastle, York and Carlisle. A further breakthrough came at Manchester Piccadilly in 2002, when Railtrack

gave the entire station a comprehensive upgrading which both restored the structure and provided stylish retail and customer facilities.

Network Rail used its new borrowing facilities to fund a progressive upgrading of all its major stations. It followed CTRL's iconic restoration at St Pancras International in 2009 with its own equally inspired upgrade at King's Cross in 2012, with a completely modern rebuild at Birmingham New Street to follow in the years 2013-15. Network Rail has also worked with train companies to co-ordinate investment at the larger franchised stations such as Wolverhampton, Derby, Bristol Parkway, Reading, Peterborough and Loughborough.

Most long-distance companies have also invested in 'line-of-route' station upgrades which have provided a smarter image for rail travel. East Coast and Great

LEFT The two-track bottleneck on the West Coast main line in the Trent Valley seen in the late 1990s. *Network Rail*

LEFT The two-track bottleneck on the West Coast main line in the Trent Valley seen in the late 1990s. *Network Rail*

Western are good examples of routes that have achieved virtually end-to-end station refurbishment, whilst West Coast has put its efforts into a series of multi-storey car parks, whilst Midland Mainline has created a new Parkway station.

This period of sustained station investment has created an image of smart customer-friendly inter-city stations which are amongst the best in Europe and which complement the image of the modern trains that use them. It is, however, surprising that East Midlands Parkway and Ebbsfleet are the only two new InterCity parkway stations to have been built since privatisation.

New-capacity investment

The huge growth in passenger demand since privatisation has created a sea-change in Whitehall's willingness to expand network capacity rather than rationalise it. Funding is now being made available for significant increases in rail capacity across the network which will allow long-distance travel to keep growing.

Table 14.14 shows the scale of change since 1996, with around £18 billion of investment now being committed to infrastructure enhancements which

will benefit long-distance operators. The creation of Network Rail as a not-for-dividend company in 2002 brought robust five year funding plans supported by the ability to raise debt borrowing to fund them and this has led to a more strategic investment policy which is increasingly focused on expanding network capacity for long-term rail growth.

The £9 billion West Coast upgrade delivered the radical remodelling of the Rugby area and the four-tracking northwards along the Trent Valley. The £7 billion Great Western upgrade will include the re-modelling of the Reading Area with grade-separated junctions and five additional platforms. The £0.5 billion

BELOW Mixed-traffic railway. On 5 April 2011, freight, intercity and interurban traffic all compete for space on a congested stretch of the West Coast main line in the Trent Valley. *Bob Sweet*

Table 14.15: The software revolution

InterCity 1984-94	Train companies 1996-2012
Access	**Access**
Station booking office or home phone	Laptop, smartphone, ipod, ipad
Public pay phone on trains	Mobile phones
Ticketing	**Ticketing**
Visit station	E-ticket via website and FastTicket machine
Phone telesales and get ticket posted	M-ticket via website and smartphone
Travel Agent	ITSO plastic card (a national 'Oyster')
Timetable information	**Timetable information**
Telephone Enquiry Bureaux (TEBs)	Laptops and smartphone to websites
Published timetables	
Real-time information	**Real-time information**
Public address at stations/ trains	Electronic station/train indicators
	Website live destination boards
	Live Twitter control desks; mobile apps

East Coast upgrade will deliver a series of capacity improvements from King's Cross to York. Indeed, the biggest single difference between BR InterCity and its successors is this welcome ability to invest in expanding the rail network rather than constraining it.

A software revolution
Since 1996 there has been a revolution in the way that inter-city passengers access both train information and ticketing. BR was ahead of its time in developing computer systems to allocate ticket revenue to business sectors and it could not have created those sectors without such processes, any more than the Government could have privatised the railway without them.

Table 14.15 shows how rapidly the new industry has built on this software legacy to put passengers in control of their information. The InterCity Telephone Enquiry Bureaux have evolved into websites which allow customers to book their own tickets on-line without speaking to anyone. Where InterCity passengers had to wait for their Telesale tickets to arrive in the post, today's passengers pick up their

E-tickets from FastTicket machines at the station – or increasingly receive them as M-tickets on their mobiles. Two-thirds of the population are likely to own a smart phone by 2013, and the rail industry is working hard to keep up with an e-ticketing revolution that has already transformed the airline business.

Free wi-fi will soon be standard on all long-distance trains, whilst smart phones give passengers in transit direct access to 'live departures' sites where they can check the running of 23,000 trains in real-time.

Robin Gisby, Network Rail's Director of Operations & Maintenance, believes that social-media networks such as Twitter and Facebook will soon provide the fastest way of keeping both passengers and staff updated on fast-changing situations. BR's computer legacy is evolving to exciting areas where passengers are increasingly being put in control of their own travel data and destinies.

Summary: The roller-coaster
All the ex-InterCity routes have been through difficult times since 1994, but the evidence shows that the long-distance train experience has improved significantly over almost all measures apart from cost. If the new companies can restore InterCity levels of cost control and transparency whilst retaining their quality of service and investment, then the InterCity legacy will be one of continuous growth after what was a difficult and decidedly rocky start.

ABOVE From mouse to my rail journey. *Arriva CrossCountry*

ABOVE Keeping connected? No problem! Passengers surf the internet on an East Coast service. *East Coast Main Line Co Ltd*

BELOW Finding a partner? No problem! Customers speed-date on a Virgin West Coast service from Euston. *Paul Bigland*

ABOVE Keeping in touch: Live progress whilst travelling. *Arriva CrossCountry*

Chapter 15
THE FUTURE

ABOVE An artist's impression of the atrium planned for Birmingham New Street in 2015. *Network Rail*

The future as at 1994

The original InterCity Story ended in 1994 with predictions that InterCity's core vision would stand the test of time, and that the future would continue to be about being 'the best, most civilised way to travel at speed from centre to centre'. It went on to suggest ways in which the future owners might choose to keep the vision alive:

- by surviving the 1994 fragmentation
- by continuously raising service standards
- by raising journey speeds
- by plugging InterCity into Europe

Twenty years on, it is clear that the first two predictions have been delivered, whilst the latter two have not. InterCity's successors did indeed survive the 1994 fragmentation and have certainly continued raising service standards but, far from delivering InterCity's vision of 160mph journey speeds, the new train companies, with the notable exception of Eurostar, have found it impracticable to raise main-line speeds above 125mph. Nor can it be said as yet that they have plugged InterCity into the wider European rail network beyond Paris and Brussels.

Current predictions

The mistake in 1994 was to assume that the InterCity vision of 'speed and civilised' could work for the foreseeable future. Circumstances changed, and the new owners quickly decided that a better vision lay in going for growth and reversing a declining market. The extra passengers were to come from higher train frequencies rather than higher train speeds and a new vision evolved of growing the market through frequency rather than speed. InterCity in 1994 was largely blind to this suppressed demand for long-distance travel as it was conditioned by Whitehall to inhabit a steady state universe rather than the expanding universe that its successors discovered.

Inter-city predictions for the next 20 years should clearly be based around an expanding universe – but it is a universe that is going to run out of room to expand, unless some radical decisions are taken. The strategic need for the next 20 years is going to be capacity, capacity and capacity. Everything else will become secondary to achieving the space to run more and faster trains across an increasingly crowded network.

A balanced prediction for the next 20 years would therefore include the following ingredients:

- new capacity for growth
- new electric fleets
- new inter-city routes
- higher service standards
- stable and affordable industry

New capacity for growth

If affordability can be restored, the initial investment will be focused on creating more capacity on an already busy railway network. Britain has become an extreme example of a mixed traffic railway in which inter-city, local and freight trains all have to be accommodated on the same tracks. The BR legacy in 1994 was a heavily rationalised rail network which had been progressively pruned to match a slow decline in demand. The privatisation legacy has been to reverse a declining trend by doubling the number of trains on this heavily

RIGHT A view of the future greets passengers as Network Rail unveils the new western concourse at King's Cross in 2012.
East Coast Main Line Co Ltd

ABOVE The new, larger footbridge at Reading will facilitate customer movement above platform level, whilst the new track and flyover arrangements are planned to give an estimated 37% improvement in train performance. *Network Rail*

Table 15.1: Future inter-city capacity schemes

Route	Extra capacity
Great Western	Four-tracking Bristol Parkway–Bristol Temple Meads Fourth platform at Bristol Parkway; extra platforms Bristol Temple Meads Double-tracking Swindon–Kemble Extra platforms at Oxford station
East Coast	Four-tracking Huntingdon–Peterborough Flyover at Peterborough Werrington Junction for freight to Lincoln More bay platforms at Doncaster
East Midlands	Double-tracking Kettering–Corby Leicester-area grade separation Faster approaches to Leicester, Derby, Nottingham and Sheffield
West Coast	Stafford congestion: flyover at Norton Bridge
CrossCountry	Double tracking Leamington–Coventry Water Orton–Tamworth capacity
East – West	New route from South West to North avoiding Birmingham

Source: DfT HLOS Proposals July 2012

rationalised network. Robin Gisby, Network Rail's Director of Operations & Maintenance, has indicated that '70% of long-distance delays are now caused by reactionary delays from other trains'. In other words, one small delay can have a domino effect across the congested network. This growing congestion will also make it ever harder to run extra trains – let alone accelerate existing services.

So the priority for the next decade will be to remove the worst bottlenecks with investment in flyovers, four-tracking, extra station platforms and multi-storey car parks. The £900 million investment at Reading is a classic example of generating more capacity on a mixed railway, but the DfT went considerably further in July 2012[1] when it announced a new list of congestion-busting investment schemes for the five years 2014-19 as summarised in Table 15.1, schemes supported by a further £4.5 billion of financial support for the railways.

But in another decade's time even this extra capacity will be exhausted – and Britain will still be running its inter-city trains at 125mph half a century after the HST was introduced. The only way forward will then be to recognise that Britain's mixed traffic model has reached its limit, and to follow the rest of Europe into a purpose-built network of high-speed lines dedicated to long-distance travel. This will in turn free up the classic network for the further expansion of regional and freight services, whilst giving inter-city services the chance to make long overdue step changes in speed, frequency and access.

[1] DfT 2014-19 HLOS (High Level Output Statement) July 2012

Table 15.2: The initial core high speed rail network

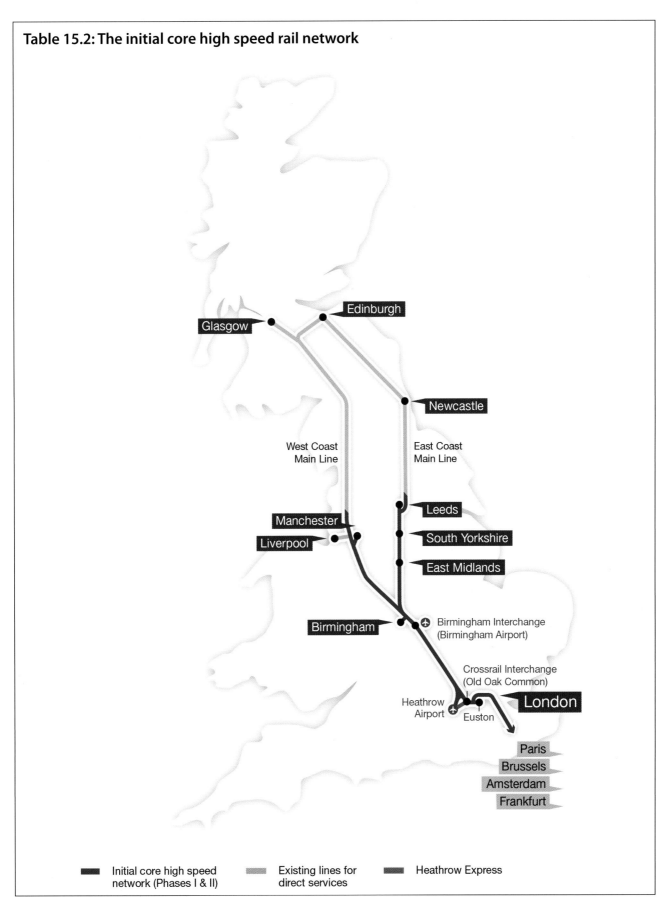

Glasgow

Edinburgh

Newcastle

West Coast
Main Line

East Coast
Main Line

Leeds

Manchester

South Yorkshire

Liverpool

East Midlands

Birmingham

Birmingham Interchange
(Birmingham Airport)

Crossrail Interchange
(Old Oak Common)

Heathrow
Airport

London

Euston

Paris

Brussels

Amsterdam

Frankfurt

■■ Initial core high speed network (Phases I & II)	■■ Existing lines for direct services	■■ Heathrow Express

ABOVE HS2 core route map. At the time of writing, the link to Heathrow Airport is on hold. *HS2*

High Speed 2

High Speed 2 will provide a new line from London to the North. It will be built in two stages, with Phase 1 planned for completion from London to Birmingham by 2026. This will reduce journey times from London to Birmingham (Curzon Street) to 49 minutes and will connect back into the classic West Coast at Tamworth. It will also provide new stations at Old Oak Common in west London (for transfer to Crossrail and Heathrow Airport) and Birmingham Interchange (for the National Exhibition Centre and the airport). Phase 2 will create two extension lines to Manchester and Leeds. These new routes will almost halve the journey times to these two cities to just 1hr 8min and 1hr 22min respectively.

HS2 will be designed to take the new standard UIC 400-metre length trains which seat more than 1,000 passengers. It will eliminate the problems of mixed-traffic railways and allow trains of identical performance to follow each other at three minute headways in Japanese 'Shinkansen' style. It will also be aligned for 215mph running to realise rail's potential for radical journey time reductions. See Factfile K for further information.

New electric fleets

Meanwhile, back on the 'classic' railway, the HSTs will be approaching 40 years old by 2015, and the DfT has taken the lead in finding a replacement for this iconic fleet. The strategy is to link the diesel-renewal plans to the progressive electrification of the core long-distance network. The resulting Intercity Express Programme (IEP) will bring further major investment in both trains and infrastructure over the next decade.

Table 15.3 illustrates the scale of the infrastructure investment over the next five years; which will increase Britain's electrified network to 53% by 2019, with 76% of trains running under electric power. There is every hope that this level of investment will keep rolling forward in future five-year electrification plans.

The Great Western electrification will trigger a new fleet of IEP electric trains, and the DfT has confirmed a £4.5 billion order for 92 IEP trains from Agility Trains which includes their ongoing maintenance together with new depots. The 596 coaches will be delivered in two tranches to the Great Western and East Coast as shown in Table 15.4. The flexibility of design allows for long and short formations, splitting and joining en route, with the bi-modal diesel engines allowing operation beyond the wire.

ABOVE Visualisation of the HS2 route as it crosses the Colne Valley. *HS2*

ABOVE Visualisation of a high-speed train as it crosses the Birmingham & Fazeley Canal. HS2

Table 15.3: New electric long-distance routes

Route	Electrification
Great Western	London Paddington to Bristol, Swansea, Oxford and Newbury
CrossCountry	Southampton–Birmingham Leamington–Coventry
East Midlands	London St Pancras to Sheffield, Nottingham and Corby
Northern Hub	Liverpool–Manchester–Leeds–York
East–West	Oxford to Milton Keynes and Bedford

Source: DfT HLOS 2014-19

Table 15.4: New IEP electric fleet

The IEP Train	Features
Initial contract	£4.5bn
Electric train sets	One diesel engine instead of batteries
Bimode train sets	Several engines underfloor
26 metre coaches	Formed into five- or nine-car sets
Manufacturer	Hitachi (Agility Trains)
Phase I: Great Western	369 cars: 21 x nine-car electric 36 x five-car bi-modal
Phase 2: East Coast	227 cars: 12 x five-car electric 10 x five-car bi-modal 13 x nine-car bi-modal
Phase 2: Unallocated	270 cars: 30 x nine-car electric

Source: DfT HLOS 2014-19 (See Factfile G5 for more details)

The IEP is due to enter service on the Great Western in 2017 on its newly electrified London–Bristol/Swansea routes with depots at London North Pole, Bristol Stoke Gifford and Swansea Maliphant. This will be closely followed by the first deliveries to East Coast in 2018 for an HST-replacement programme based around new depots at Doncaster and Bounds Green, London. This will leave a final tranche of 30 nine-car IEPs available for HST replacement to the West of England or IC225 replacement on the East Coast.

The electrification of the Midland main line by 2020 has also been announced and could be achieved with a mix of electric 'Meridians' and further IEPs.

The core CrossCountry network should also be largely electrified by 2020. The flexibility of the IEP may well lead to a second tier of semi-fast five-car IEPs which could develop the secondary markets. These will be five-car IEPs with one-third/two-third doors to minimise station times but with inter-city seating and catering. They would be ideal for intermediate services such as TransPennine, London–Norwich and perhaps even London–Southampton. See Factfile G7 for further information concerning rail electrification.

ABOVE The InterCity Express Programme (IEP) is a major project to replace the HST fleet with a modern electric train and with a programme of rolling electrification. *IEP/Hitachi Europe*

BELOW The Chiltern main line gained InterCity status in December 2012 with the introduction of an hourly service of 100mph locomotive-hauled expresses between London and Birmingham. Here DVT 82305 passes Hatton at the head of the 1425 from Birmingham Moor Street. *Bob Sweet*

ABOVE TransPennine Express should achieve InterCity status in 2016 when it is upgraded to a 100mph electric east–west service. 'Adelante' units Nos 185112 and 185104 are pictured working empty-stock from York to Ardwick on 18 August 2006. *Bob Sweet*

New inter-city routes

There is no reason why the former InterCity routes should remain frozen around the 1994 map. A whole series of new opportunities for quality long-distance services will emerge as extra capacity allows services to be accelerated and upgraded. Open access operators such as Hull Trains and Grand Central have already shown how new inter-city markets can be developed with quality services, but many other opportunities exist to upgrade existing franchises.

The Chiltern main line has been dramatically upgraded from a suburban railway to an alternative main line between London and Birmingham with continuous 100mph running over most of the route. Under a new 'Chiltern Mainline' brand, it offers an hourly service of wi-fi-equipped, air-conditioned Mk3 coaches with a Business Coach offering an at-seat service of hot food and drinks. The quality of service is certainly equal to the Anglia expresses and the fastest journey time of 95 minutes with two stops is close to the West Coast in 1994. 'InterCity Chiltern' has surely arrived.

TransPennine nearly made it into the InterCity business in 1985 but was rejected because of the quality of the product and the lack of profit. First TransPennine brought InterCity standards to the route and was rewarded with an additional long-distance service from Manchester to Scotland, but it was unable to get Government support to resolve the chronic overcrowding on TransPennine. The situation should radically change with the electrification of the Liverpool–Manchester–York route, together with re-signalling and line speed improvements. If the new electric trains offer the service standards of the existing fleet, then Britain could be celebrating 'InterCity TransPennine' as soon as 2016.

The 'Javelin' services run by Southeastern are currently a 'near miss' for inter-city status. The Ashford services are able to exploit the new HS1 opportunity to run at 140mph for their 37-minute journey, but they fall short of full inter-city badging. Nonetheless, they could easily be upgraded with First Class accommodation, seat reservations, at-seat catering trolleys and acceleration to Ramsgate and Dover. The 'Javelins' could also be projected north of London to provide a long-overdue 'InterCity Kent' service across the South East.

The new East–West railway will re-open as a double-track electrified main line by 2019 and could evolve to provide an alternative CrossCountry inter-city service avoiding Birmingham. Possible services would be Bristol–Oxford–Bedford–Sheffield and

ABOVE Southeastern Trains''Javelin' services are a 'near miss' for inter-city status. Further enhancement of line speeds south of Ashford and the provision of on-board services could help to achieve the standard. *Southeastern Trains*

Southampton–Oxford–Milton Keynes–Manchester. The growth of CrossCountry since 1985 has shown the size of the potential rail market for fast InterCity links across the heart of Britain.

Continental Europe probably offers the most dramatic opportunities for future inter-city-style services. Eurostar offered a brand new InterCity experience in 1992 with its new 'top of the range' London–Paris/Brussels services, but it remains a self-contained shuttle service which does not penetrate beyond those three cities. The next decade should finally see London services extended to Amsterdam, Marseilles, Frankfurt and Geneva – either as Eurostar trains or as new 'open-access' DB services, with both contenders using

ABOVE There are still no through trains beyond Paris or Brussels in 2013, almost 20 years after the Channel Tunnel was opened by HM Queen Elizabeth II and the French President, Francois Mitterrand, at Calais on 6 May 1994. *Colin J. Marsden*

brand new e320 Valero trains. In two decades' time it should be possible to extend some of these services onto Britain's new High Speed 2 line which would finally give Birmingham, Manchester and Leeds direct inter-city services into the European network.

Higher service standards
Long-distance passengers will always have a choice of mode and there will always be competition between car manufacturers, domestic airlines and inter-city rail services to meet rising customer expectations. InterCity was good at providing pro-active customer service within the technology of the day, and its successors have made further strides. The future will clearly see further quality upgrades of stations,

LEFT Opened in November 2007, St Pancras International is the perfect gateway for through services to continental Europe. *Network Rail*

interchange facilities and trains – but the new ingredient will lie in the software revolution.

The challenge will be to use software to put customers and staff in even greater control of their information. This will require new levels of co-operation, as much of the information lies within national computer systems which will have to be brought together to provide real-time links – for example, between a blocked line and alternative journey plans. Electronic indicators at stations and trains will be upgraded to 'smart' indicators which will be linked to a central information system, rather than just to the local route. Individual indicators will then extract fuller information on perturbations down the line and offer alternative travel plans. Smart phones will effectively become personal electronic indicators and will be continuously updated to keep both passengers and staff informed of their individual journeys or activities.

Ticketless travel will radically improve access to the network with electronic M-tickets displaying barcode authority on a mobile phone screen. The use of

RIGHT The ultimate inter-city journey for Britain was Eurostar's world-record-breaking run from London to Paris on 30 July 2003, in just 2hr 3min 36sec. This is the evidence as seen from the train. *Colin J. Marsden*

BELOW The traincrew pose for the traditional post-record photograph. *Paul Bigland*

contactless M-ticketing is set to quadruple by 2016[2] and this will radically improve access to the network with electronic authority to open ticket barriers. Advance Purchase with a free seat reservation will increasingly cover the majority of inter-city journeys as the pressures increase to improve Britain's low load factors, but customer-friendly ways will be needed to allow passengers the flexibility of changing their reservations at the last minute, through on-line M-ticketing or machines at stations. There will always be a market for walk-up tickets, and ticketing will move towards a national 'Oyster' pay-as-you-go system, involving

[2] Mobile Ticketing Evolution NFC: forecasts & markets 2011-16

either the proposed ITSO ticket or simply touching in and out with 'smart' credit cards which will extend the journey to trams, buses and even taxis.

A stable and affordable industry

But none of these exciting predictions will occur unless a stable and affordable rail industry can be delivered. The McNulty report made it clear that the industry had to earn the right to grow – so future investment in rail growth is going to be conditional on reducing cost levels by almost a third by 2018/19. This condition will be especially important to the long-distance companies that need the extra capacity most, as Government has also warned that inter-city franchisees will need to be lean enough to operate without subsidy or inflationary fare increases. This new focus on cost control is likely to concentrate minds on eliminating the worst excesses of rail privatisation over the next five years and it is encouraging that Network Rail has set the example by committing to 20% efficiency savings in the 2014-19 Control Period with 'best endeavours' to find the remaining gap.

ABOVE Passengers judge the rail industry on its speed of recovery from incidents. With all services shown as cancelled, 26 June 2006 was clearly a difficult day at King's Cross. *Paul Bigland*

ABOVE New generations of customers have higher expectations around customer service. *Arriva CrossCountry*

ABOVE Inter-city operators will need to be more and more resourceful in meeting increasingly diverse and sophisticated expectations. *East Coast Main Line Co Ltd*

The Brown Report demonstrated that the franchise process had served the industry well and can continue to do so once some urgent repairs have been made. The recommendations should lead to a more robust and transparent franchising process, in which a maximum of four franchises are re-let every year. An important win for the InterCity franchises is the endorsement for longer fifteen year franchises, but with the proviso that break points must be provided for the operator to demonstrate evidence of delivery.

These measures should restore stability and confidence in the InterCity franchises, which can now expect the government to take back some of the risks which are outside the owner's control, such as changes in the national economy. The ability to extend franchises to fifteen years should lead to a renewed interest in longer term investment in the InterCity business.

Conclusions

The InterCity story has been one of steady improvement since its inception in the 1980s. Where other countries have focused on new high-speed lines, Britain has developed a national web of frequent, modern long-distance services which offers consistently high standards across the nation. The evolution of these services has been like a relay race, in which each generation has made its own contribution to growth and development despite the obstacles thrown in their path.

BR InterCity

BR held the baton first, and its outstanding achievement was to establish InterCity as an internationally-recognised brand for fast, civilised rail travel. It was so successful in doing this that the name 'InterCity' was adopted in countries as far apart as Germany and Australia with the new brand being successful because it was under-pinned with consistent and specific standards for speed, comfort, customer service and marketing presentation.

But BR did not just create a marketing brand: it also demonstrated that high service quality could be delivered in an affordable way. BR InterCity became one of the most cost-effective networks in Europe because it was forced to inhabit a steady-state universe in which investment and expansion were not on the cards, and every penny had to be made to count. Philip Beresford summarised the situation perfectly at the time in 'Management Today': '… by comparison with other European railways, BR is a paragon of financial virtue, taking just 0.14% of GNP against a European average of 0.72%'.

Privatised InterCity

The baton was then passed to the private owners, whose outstanding achievement was to transform the steady-state InterCity universe into an expanding one. At a stroke it became acceptable and desirable to double train frequencies to half-hourly and to restore services to new destinations. This in turn, helped to trigger the awesome doubling of passenger numbers that has been achieved on almost every InterCity route since privatisation.

The private owners also delivered long-overdue investment in the fabric of an ageing InterCity product. New trains were bought to increase frequencies. Whole fleets were either renewed, or refurbished to very high standards. New investment was targeted at stations to bring them up to a higher standard across the network, whilst software investment brought website ticketing, wi-fi and electronic indicators on both trains and stations. The only irony is that this reversing of InterCity's investment fortunes has also been accompanied by the wanton loss of BR's iron grip on costs.

Future inter-city

Looking to the future, the evidence suggests that inter-city travel will continue to expand over the next 20 years – and could even double for a second time. The outstanding achievement of the next two decades is likely to be the long-overdue creation of new capacity to allow inter-city to expand and accelerate. In the first decade, this will mean removing bottlenecks on the existing network, and completing the electrification of the core inter-city network. Nevertheless, the second decade should bring the ultimate prize of the new High Speed 2 line between London and the North, which will create a step-change in journey times whilst also releasing significant capacity on the classic network.

A final thought

The InterCity Story is an encouraging tale of continuous improvement: a baton race in which each era developed and improved on the work of its predecessors. Interestingly, both the public and private sectors have played their part in the race. The only unanswered question is whether the InterCity name will be reunited with its diversifying product in the future. It is unlikely that Britain's entire inter-city network will ever be put in the hands of a single monopoly owner – but is it too much to hope that the InterCity name might one day be applied again to all long-distance services? After all, Britain did give the InterCity name and brand to the world!

LEFT Inter-City 1975: the gas-turbine APT-E stands next to pre-production HST set No 252001 at Swindon on 7 August.
Colin J. Marsden

RIGHT The 15.13 Eurostar from Paris Midi to St Pancras International has emerged from the Thames Tunnel at West Thurrock and, with unit No 3005 leading, now slices through Essex on its way to its London terminus. *Brian Morrison*

LEFT Inter-city 2015: DB has announced its intention of providing through eValero services from London to Frankfurt by 2015. Here DB's Inter-City Express set No 4685 enters the French portal of the Channel Tunnel on 13 October 2010 – the first time an ICE had ever done so on test. *Bob Sweet*

RIGHT High speed travel, Chinese style.

FACTFILES

ABOVE 'Javelin' No 395028 about to depart St Pancras International on the 2055 service to Faversham on 26 August 2010. *Antony Christie*

Factfile A: **Chronology**

Year	InterCity event
1950	October: first use of 'Inter-City' – on Paddington–Wolverhampton train
1957	January: Edinburgh–Glasgow DMUs described as 'first inter-city express diesels'
1960	July: 'Blue Pullmans' introduced on London Midland and Western Regions
1962	May: 100mph 'Deltic' locomotives introduced on East Coast route
1963	April: 'inter-city' used in Beeching Report to describe long-distance services
1964	June: 'XP64' project produced prototype InterCity vehicles
1966	April 18: Euston-Manchester-Liverpool electrification uses InterCity brand name for new services December 5: extended to Euston-Birmingham-Manchester-Liverpool electric services (via Birmingham)
1967	March 6: Reading–Heathrow Airport coach service introduced
1969	April: 'InterCity Sleeper' branding introduced June 30: Rail Drive car hire introduced with Godfrey Davis at 70 InterCity stations September: BR announce all new InterCity coaches will have air-conditioning North East–South West route given InterCity status
1970	InterCity fares raised with first examples of selective pricing February 23: Government approves Crewe–Glasgow electrification
1971	January: BRB first corporate plan – InterCity targeted with 25% increase in revenue May: Half-hourly InterCity service introduced between Edinburgh and Glasgow May: Air-conditioned Mk2d coaches introduced September: DB (German Federal Railways) brands its express-train network 'InterCity'
1972	May 1: Bristol Parkway becomes first purpose-built Parkway station to open May: Euston–Birmingham half-hourly service introduced May: New North East–South West timetable builds hub at Birmingham July 25: Experimental gas-turbine-powered Advanced Passenger Train (APT) runs

Year	InterCity event
1973	January: 125mph prototype High Speed Train (HST) begins trials May 7: Alfreton & Mansfield Parkway opened June: Air conditioned Mk2e coaches introduced on Bristol/Swansea routes July 16: Rebuilt Stevenage station promoted as InterCity (London) peripheral hub
1974	May 5: Prototype HST enters service on London–Bristol route May 12: Mk3 coaches introduced on the London (Euston)–Liverpool route. May: Mk3 coaches first to permit wheelchairs by removal of seat and table
1976	January: Birmingham International station opened April 1: Senior Citizens' Railcard introduced October 4: New HSTs on Bristol/Swansea routes marketed as 'Inter-City125' (IC125) December: Business up 35% within 10 years of marketing InterCity name
1977	September: Big City Saver fares introduced on Midland main line to Scotland October: Full InterCity service introduced on Bristol/Swansea routes
1978	May 8: Initial InterCity trains into service on East Coast to Edinburgh December: travel up 33% in first two years of InterCity125 on Bristol/Swansea routes
1979	May 14: 0800 and 0905 HSTs ex King's Cross become third-fastest trains in world June 17: Family Railcard introduced September: First major joint promotion – free train tickets with Persil coupons October: HSTs start operating London–Penzance services December: HST concept and technology sold to Australia
1980	January: Minister of Transport calls for InterCity to operate without subsidy May 12: Full IC125 service on the London (Paddington)–Penzance route. May 19: East Coast HST units increased from eight to nine coaches
1981	January 5: HSTs introduced on Humberside and Teeside services July 27: Smoking banned in refreshment vehicles on WR IC125 services

Year	InterCity event
1981	September: North East–South West route branded 'Cross-Country' with first HSTs September: Saver Fares introduced on the Liverpool–London service December 7: APT enters revenue-earning service
1982	January 4: Sector Management introduced by British Railways Board 'InterCity' adopted as the name for the long-distance passenger sector Cyril Bleasdale appointed first InterCity Sector Director January: Saver Fares introduced nationally May 17: Full IC125 service on Cross-Country route October 4: IC125 trains introduced on the London (St Pancras)–Sheffield route Swiss Railways adopts Inter City as brand name for its express services
1983	January 20: Serpell Report saw no prospect of getting InterCity out of subsidy by 1985 July: £18 million refurbishment programme of 1,300 coaches announced October 1: Selby Diversion opened, reducing East Coast journey times October: InterCity sector reveals new InterCity livery based on APT colours
1984	January 5: On-train public telephones introduced on London–Swansea trains May 14: Maximum speed on West Coast main line increased from 100mph to 110mph New InterCity station opened at Sandwell & Dudley May: New InterCity livery applied to Gatwick Express trains July 27: £306 million East Coast electrification scheme authorised by Government October: 'InterCity into Profit' proposes turning £107m loss into £5m profit by 1989 December: Charter Train Unit incorporated into InterCity Sector
1985	April: InterCity Charter Train Unit launched InterCity takes Gatwick Express; London–Norwich/Harwich boat trains May: Pullman concept re-launched on East and West Coast routes July 29: Didcot station designated Parkway December: 130 InterCity services have on-board telephones
1986	February: Dr John Prideaux takes over as Sector Director March 6: New InterCity services introduced from Brighton to the North via Kensington Olympia May 12: Introduction of prestige Lancashire Pullman linking Blackpool, Preston and London: Tiverton Parkway opened next to M5

Year	InterCity event
1987	May 1: InterCity's 21st birthday brings new swallow logo and typeface May 6: InterCity Sleeper re-launch with Lounge Cars and Sleeper Check-in May 11: Second Class re-designated Standard December 2: APT project abandoned December: InterCity owns own train fleets when rolling stock allocated to sectors
1988	February 1: Silver Standard introduced for Standard Class customers October 3: Train Crew Agreement for new 'Senior Conductor' grade on InterCity December 14: Push-pull working on WCML Wolverhampton service December: All InterCity trains have on-board telephones
1989	Financial year 1988/89: InterCity achieves profitability one year earlier than expected May: Senior Conductors introduced with new uniforms and high-profile image October 2: New InterCity 225 electric service on Leeds route with Class 91 locomotives
1990	May 14: InterCity high-density commuter trains London–Peterborough/Derby June: £800m WCML upgrade announced (cancelled in July 1992 with privatisation)
1991	March: Refurbishment of Gatwick fleet announced September: First Boots' promotion generates £16m income and 4m journeys September 26: Record-breaking InterCity 225 run from London to Edinburgh September 30: HST units begin work on London–Holyhead route
1992	January 6: Chris Green appointed Managing Director, InterCity January: Free reservations for First Class and free tea/coffee for Pullman customers April 6: BR Organising for Quality Programme (OfQ) begins OforQ gives InterCity ownership of own infrastructure, fleet and staff May 11: Stagecoach leases six coaches for use on overnight Aberdeen services June: Richard Branson discusses Virgin running trains in partnership with InterCity; raises idea of Virgin taking over a number of InterCity's routes July: Government publishes White Paper on rail privatisation September 16: Major InterCity anti-recession marketing campaign November 1: Stagecoach withdraws from lease of coaches on Aberdeen service

Year	InterCity event
1992	December 9: All-party Parliamentary group formed to lobby for WCML upgrade Sleeper and Motorail services combined to form new InterCity Overnight Services
1993	February 3: Railways Bill receives second reading February: First three franchises will include East Coast, Great Western and Gatwick Express June: West Coast, Midland Main Line, Cross Country and Anglia in second tranche October 4: London–Bristol/Swansea service becomes InterCity Shuttle October 10: Gatwick Express established as first full shadow franchise October 31: Stagecoach joint marketing arrangement cancelled completely November 30: Chancellor announces £600m WCML upgrade in private sector
1994	January 3: InterCity's last TV advertisement – 'Get Motoring' January 13: £17m central door-locking project launched on Great Western February 14: InterCity first credit card machines piloted at Euston

Year	InterCity event
1994	March 26: InterCity's final naming ceremony at Paddington – HST *InterCity* March 31: InterCity closes as corporate business with final profit of £100m April 1: Railways Act takes effect with new Railtrack plc May 28: Motorail services withdrawn
1995	March: Special Trains unit sold to Pete Waterman On Board Services unit sold to management buyout
1996	February 4: Great Western Franchise starts trading (GW Holdings) April 28: Gatwick Express franchise starts trading (National Express) Great Western Franchise starts trading (GW Holdings) East Coast franchise starts trading (Sea Containers) Midland Mainline franchise starts trading (National Express)
1997	January 5: Anglia Railways franchise starts trading (GB Railways) January 5: CrossCountry franchise starts trading (Virgin 51%, Stagecoach 49%) February 25: final franchise awarded with National Express winning ScotRail March 9: West Coast franchise starts trading (Virgin) March 31: British Rail runs its final train – sleeper from Glasgow to London May 1: General Election won by Labour September 19: Southall high-speed collision October: Stagecoach acquires 49% shareholding in Virgin Rail

BELOW A line-up of top-flight motive power at Didcot Railway Centre, comprising (from left to right) GWR '43xx' 2-6-0 No 5322; 'King' 4-6-0 No 6023, WR gas-turbine locomotive No 18000 and BR HST power car No 43024. The occasion was the naming of the last-mentioned as *Great Western Society 1961-2011 Didcot Railway Centre* on 10 September 2011 *Antony Christie*

Year	InterCity event
1998	Sandy derailment when wheel disintegrates on GNER train
1999	January: PUG2 West Coast Upgrade contract signed by Virgin/Railtrack January: Virgin introduces first airline-style at-seat meal service February 25: Virgin launches new £10m Trainline internet ticketing project July 26: Advanced Tilt Train renamed 'Pendolino' October 5: Ladbroke Grove high-speed collision: 31 dead and 520 injured December: Railtrack withdraws from PUG2 140mph running and ECTS signalling

Year	InterCity event
2000	Anglia Railways doubles London–Norwich service to half-hourly May 30: Anglia introduces new Ipswich–Basingstoke service (withdrawn September) October 17: Hatfield derailment leaves four people dead December 6: Bombardier hands over first 'Voyager' train at Brugges November 22: Virgin £43m order to lengthen all 'Pendolinos' to nine-car
2001	Great Heck derailment leaves 10 people dead First 'Voyager' into passenger service – Birmingham–Bournemouth
2002	Railtrack goes into Administration March: Virgin and Railtrack in Administration sign £200m CrossCountry upgrade September: CrossCountry launches intensive 'Cinderella-Princess' timetable Network Rail created as not-for-dividend company July 9: 'Red Revolution' media launch of 'Pendolino' at test track July 25: first 'Pendolino' in passenger service August 31: 'Pendolino' achieves 145mph on test run West Coast: Virgin negotiates a management contract for its franchise Hull Trains awarded access rights for 10 years by ORR FirstGroup buys out GB Railways and acquires 80% of Renaissance Trains September 20: 'Operation Princess' launched 'White Rose' service to York and Leeds starts using Regional Eurostar trains
2003	March 31: Anglia Railways absorbed into new National Express Greater Anglia franchise GNER invites HM Queen to launch first 'Mallard' Mk4 refurbishment Second East Coast franchise: reduced from 20 to two years; won by GNER May: revised CrossCountry timetable launched May: 'Project Rio' HST service between St Pancras and Manchester during WCML upgrade
2004	April 1: Greater Eastern franchise (to 2012) absorbs InterCity into regional network September 20: New 125mph tilting 'Pendolino' timetable launch with Prime Minister September 20: Non-stop run London–Manchester and back (1hr 53min each way) September 24: New 125mph tilting 'Pendolino' timetable launched (36 tilting trains) November 6: Ufton Nervet level-crossing accident kills seven people
2005	Third East Coast franchise (10 years) won by GNER

ABOVE BR's Advanced Passenger Train passes Banbury Lane Crossing on the West Coast main line. *Antony Guppy*

ABOVE East Coast's Skyfall train crosses the Royal Border Bridge at Berwick-upon-Tweed on its maiden journey from London King's Cross to Edinburgh Waverley on Saturday 16 February 2013. *East Coast Main Line Co Ltd*

Year	InterCity event
2006	April 1: Second Great Western franchise (10 years); InterCity absorbed into regional franchise Renaissance Trains and Laing Rail create Wrexham & Shropshire 'Pendolino' record run London–Glasgow in 3hr 55min, averaging 102.4mph
2007	February 22: 'Pendolino' derailed on faulty points – one passenger dies November 11: CrossCountry franchise won by Arriva Trains (until 2016) November 11: East Midlands Trains franchise (to 2015) won by Stagecoach December 9: Fourth East Coast franchise (10 years) won by National Express December: Launch of Virgin high Frequency (VHF) timetable
2008	Hull Trains''Pioneer' fleet replaced by four five-car Class 180 'Adelante' units April 28: Wrexham & Shropshire wins seven-year track-access rights to London July: Grand Central runs three Sunderland–King's Cross trains daily – the 'North Eastern' service December 2008: Virgin trains introduces new Wrexham–London service via Chester
2009	Virgin orders four new 'Pendolinos' and extra coaches to lengthen 31 sets to 11 cars January 26: East Midland Parkway station opens February: Grand Central awarded three return services to Bradford Interchange

Year	InterCity event
2009	April: New Corby station opens with direct service to London August: Grand Central introduces fourth return service from Sunderland to London Hull Trains' access rights to London extended to 2016 DfT announces Great Western electrification by 2017 September 20: Greater Southern Franchise (10 years) absorbs Gatwick Express November 14: Directly Operated Railways takes over management of East Coast franchise December: London–Sheffield service doubled to twice-hourly
2010	May 23: Grand Central introduces new 'West Riding' services to Bradford via Pontefract
2011	March: DfT announces £5bn Great Western upgrade January 28: Last Wrexham & Shropshire train runs; transferred to Chiltern Railway
2012	Alliance Rail Holdings bids for paths for new services February 5: Greater Anglia franchise awarded to Abellio to 2014 December 9: Virgin West Coast franchise extended until 9 November 2014
2013	Following publication of the Brown Report, DFT gives amended start dates for inter-city franchises as follows: East Coast February 2015, Great Western July 2016; Greater Anglia October 2016; West Coast 2017; East Midlands October 2017 and CrossCountry November 2019

Factfile B: **Performance**

Table B1: Passenger satisfaction (%)

Year	Anglia (inter-city)	Cross Country	East Coast	Great Western	MML (inter-city)	West Coast	Total inter-city
2000/01	87	77	85	80	81	81	**82**
2001/02	76	72	84	73	80	70	**76**
2002/03	88	80	84	81	81	75	**82**
2003/04	79	81	84	80	76	76	**79**
2004/05	82	81	84	83	80	78	**81**
2005/06	n/a	83	86	81	86	81	**83**
2006/07	75	82	89	77	87	88	**85**
2007/08	80	83	85	73	88	87	**83**
2008/09	75	84	87	77	84	85	**83**
2009/10	80	85	88	82	83	88	**85**
2010/11	83	85	88	83	87	90	**87**
2011/12	83	84	87	82	87	89	**86**

Source: **Passenger Focus**

Table B2: Passenger journeys (000,000)

Year	Cross Country	East Coast	Great Western	MML (inter-city)	West Coast	Total inter-city
1994/95	10.4	12.5	n/a	5.3	13.1	54
1995/96	11.2	12.6	n/a	5.2	13.2	56
1996/97	12.0	12.8	n/a	n/a	13.4	59
1997/98	12.6	13.7	n/a	5.8	13.6	64
1998/99	n/a	14.1	n/a	6.3	15.5	67
1999/00	n/a	14.8	n/a	6.8	15.5	72
2000/01	15.0	13.6	n/a	8.2	15.3	70
2001/02	n/a	14.5	19.2	8.6	14.7	74
2002/03	n/a	14.7	20.2	9.3	14.1	77
2003/04	19.2	15.7	21.1	9.0	14.1	81
2004/05	19.3	16.8	22.3	10.5	15.1	84
2005/06	20.6	17.0	23.1	10.7	18.7	90
2006/07	23.2	17.6	25.3	10.8	19.0	99
2007/08	23.3	18.2	29.6	11.6	21.0	104
2008/09	24.7	18.9	31.2	12.1	22.5	109
2009/10	25.6	18.2	30.8	12.6	26.0	112
2010/11	26.7	18.5	32.7	12.2	28.9	119
2011/12	27.6	18.8	34.6	12.9	30.0	124

Sources: **SRA (1994-2003); ORR (2004-11)**

Table B3: Trains run daily (Monday-Friday)

Year	Anglia (inter-city)	Cross Country	East Coast	Great Western	MML (inter-city)	West Coast	Total inter-city
1997/98	48	94	93	134	59	152	580
1998/99	56	107	99	153	59	160	634
1999/00	60	107	102	158	110	170	708
2000/01	58	103	102	159	114	152	688
2001/02	64	123	107	175	123	162	754
2002/03	64	172	112	176	124	160	809
2003/04	63	167	112	165	130	157	793
2004/05	75	168	111	165	126	171	815
2005/06	83	170	111	172	122	193	850
2006/07	81	167	113	178	122	192	853
2007/08	88	202	118	193	161	205	967
2008/09	89	268	122	194	171	331	1,175
2009/10	87	274	120	196	188	331	1,196
2010/11	83	278	119	194	194	331	1,199
2011/12	72	281	154	195	195	331	1,228

Source: **ATOC**

Table B4: Punctuality (%) – arrivals within 10 minutes of scheduled time

Year %	Anglia (inter-city)	Cross Country	East Coast	GW (inter-city)	MML (inter-city)	West Coast	Total inter-city
1989/90	84	75	81	86	91	77	84
1990/91	84	78	80	88	89	78	85
1991/92	86	80	81	88	88	76	84
1992/93	85	81	88	87	89	83	87
1993/94	85	80	85	84	86	79	85
1994/95	n/a	n/a	n/a	n/a	n/a	n/a	n/a
1995/96	n/a	n/a	n/a	n/a	n/a	n/a	n/a
1996/97	n/a	n/a	n/a	n/a	n/a	n/a	n/a
1997/98	87	83	84	77	87	80	82
1998/99	90	74	85	81	86	77	81
1999/00	87	78	87	85	86	81	84
2000/01	78	55	71	76	76	63	69
2001/02	77	63	70	72	74	69	70
2002/03	77	62	71	72	74	74	71
2003/04	78	72	74	74	70	75	73
2004/05	85	78	78	80	88	72	79
2005/06	81	83	84	75	93	84	82
2006/07	83	85	83	76	93	86	85
2007/08	87	87	83	77	90	86	86
2008/09	86	90	87	86	91	80	87
2009/10	86	90	87	88	93	85	89
2010/11	85	88	83	84	93	87	88
2011/12	86	89	86	85	94	86	89

Note: Pre 1994 was measured on arrivals within 10min 59 seconds of schedule; post 1994 measured on arrivals within 9min 59 seconds.

Sources: **InterCity (pre-1994); ATOC (from 1994)**

Table B5: Train catering

Number of weekday trains serving hot meals

Year	Anglia	Cross Country	East Coast	Great Western	Midland Mainline	West Coast	Total inter-city
1993/94 Restaurant cars	22	0	60	28	13	117	249
2011/12 At seat (First Class)*	0	92	142	29	125	151	539

* excludes Hull Trains 14 daily and Eurostar 48 daily

Source: **Barry Doe**

Table B6: Speed v frequency

Daily services, Monday–Thursday service, 0700–2000hrs

London to:	Frequency Trains Run		Journey Time Average		Speed Average (mph)	
	1992	**2012**	**1992**	**2012**	**1992**	**2012**
East Coast						
Peterborough1	29	41	0hr 46	0hr 45	99	101
Doncaster2	28	54	1hr 42	1hr 37	92	95
York2	25	37	1hr 56	2hr 00	97	94
Leeds	16	27	2hr 22	2hr 17	79	81
Hull2	3	8	2hr 49	2hr 38	73	78
Newcastle-upon-Tyne	23	27	2hr 57	3hr 03	91	88
Edinburgh	14	19	4hr 22	4hr 33	90	86
West Coast						
Birmingham New St	26	39	1hr 38	1hr 23	69	81
Manchester Piccadilly	15	39	2hr 35	2hr 08	71	86
Liverpool Lime St	12	15	2hr 38	2hr 08	73	91
Chester	3	12	2hr 24	2hr 01	75	89
Preston	14	16	2hr 38	2hr 20	79	96
Warrington Bank Quay	10	15	2hr 11	1hr 44	83	105
Glasgow Central	5	12	5hr 17	4hr 32	76	88
Great Western						
Reading1	52	90	0hr 24	0hr 26	90	83
Swindon	40	59	0hr 54	0hr 58	86	80
Bristol Parkway	19	24	1hr 17	1hr 24	87	80
Bristol Temple Meads	21	27	1hr.37	1hr 43	73	69
Cardiff Central	18	24	1hr 57	2hr 04	74	70
Exeter St Davids	11	17	2hr 16	2hr 22	77	73
Plymouth	11	13	3hr 26	3hr 21	66	67
Midland Mainline						
Leicester	30	52	1hr 14	1hr 14	80	80
Derby	16	26	1hr 45	1hr 41	73	76
Nottingham	13	26	1hr 41	1hr 53	75	67
Sheffield	14	26	2hr 22	2hr 22	70	70
Anglia						
Norwich	15	29	1hr 44	1hr 54	66	60
CrossCountry Ex Birmingham						
Reading	14	26	1hr 51	1hr 35	53	62
Bournemouth	8	13	3hr 43	3hr 07	47	56
Bristol Temple Meads	14	26	1hr 33	1hr 27	60	64
Plymouth	9	13	3hr 55	3hr 34	56	62
Manchester Piccadilly	13	26	1hr 38	1hr 35	50	52
Glasgow (West Coast)	6	73	4hr 30	3hr 57	66	74
Newcastle-upon-Tyne	8	25	3hr 34	3hr 22	59	62
Edinburgh (East Coast)	2	12	5hr 25	5hr 04	61	66
Edinburgh (West Coast)	4	6	4hr 58	4hr 02	59	73
Eurostar						
London – Brussels	5	9	3hr 17	2hr 05	63	112
London – Paris	9	15	3hr 00	2hr 19	102	132

1 long-distance services only 2 includes open-access services 3 operated by Virgin West Coast

Source: **Gordon Pettitt**

Table B7: World's fastest journeys, 2011

Train	From	To	Average speed (mph)	Operator
Britain				
Hourly	London Euston	Stafford	107.4	Virgin Trains
0948hrs	London King's Cross	Grantham	107.8	Hull Trains
Four Class 395s	Ashford International	Stratford Intl	108.3	Southeastern Trains
1942hrs	Stafford	Watford Jct	109.5	Virgin Trains
0744hrs	Stevenage	Grantham	111.9	Hull Trains
Italy				
Four services	Roma Termini	Napoli Centrale	122.0	FS
Eurostar				
Eurostar 9112	St Pancras International	Brussels	123.8	
13 services	St Pancras International	Paris	136.8	Eurostar
Germany				
ICE 828	Frankfurt Flughafen	Bonn/Siegburg	149.3	ICE
Spain				
AVE 5340	Madrid	Valencia	154.4	RENFE
Japan				
Nozomi 1/95	Hiroshima	Kokura	160.0	JR West
France				
TGV 5401	Lorraine TGV	Champagne-Ardenne	169.9	SNCF
China				
Four G class	Wuhan	Guangzhou Nan	192.5	China Railways

Source: **Railway Gazette International, September 2011**

Table B8: Inter-city train reliability

Company	Train type	Miles per technical incident MAA 2011/12
CrossCountry	Class 220 'Voyager'	38,273
CrossCountry	Class 221 'Super Voyager' (non-tilt)	31,534
Cross Country	HST sets	22,741
Grand Central	HST sets	17,050
East Midlands Trains	Class 222 'Meridian'	15,594
Virgin Trains	Class 221 'Super Voyager' (tilt)	15,391
National Express East Anglia	Class 90 + Mk3 sets	14,783
East Midlands Trains	HST sets	13,985
East Coast	HST sets	11,258
Virgin Trains	Class 390 'Pendolino' (tilt)	9,972
Hull Trains	Class 180 'Adelante'	9,437
East Coast	Class 91 + Mk4 sets	8,325
First Greater Western	HST sets	7,417
Grand Central	Class 180 'Adelante'	5,589
Chiltern Trains	Class 67 + Mk3 sets	5,490

Table B9: Domestic passenger journeys by air to/from London Heathrow, Gatwick, Stansted, Luton, City & Southend

London East Coast flights (both directions)

000 trips	Edinburgh	Newcastle	Leeds/Bradford	Durham /Tees Valley	Total
2000	3015	710	228	173	**4126**
2001	3088	730	209	156	**4183**
2002	3437	896	217	153	**4703**
2003	3533	1050	189	146	**4916**
2004	3580	1087	189	144	**5000**
2005	3646	1067	186	159	**5058**
2006	3476	1013	148	151	**4788**
2007	3419	906	137	88	**4550**
2008	3157	764	126	81	**4128**
2009	2969	727	52	14	**3762**
2010	2755	643	51	-	**3449**
2011	2935	597	11	-	**3543**
2000-11	-2.7%	-15.9%	-95.2%	-100%	**14.1%**

Source: **CAA Airport Statistics**

London West Coast flights (both directions)

000 trips	Glasgow	Manchester	Prestwick	Liverpool	Blackpool	Total
2000	2426	1850	441	201	-	**4918**
2001	2552	1798	627	49	-	**5026**
2002	2631	1782	694	1	-	**5108**
2003	2733	1950	721	0	69	**6273**
2004	2799	1987	591	68	128	**6354**
2005	2693	1890	505	72	131	**6244**
2006	2598	1795	470	49	122	**5912**
2007	2723	1596	427	17	43	**5502**
2008	2499	1366	403	-	-	**4926**
2009	2342	1225	278	-	-	**3472**
2010	2160	1051	225	-	-	**4031**
2011	2158	1007	89	-	-	**4031**
2000-11	-11%	-45.6%	-79.8%	-100%	-100%	**-18.0%**

Source: **CAA Airport Statistics**

Other domestic flights (both directions)

000 trips	Edinburgh–Manchester	Edinburgh–Leeds Bradford	Edinburgh–Birmingham	Glasgow–Manchester	Glasgow–Birmingham	Total
2000	172	31	287	178	284	**952**
2001	175	34	288	175	277	**949**
2002	148	50	334	148	315	**995**
2003	176	55	373	176	363	**1143**
2004	189	57	387	189	345	**1167**
2005	179	52	471	179	324	**1205**
2006	200	51	495	200	326	**1272**
2007	180	51	436	180	346	**1193**
2008	152	41	401	152	337	**1083**
2009	104	19	337	104	269	**833**
2010	79	15	288	79	212	**673**
2011	59	12	289	59	212	**631**
2000-11	-65.7%	-61.3%	+0.7%	-66.9%	-25.4%	**-33.7%**

Source: **CAA Airport Statistics**

Table B10: EU safety performance

Fatality rates 2007-10 (passenger and workforce)

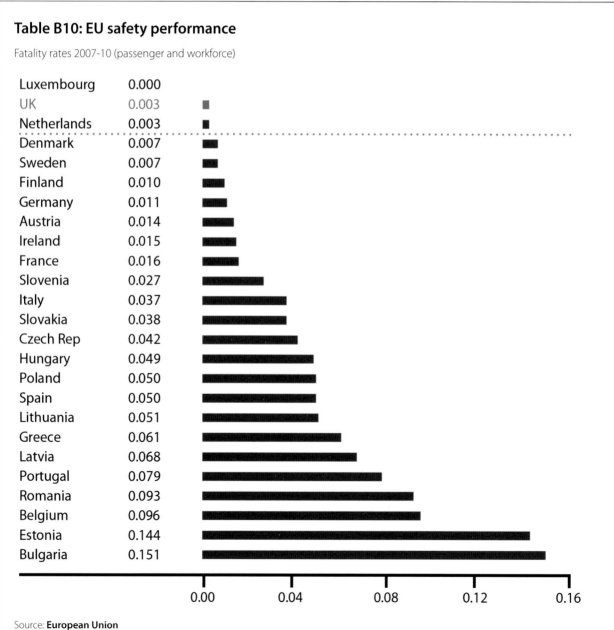

Luxembourg	0.000
UK	0.003
Netherlands	0.003
Denmark	0.007
Sweden	0.007
Finland	0.010
Germany	0.011
Austria	0.014
Ireland	0.015
France	0.016
Slovenia	0.027
Italy	0.037
Slovakia	0.038
Czech Rep	0.042
Hungary	0.049
Poland	0.050
Spain	0.050
Lithuania	0.051
Greece	0.061
Latvia	0.068
Portugal	0.079
Romania	0.093
Belgium	0.096
Estonia	0.144
Bulgaria	0.151

Source: **European Union**

LEFT 'Heading towards Chester, Crewe and the West Coast main line, 'Super Voyager' No 221102 approaches Llandudno Junction on its way east with the 1150 Holyhead–Euston on 27 March 2011. *Antony Christie*

RIGHT Virgin people made the ultimate difference. Customer Service Values in action at Stoke-on-Trent. *MP92½*

Table B11: Vision, strategy and values, 1992-2012

Vision	Strategy	Values/Behaviours
InterCity 1992		
To be the most civilised way to travel at speed from centre to centre	To focus on quality as seen by our customers and deliver a consistent, safe and relaxing service. To improve efficiency and reduce unit costs. To grow profitably in an open, competitive environment. To provide an environment where our people can achieve their potential and enhance our competitive advantage.	Visibility Courtesy Personal discipline Teamwork Respect Empathy Enjoyment
GNER 1998		
Creating the ultimate travel experience for you	Through our people, GNER will create a golden era of rail travel. We will do this together by setting the highest standards of service, convenience and quality in the UK. We will be the ultimate travel experience for every customer	People Customer focus Safe Progressive Pride in our work
Virgin Trains 1999		
To provide a world-class travel experience	Safe and reliable Transforming our railway Developing our people Memorable customer service Growing our business World-class delivery	Customer focus Active listening Teamwork Empathy Empowerment Dressed smartly Walking the Talk
Midland Mainline 1996		
A recognised leader in Customer Service	Renowned for warmth of welcome and enabling every customer to feel treated as an individual To be one team in which everyone enjoys playing a part in serving our customers and shares in success To grow profitably by consistently delivering promises to customers and stakeholders and improving effectiveness To develop, recognise and reward our people within learning culture	People who feel good about themselves do good things. Put customers at heart of everything we do. Value people and build their self-esteem. Harness creative talent of our people. Empower people and teams with responsibility and accountability. Behave with clarity, trust and openness. Be ambassadors for our business.

Source: **Chris Green**

Factfile C: **InterCity 1982-1993**

InterCity Routes

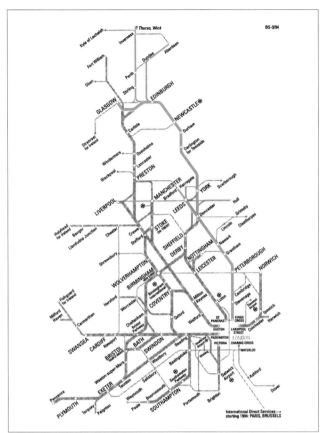

ABOVE InterCity emphasises its 'fast and civilised' brand values by using A4 Class locomotive *Mallard* on a special train from London King's Cross to Scarborough on 3 July 1986. *David Ward*

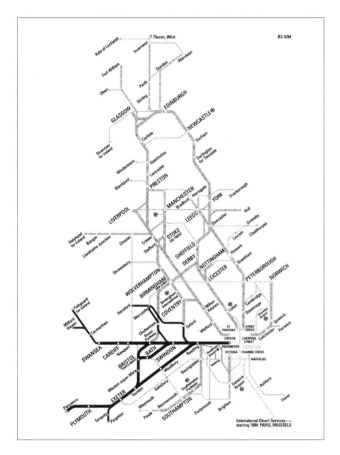

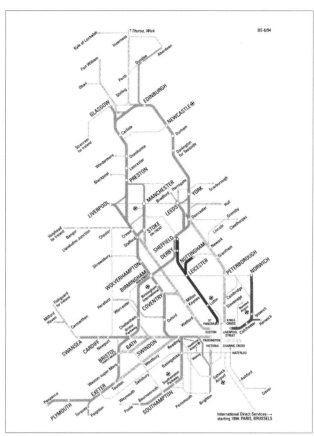

InterCity Route by Route

+ Owned by Network South East   Source: The InterCity Story 1994

	Anglia	East Coast	Great Western	Midland	West Coast	Cross Country	InterCity Total
System							
Route Miles	125+	493	467	161	531	213	**1865**
% Electrified	100+	100	0	33	94	2	**58**
Track Miles	250+	1309	1557	548	1446	476	**5336**
% Electrified	100+	97	0	40	93	3	**53**
Trains operated Mon-Fri	47	104	135	68	174	102	**630**
Infrastructure							
Bridges & Culverts	+	2353	1748	1500	3373	1300	**10274**
Tunnels	+	42	33	28	31	14	**148**
Signalboxes	+	9	20	5	45	13	**92**
Points & Switches	+	1193	1860	985	2148	1263	**7449**
Signals	+	3292	3479	890	3580	873	**12114**
Stations	3	13	21	8	22	1	**68**
Carriage Washing Machines	1	2	12	2	6	1	**24**

InterCity People

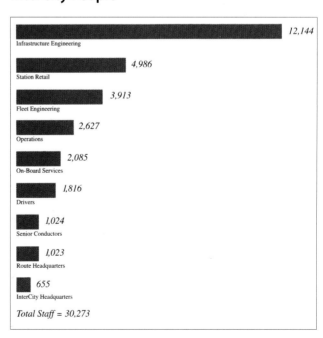

Infrastructure Engineering — 12,144
Station Retail — 4,986
Fleet Engineering — 3,913
Operations — 2,627
On-Board Services — 2,085
Drivers — 1,816
Senior Conductors — 1,024
Route Headquarters — 1,023
InterCity Headquarters — 655

Total Staff = 30,273

InterCity People

ABOVE From 1992 InterCity's workforce was led by Managing Director Chris Green who is seen here with his fellow directors from the headquarters functions and the operating routes. From left to right (back row): Ivor Warburton, Geoff Ashton, Richard George, Barry Woledge, Terry Coyle, Andy Cooper, Richard Brown, David Ward, John Cimelli. Front row: Brian Burdsall, Bob Brown, Chris Green, John Ellis, Brian Scott

---

INTERCITY ORGANISATION

a) Unified Business 1992-94

Managing Director
Chris Green

Route Directors | HQ Directors

Anglia & Gatwick
Andy Cooper

East Coast
Brian Burdsall

Great Western
Brian Scott

Midland Cross Country
Richard Brown

West Coast
Ivor Warburton

Special Trains
David Ward

Finance
Geoff Ashton

Fleet
Brian Clementson

Human Resources
Barry Woledge

Infrastructure
Bob Brown

Marketing
John Cimelli

On Board Services
Terry Coyle

InterCity Customers

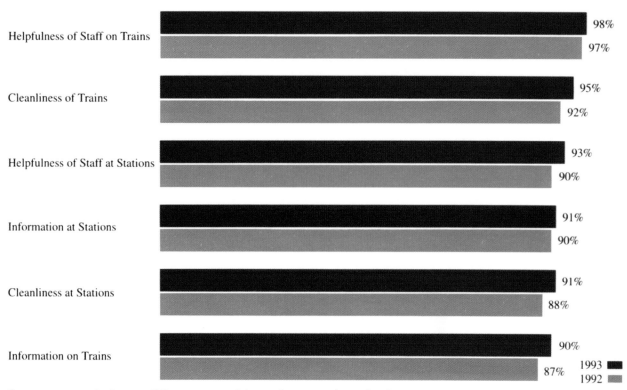

Customer Satisfaction Scores

	1993	1992
Helpfulness of Staff on Trains	98%	97%
Cleanliness of Trains	95%	92%
Helpfulness of Staff at Stations	93%	90%
Information at Stations	91%	90%
Cleanliness at Stations	91%	88%
Information on Trains	90%	87%

Customers were asked to rate different aspects of the service on a scale ranging from very poor to very good. The results show the percentage of InterCity customers who rated each aspect as at least "satisfactory" (covering adequate, good or very good).

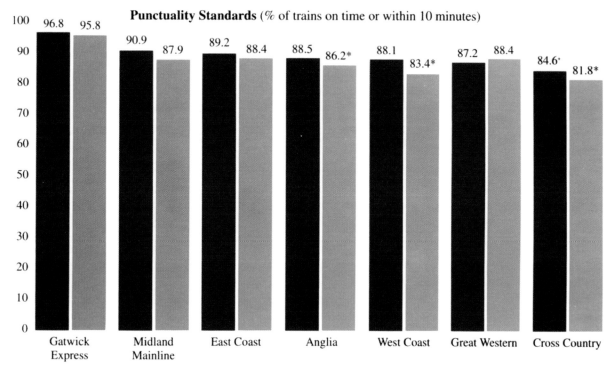

Punctuality Standards (% of trains on time or within 10 minutes)

	1993	1992
Gatwick Express	96.8	95.8
Midland Mainline	90.9	87.9
East Coast	89.2	88.4
Anglia	88.5	86.2*
West Coast	88.1	83.4*
Great Western	87.2	88.4
Cross Country	84.6ʼ	81.8*

Notes
1. These are 52 week moving averages as at 4 December 1993 and 5 December 1992.
2. * = Season ticket discount triggered in December 1992   + = Season ticket discount triggered in December 1993
3. Target is 90%. Discounts are triggered below 87%.

InterCity Finance and Investment

		1982	1983	1984/85†	1985/86	1986/87	1987/88	1988/89	1989/90	1990/91	1991/92	1992/93
Income/Turnover	£m	350	439	685	613	658	733	803	833	892	897	889
Operating (loss) (as published)	£m	(196)	(159)	(172)	(117)	(99)	(86)	–	–	–	–	–
Operating profit (at 1993/94 conventions)	£m		–	–	–	–	–	153	149	132	102	82
Receipts per train mile	£	na	na	14.65	16.18	17.16	18.19	18.69	18.69	18.33	17.69* [17.27]	17.54
Receipts per passenger mile	pence	na	na	9.82	10.36	10.71	10.73	11.17	11.63	11.68	11.37* [11.10]	11.20
Passenger miles per loaded train mile	passengers	na	na	155	161	165	175	174	167	162	160	161
Total operating expenses per train mile	£	na	na	20.93	19.88	20.20	19.70	17.42	18.68	18.01	15.64* [17.64]	16.00

* restated 1991/92, originally reported figures in [square] brackets
† 15 month period (change from calendar to fiscal year accounting)

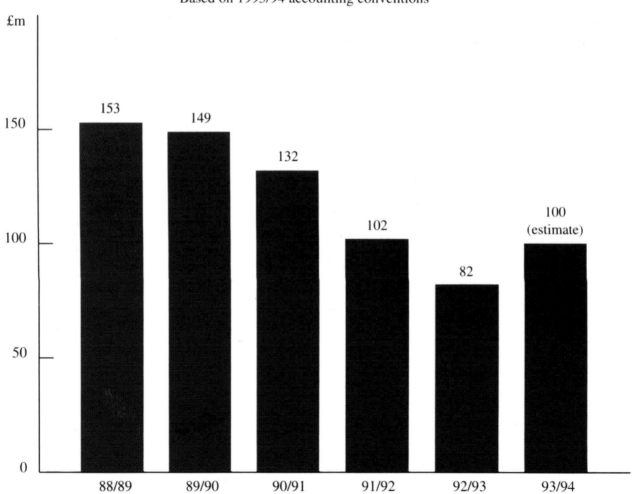

InterCity Profit
Based on 1993/94 accounting conventions

ABOVE InterCity: A railway business under one overall roof.

InterCity's 1993/4 Investment Plan

	£m
Track Renewals	41.0
Signalling and Track Projects	5.8
Electrification Projects	0.1
Telecommunications	0.9
Engineering Equipment	1.1
Road Vehicles	1.5
Traction and Rolling Stock	4.9
Terminals and Facilities	11.2
Stabling and Servicing Facilities	1.0
Computer and Other Projects	2.5
Total	**70.0**

InterCity Investment (total, including track renewals)

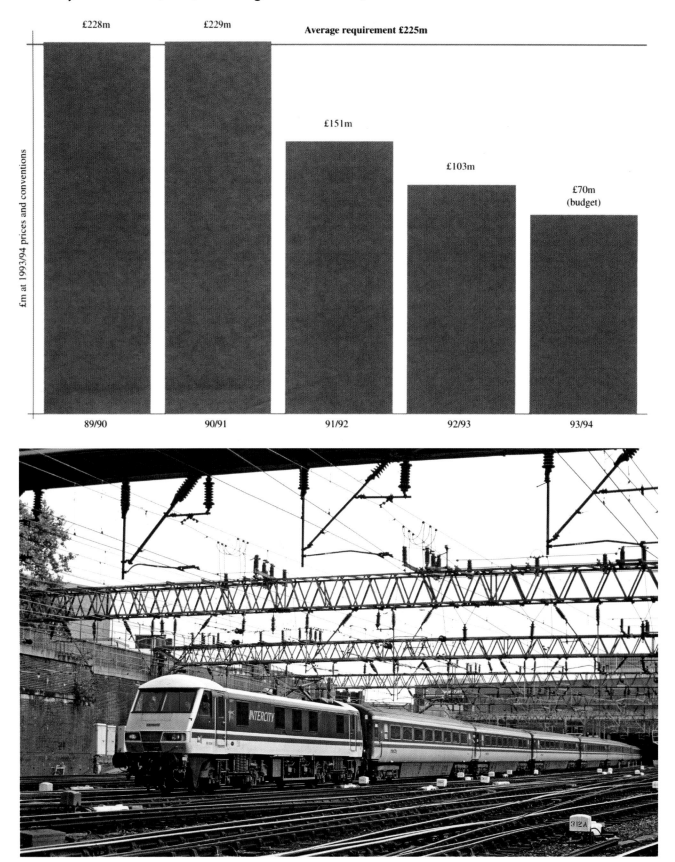

£228m £229m Average requirement £225m

£151m

£103m

£70m (budget)

£m at 1993/94 prices and conventions

89/90   90/91   91/92   92/93   93/94

ABOVE Heading north with a rake of Mk3s, 90004 departs from London Euston on 7 September 1988 *Brian Morrison*

InterCity Brands

InterCity has a broad customer base

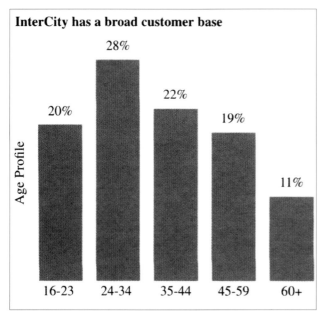

InterCity Brand Awareness

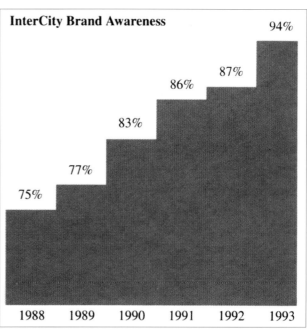

Long distance travel market in Britain

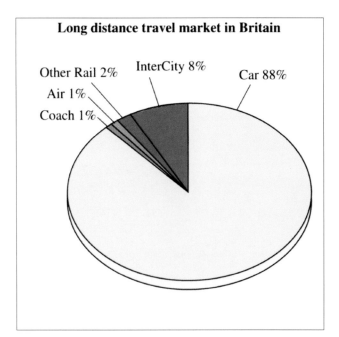

Other Rail 2%
InterCity 8%
Air 1%
Coach 1%
Car 88%

Journey purpose on InterCity

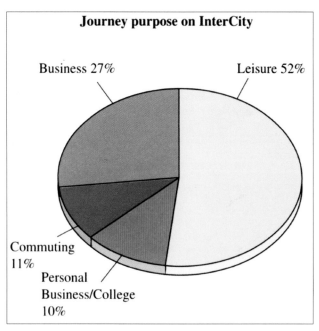

Business 27%
Leisure 52%
Commuting 11%
Personal Business/College 10%

	1987/88	1988/89	1989/90	1990/91	1991/92	1992/93
Passenger Journeys (million)	75	72	71	70	66	62
Passenger Miles (million)	8200	8300	8100	7900	7800	7600
Average Journey Length (miles)	109	115	114	113	118	122
Customers per day (000's)	207	198	195	191	182	171
Trains per day	–	–	–	–	780 *	775 *

* Includes Gatwick Express

Journeys by ticket type

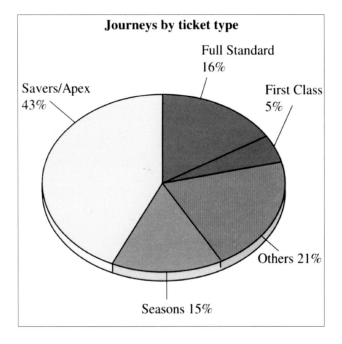

Full Standard 16%
Savers/Apex 43%
First Class 5%
Others 21%
Seasons 15%

Income by ticket type

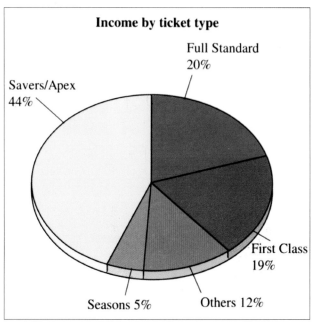

Full Standard 20%
Savers/Apex 44%
First Class 19%
Others 12%
Seasons 5%

InterCity Brand Delivery

ABOVE This First Class mock-up of the IC250 should have been in service by 1995. However, recession and privatisation both ensured that these vehicles never saw service. *Authors*

ABOVE Senior conductors with their high profile image and smart new uniforms were introduced in May 1989. *Authors*

Factfile D: **Eurostar**

ABOVE Eurostar's current logo *Eurostar International Ltd*

Introduction

Richard Brown, Eurostar's Chairman, believes that his company 'might best be described as the Continental first cousin of InterCity'. Although never formally part of the InterCity network, it nonetheless conforms to the original InterCity vision, with similar brand and customer service standards. Eurostar has become one of the most widely recognised and respected travel brands in the United Kingdom and provides a very real physical and cultural link between Britain, France and Belgium – where it is an umbilical cord to over 300,000 French nationals living and working in London.

In 2011 the company carried 9.7 million passengers on its 27 Class 373 'InterCapital' trainsets. It has largely replaced the airlines between London and Paris/Brussels and currently has roughly 80% of the market on both routes. This market has doubled in size since Eurostar's early days because of the faster city-to-city travel experience by high-speed rail.

Eurostar International Ltd (EIL) – the joint venture TOC that since September has operated the service in all three countries – reported punctuality at 92.7% in 2011, together with a net profit of £20.8million despite exceptionally high access charges. Today Eurostar can legitimately be regarded as a great success story for high speed international passenger rail travel. But it has not always been so.

Partners: past and present

Eurostar started life as European Passenger Services (EPS) – a separate division of British Rail – hived off as a stand-alone Government-owned company prior to rail privatisation. Working in partnership with SNCF and SNCB, EPS inaugurated its high-speed operation in 1994, initially only on France's 'Ligne 3', between Calais and Paris. Each partner contributed a number of trainsets and train crews and each took responsibility for operations, safety and costs within their own territory. Revenues and certain costs were shared according to pre-agreed protocols, but these arrangements were the sum total of the formal relationships between the partners.

This loose partnership remained in place right through to 2010, when Eurostar International was eventually formed as a formal joint venture, each partner taking a shareholding and with the previous pooling arrangements coming to an end. SNCF has 55% of the shares, the UK through London & Continental Railways (LCR) 40%, and SNCB 5%, the percentages broadly reflecting each railway's participation in the previous pooling arrangements. On the UK side, EPS was transferred to LCR ownership in 1996 when its consortium won the concession to build the Channel Tunnel Rail Link. LCR changed the name to Eurostar (UK) Ltd (EUKL), making EPS's founding Managing Director, Richard Edgeley, and most of his management team redundant. Initially it ran EUKL directly with a number of Virgin managers parachuted in to strengthen the marketing function. Adam Mills, Chief Executive of LCR, doubled as Managing Director of EUKL until Hamish Taylor was recruited from British Airways to take over that role.

Virgin had very different views from EUKL's continental partners, including an expectation to re-brand the trainsets. In 1998 Virgin was subsequently bought out of the LCR consortium, and in the same year LCR had to be refinanced due to over-optimism in its financial bid for the CTRL concession.

Part of the resulting restructuring included contracting-out responsibility for managing EUKL to another consortium namely, InterCapital and Regional Rail Ltd (ICRRL). This grouping was made up of National Express (40%); SNCF (35%); SNCB (15%) and British Airways – always a sleeping partner – securing a share of 10%. From then on ICRRL effectively appointed EUKL's senior management and oversaw its operation until the formation of Eurostar International Ltd in 2010. In 2002 ICRRL appointed as CEO Richard Brown, who then served until EIL was formed in 2010 providing much needed stability of direction.

Table D1: Eurostar Managing Directors and Chief Executives

1994	Richard Edgeley, MD European Passenger Services
1996	Andrew Mills MD, Eurostar (UK) Limited (EUKL)
1997	Hamish Taylor
1999	Gordon Bye
2002-10	Richard Brown CEO, EUKL and Eurostar Group Ltd (Chairman from 2010)
2010-	Nicholas Petrovic CEO (EIC)

Difficult days, 1996-2002

Eurostar's first few years of operation were undoubtedly difficult. Passenger growth was much slower than expected, and, in 1996 after the first Channel Tunnel fire, operations were suspended for several months. In turn, the service suffered from lack of continuity of both purpose and personnel with the three national stakeholders struggling to find good working relationships.

In addition, Eurostar's early days generated several proposals which turned out to be non-starters. The North of London services which would have seen Eurostar trains directly linking key cities such as Newcastle, Manchester and Birmingham with Paris and Brussels were included as part of the overall Channel Tunnel Act package in order to secure support from northern MPs with seven specially configured 14 coach trainsets being included in the initial train fleet order. However, the economic case had not been properly established and, following the restructuring of LCR, studies showed that these services would have been hopelessly uneconomic in the then emerging world of low-cost airlines. Preparations for North of London services were therefore cancelled in 1999, some of the sets being subsequently rented to GNER (see Chapter 10) before being leased to SNCF to help operate the Nord Pas de Calais–Paris service group.

Even more ill-fated was the proposed NightStar sleeper-train network, which would have provided direct night services from Scotland, Wales and a number of northern cities to the continent. Again no real attention was paid to potential economics when planning the services and the sleeper cars were not even completed before the project was cancelled and the coaches ultimately sold to owners in Canada and the Middle East.

More high-profile evidence of short-term planning is apparent in the shape of the now disused international terminal at Waterloo. This magnificent station within a station was designed by Nicholas Grimshaw, and was home to Eurostar in its first 13 years of life. However, the expense of operating two city centre stations; the potential confusion for passengers in splitting the service between the two stations; and the fact that St Pancras International used the much faster HS1 route meant that the decision was taken to withdraw from Waterloo once HS1 was fully open.

Less visible but equally unfortunate is Eurostar's disused maintenance facility on the approach to London Paddington at North Pole International depot. Originally the intention was to continue to use this as Eurostar's London maintenance base after the opening of HS1, but too little attention had been paid to the practicalities of accessing North Pole via the North London line. A new maintenance facility was finally built at Temple Mills, near Stratford, with one benefit being that learning from 13 years' experience at North Pole meant that many of its design shortcomings could be remedied at Temple Mills. A second benefit is that North Pole will provide the perfect site for a new IEP depot outside Paddington.

ABOVE The last Eurostar train prepares to leave Waterloo International on 13 November 2007, before the successful transfer of the service to St Pancras International *Eurostar International Ltd*

Growing the business, 2003-7

The early years of Eurostar were not easy. For example, the initial pricing strategy proved to be ill-conceived and, on occasions, the different partners were quoting different fares for exactly the same journey. Growth stalled in 2000 with the onset of recession and passenger numbers actually declined for the following three years.

In 2001 the service lost market share too – partly because of poor punctuality and partly because of a confused commercial strategy. In some ways, this was unsurprising in that EUKL had seen five different managing directors in its first years of operation along with three different controlling entities: the DfT in the days of EPS; LCR with a strong Virgin involvement and finally, ICRRL from 1998.

The opening in 2003 of the southern section of the newly-named HS1 marked the turning point in Eurostar's fortunes. London to Paris journey times were reduced by 20 minutes to 2hr 35min to Paris, and punctuality improved through having to share less of the old Southern Region's infrastructure. Opening of the new line was used as an opportunity to re-launch the service.

Equally important was a concerted drive to capture the business travel market. Whilst Eurostar had always carried the lion's share of leisure travel on its core routes, it had not successfully appealed to business travellers. Whilst its share of leisure travel was already approaching 80% by 2001, business travel was still only around 30%. The breakthrough came in 2005, when First Class was split into Business Premier and Leisure Select. With these new marketing arrangements in place, combined volumes in the two new classes grew by over 40% in the following two years.

A new approach to pricing also had a large impact when Eurostar abandoned its traditional railway fares' structure in 2003 for a low-cost airline model, in which the price of leisure fares depended on how long ahead customers booked and how busy their intended train was likely to be. At the same time the lead-in fare was reduced to £59 return and then held for six years. These changes were followed in 2005 with the implementation of a sophisticated income management system allowing fine tuning of transferability and loadings on a train-by-train basis. Nowadays, Eurostar's year-round load factor consistently exceeds 70% compared to 45-50% for a UK inter-city train company.

Table D2: Eurostar annual passenger volumes, 1994-2012

Year	Passenger Volumes
1994	155,000*
1995	2.9m
1996	4.9m
1997	6.0m
1998	6.3m
1999	6.6m
2000	7.1m
2001	7.0m
2002	6.6m
2003	6.3m
2004	7.3m
2005	7.5m
2006	7.9m
2007	8.3m
2008	9.1m
2009	9.2m
2010	9.5m
2011	9.7m
2012	9.9m

* for 2 months only, passenger service having started in November 1994

Source: **Eurostar International Ltd**

Coming of age, 2007

The final step in Eurostar's turnaround of fortunes came with the opening of the second section of HS1 and the switch to St Pancras International in November 2007. This enabled a further cut of 20 minutes journey time to be made, thus reducing the fastest run to Paris to just 2hr 15min and 1hr 51min to Brussels. Use of HS1 enabled a further improvement in punctuality to be made through self-contained infrastructure and an absence of weekend engineering work with all HS1 track maintenance being carried out within night-time possessions.

The icing on the cake for Eurostar was the opening of St Pancras International itself, justly dubbed 'Europe's most beautiful station' by Guillaume Pepy, President of SNCF. Knowing that the opening of HS1 and St Pancras International would attract huge media attention, Eurostar chose the risky but highly successful strategy of using both the move and the opening as the principal means of advertising the improved service. Defying fate, it chose its 13th birthday to undertake the transfer. Four years of detailed planning ensured it went extremely well. With much media acclaim, this was to prove a powerful contrast to the later, and altogether far less successful, BA move to Heathrow's Terminal 5.

ABOVE On 7 October 2010 a mock-up of the new Eurostar e320 was placed on display in London's Hyde Park *Eurostar International Ltd*

ABOVE Eurostar's Premier Business Lounge at Paris Gare du Nord
Eurostar International Ltd

LCR and Eurostar realised that the success or failure of HS1 would directly influence the wider debate around high-speed rail in the UK. Their decision to rename the rather clumsy CTRL as High Speed 1 was intended to suggest that it should be but the first of several high-speed lines in the UK.

Eurostar's fleet

When built, Eurostar's Class 373 trainsets were a triumph of design ingenuity – configured to operate with four different signalling and electrical supply systems. Furthermore, all this complexity was contained within a UK gauge profile so that the trains could initially operate over the former Southern Region route into Waterloo. The complex trains have proved difficult to maintain and reliability has been a significant problem. Indeed, it is only in the last two or three years that many of the original design issues have been mastered with the Eurostar fleet now at comparable levels of reliability as several of the TGV fleets.

With the establishment of Eurostar International in 2010 as a truly integrated company, it could now raise finance in its own name. Its first act was to order 10 new Siemens e320 trainsets, based on the successful Velaro series. The new trains will give capacity for expansion as well as replacing some existing Class 373 sets. They are due for delivery in 2014/15, and will give an extra 150 seats per train. With much lower maintenance costs as well as giving better availability and reliability, they will be designed by Pininfarina, the Italian design house best known for its association with Ferrari. A comprehensive programme of refurbishment for all existing, retained trainsets started in late 2012.

In September 2010 Standard Premier – a class essentially designed for cost-conscious business travellers and others who want the same legroom as Business Premier as well and some at-seat service – was also introduced. Eurostar's on-board catering is not operated by the company but is contracted out to Momentum, a joint venture between Cremonini of Italy and Select Service Partners.

In 2011 Eurostar also offered a range of enhancements to its flagship Business Premier class, including new menus developed in collaboration with Michelin Three Star chef, Alain Roux, a new guaranteed boarding service, a mobile app for iPhone and Android users including new mobile M-ticketing, on-board taxi bookings and enhancements to business travel facilities in Paris and Brussels.

Future developments, 2012-15

Eurostar is structured on a pure open-access basis in all three countries of operation. Not being a franchise operator, and having no grandfather rights or public service obligation to deal with, it is now free to develop and expand wherever there is a commercial case. An important priority is to grow the market in travel on the

continent beyond Paris and Brussels and, in the UK, beyond St Pancras International. Since 2007, Eurostar has offered through fares from a wide range of UK towns and cities – particularly working alongside intercity and UK TOCs and it is now developing similar contractual partnerships for instance with Thalys to Holland and Germany and to Switzerland with Lyria.

Eurostar's new Velaro e320 trains are specified to run through to other continental countries and the company will be evaluating the business case for new through services from 2014. However, open access also means open competition, and Eurostar faces the prospect of head-to-head competition in the next few years. Deutsche Bahn has already announced its intention of running directly to London from Frankfurt and Amsterdam (via Brussels), offering direct competition to Eurostar on the Brussels–London route.

Table D3: Eurostar timeline

1994	November 14: Eurostar launched by French, British and Belgian railways
1996	First Eurotunnel fire halts initial momentum of Eurostar's growth trajectory UK interests vested in London & Continental Railways (LCR)
1998	InterCapital & Regional Railways Ltd (ICRR) – a conglomeration of National Express, SNCF, SNCB and BA – awarded 12-year contract to manage Eurostar (UK) Ltd (EUKL)
1999	Eurostar Group Ltd formed to lead marketing and sales in all three countries
2003	First section of Channel tunnel rail link (CTRL) opened from Eurotunnel to Fawkham Junction – cuts journey time by 20 minutes. New UK speed record of 334 km/h on 30 July 2003
2003	First refurbishment of train interiors carried out – work designed by Philipe Starck. First Class split into Business Premier and Leisure Select in 2005
2006	August: second Eurotunnel fire
2007	November 14: HS1 and St Pancras International opened. Eurostar switches services from Waterloo International. Further 20-minute acceleration with London–Paris journey time now 2hr 15min and London–Brussels 1hr 51min
2007	'Tread Lightly' initiative to cut carbon emissions per passenger by 25% by 2012
2008	September: third Eurotunnel fire leading to partial closure until February 2009 – there had been a second, smaller fire in August 2006
2009	December: severe snow in Northern France brings Eurostar services to a stand. £20m package implemented to further immunise fleet from the impact of snow and condensation. Eurotunnel rescue resources further increased
2010	September: Eurostar International Ltd (EIL) formed from merger of EUKL, Eurostar Group, and SNCF and SNCB interests – Standard Premier replaces Leisure Select
2010	October: EIL orders 10 new Velaro e320 train sets from Siemens with 320km/h capability and 150 additional seats. Part of £700m fleet upgrade package which includes full refurbishment of existing fleet
2010	'Tread Lightly' target raised to 35% carbon dioxide reduction by 2012 London–Paris and London–Brussels market shares both reach 80%
2011	EIL achieves net profit of £20.8m

trains a day on a virtual two-hourly headway, with five return trips at weekends.

Hull Trains has always been focused on delivering high levels of customer service and, for a time, it was the only train company to be offering a hot meal seven days a week. In 2012 it is still offering an at-seat service in First Class with a trolley service in standard.

By 2006 the company was achieving 94.8% punctuality – the second best of all long-distance operators. By July 2011 – now operating as First Hull Trains – it had become one of the most successful passenger operator in the country with a 95% customer satisfaction rating for its seven return services a day. However, in the same month the company suffered severe problems with its 'Adelante' fleet leading it to run a much-reduced timetable whilst, at the same time, forcing it to make a public apology for its problems. In the same year, Catherine Proctor from Chiltern Railways was appointed Managing Director.

Hull Trains has increased its passengers tenfold since it launched its open-access service, carrying 80,000 in 2000 and 777,000 in 2010. Nonetheless, the collapse in train performance that followed the arrival of the 'Adelante' fleet is a reminder of how fragile finances can be in open-access companies.

Even a small, self-contained company such as Hull Trains has gone through four fleet changes in a little

ABOVE A Grand Central HST set headed by power car No 43 drops passengers at York on its way from King's Cross to Sunderland on 7 November 2010 *Dennis Lovett*

over 12 years, and it has done well to have wea the disruptions and expenses that have followed Open access remains a risky business and, follow problems with the 'Adelantes', the £3.3 million p 2008/09 changed into a loss of £1.9 million a yea

Grand Central

Founded in 2007, Grand Central was the second open-access operator in the UK after Hull Tr proved very difficult to get its paths agreed a rolling stock operational, and in December 2007 Eagle – then the company's major shareholder its shareholding to Equishare, which included Fearnley and Bob Howells, an ex-Prism team company was bought by Arriva in 2011 – no of Deutsche Bahn – and is currently run by man director, Richard McLean (ex GNER).

In spite of opposition from GNER, the decided to allow Grand Central to start running return services a day in 2008 between Sund and London King's Cross, with calls at York. A return service was agreed in 2009 along wit

ABOVE Logo resplendent, a Eurostar set sits comfortably alongside other members of the European high-speed rail club at Paris Gare du Nord *Eurostar International Ltd*

Factfile E: **Open Access**

Introduction

Open-access operators have to identify a gap in the franchise market and then negotiate track-access 'slots' with Network Rail before demonstrating to the ORR that their income will be predominately new to rail and not just abstracted from existing franchisees. Open-access operators do not pay full fixed track-access charges but only the variable track portion. This provides a 'start up' market for new operators enabling them to charge lower fares.

In reality, very few open-access operations have developed in Britain because the national inter-city network is one of the most comprehensively developed in Europe. In 2012 Hull Trains and Grand Central were the only two open-access operators in business – with a total of 28 trains a day out of the 23,000 run on Network Rail. Of the other players, Wrexham & Shropshire ceased to trade in late 2011, and Alliance Rail Holdings has yet to turn a wheel in revenue-earning service.

First Hull Trains, 2002-16

In 2000 John Nelson and Mike Jones formed access company called Renaissance Tra focused on winning access rights for dire from Hull to London with the ORR awar rights for 10 years from 2002 to 2012. An ini was operated by three 100mph 'Turbostar these were upgraded to four 125mph 'Pior in 2005.

Services were increased to six a day by schedules accelerated by 125mph running. I exchanged its 'Pioneer' trains for the long 'Adelante' trains from First Great Westerr and committed to refurbishing the 125mp exchange for an extension of access rights t 2016. By 2011 Hull Trains was running se

BELOW Open access in action. Forming the 1537 Hull–I Hull Trains 'Pioneer' No 222102 approaches Selby on 2(2009 *Gavin Morrison*

ABOVE The departure of the last Wrexham & Shropshire service north to Wrexham General, on 28 January 2011, was preceded by a farewell staff gathering at Marylebone beside Class 67 No 67013 *Dyfrbont Pontcysllte. Antony Christie*

introduction of three new return West Riding services between Bradford and King's Cross.

Grand Central acquired three High Speed Train sets for the initial Sunderland services in 2008, but subsequently sold these to Angel Trains in 2010 in a lease-back deal. Angel then fitted the power cars with MTU engines and refurbished the sets including the provision of wi-fi facilities. Grand Central leased five Class 180 'Adelante' sets for the new additional Sunderland and new West Riding services in 2010. Known as 'Zephyrs' in Grand Central service, these are maintained along with the HST fleet at Heaton depot.

As well as covering its start-up costs, Grand Central has invested £40 million in training people and in improving stations, car parking, customer information systems and CCTV security. It has made a virtue out of offering passengers a simplified pricing structure in which the ticket price is identical whether it is bought on-line, on-station or on-train, although it now also offers a range of cheaper 'booked in advance' fares. Seat reservations are free, as are tea and coffee, which are served throughout the train. The combination of simple pricing, direct services and friendly staff has enabled Grand Central to deliver a very high 95% customer-satisfaction level.

Despite its market popularity, Grand Central made a loss of £7.6 million in 2008 and a further loss of £6.4 million in 2009. It had planned to breakeven by 2012 but it was sold to Arriva in 2011. It has brought a new direct service from London to Sunderland and a more frequent service to Bradford but, in seeking to call at intermediate stations such as York and Doncaster, it

has sharply demonstrated the intrinsic conflict between franchise and open-access operations.

Wrexham & Shropshire

After Virgin Railways withdrew the only direct service from Shrewsbury to London Euston in 2000, Renaissance Railways decided to experiment with new through services from Wrexham General, Ruabon, Chirk, Gobowen, Shrewsbury, Wellington and Telford Central to London Marylebone. To achieve this aim, they formed a partnership with Laing Rail, the owners of Chiltern Railways.

The company's original intention had been to use either Class 158 or Class 170 diesel units, but none was available, and the service had to be operated by five Class 67 diesel locomotives with three (later four) Mk3 coaches and a Driving Van Trailer. There were four complete trainsets, with the coaches hired from DB Regio UK and the locomotives from EWS.

In 2008 DB Regio UK acquired Laing Rail, together with its interests in Wrexham & Shropshire. The new service was introduced in April 2008 with five return trains every weekday between Wrexham and London. Virgin Trains responded by introducing a rival morning service in December 2008 by extending a Chester–London Euston via Crewe service back to Wrexham, which offered a 2½-hour journey time. With its four-hour journey time, Wrexham & Shropshire met disappointing demand and the service was reduced to four return trips in March 2009 and just three in December 2010.

In spite of its record 99% customer-satisfaction score, the highly positive personal leadership of the company's managing director Andy Hamilton, and the commitment of the company's 55 staff, the service was withdrawn on 28 January 2011. At its demise the Chairman, Adrian Shooter, stated that there was no prospect that the business could ever be profitable.

Alliance Rail Holdings Proposals

Alliance Rail Holdings is a new open-access company formed and led by Ian Yeowart, the founder and former managing director of Grand Central Railway. Supported by Arriva UK Trains/Deutsche Bahn, the company is planning to introduce new routes on both the West Coast and the East Coast through two subsidiaries — Great North Western Railway Co Ltd (GNWR) and Great North Eastern Railway Co Ltd (GNER).

Reflecting the scale of the investment involved, it is seeking a contract of up to 30 years and is working closely with Network Rail, the ORR and existing train companies to identify activities which complement, rather than challenge, franchised services.

At the time of writing Alliance is planning to run up to 60 trains a day on the WCML from the 2015 timetable. Trains will be operated by the Great North Western Railway Co. Ltd. (GNWR) and will be operated by brand new trains capable of the maximum line speed.

ABOVE Future open-access operators could include Alliance Rail. This artist's impression shows its proposed 'Polaris' train in GNWR livery. *Ian Yeowart*

Trains are due to operate between:
- Leeds and Huddersfield to London Euston
- Bradford, Halifax and Rochdale to London Euston
- Blackpool to London Euston
- Barrow in Furness and the Cumbrian Coast to London Euston

A Special Trains' Land Cruise offered its clients
spectacular Highland views *David Ward*

Factfile F: **Charter and Special Trains**

Introduction and history

Apart from the sale of British Rail's ballast quarries, the InterCity Special Trains' sub sector, formerly InterCity (Charter Train Unit), was the first sale to be made by the new BR Vending Unit. The original plan was for Special Trains to be merged with Rail Express Services (RES), its operational contractor, but this was soon dropped in favour of a direct sale (after an MBO was ruled out). The sale itself nearly did not take place when the Vending Unit itself came under Government pressure to stop it going through– presumably because it would create an alternative supply of traction and rolling stock to the then newly-formed ROSCOs.

The Special Trains Unit was sold on 1 April 1995 to Flying Scotsman Railways (FSR). A partnership arrangement established between Pete Waterman (50%) and Sir William McAlpine (50%), FSR traded under the Waterman Railways' banner, but this promising partnership was short-lived and ceased operations in 1996 after Pete Waterman decided to focus on train maintenance.

Once FSR came to an end, McAlpine went on to form his own Rail Charter Services (RCS) train hire company, this being launched on 22 September 1996. From 19

ABOVE This unusual picture taken in 1995 shows the Special Trains livery and logo employed by the company during the brief period between the end of InterCity and the sale of Special Trains to Pete Waterman. *Ian Osborne*

March 1997, RCS joined with English, Welsh & Scottish Railway (EWS) in a new 'Rail Charter Partnership' with the latter then providing the required motive power. From the early days of the sale, there has been a wide variety of companies involved in the charter and special trains' marketplace. The list below – although certainly not exhaustive – provides a flavour of businesses, both current and extant, whose names are associated with the sector:

- Compass
- Cruise Saver Travel
- DB Schenker
- Direct Rail Services
- Hertfordshire Railtours
- Merlin Rail
- North York Moors Railway
- Pathfinder
- Queen of Scots (now part of West Coast Railway Company)

LEFT The Venice Simplon Orient Express: 'Western' diesel-hydraulic No D1015 in charge of the VSOE train on 14 September 2007. *Bob Sweet*

- Railway Touring Company
- Riviera Trains
- Royal Scotsman (now part of Venice Simplon-Orient Express)
- Scottish Railway Preservation Society
- Statesman
- Steam Dreams
- Venice Simplon-Orient Express
- West Coast Railway Company

Companies contained within this list often play a combination of many different roles including those of operations, stock provision, traction provision and services in retail, sales and marketing. Some members embrace all of these relevant roles. However, the detail of this market place – although truly fascinating and worthy of a title in its own right – lies beyond the scope of this particular book.

Summary

Although there are notable high-quality exceptions, InterCity's first trade sale has proved no more than a moderate success. In many ways, it was quickly destroyed and left entrepreneurial followers to pick up the pieces. Indeed, the overall charter/special trains' market has faced a heavy loss of traffic within the business hospitality and high-quality events sectors. At the present time further difficulties concerning the true running operating costs of running trains in this market, along with associated insurance and compensation issues, are making the future even more financially precarious financially.

Nonetheless, charter and special trains' operations are driven by passionate and enthusiastic owners, managers and volunteer staff and – despite Network Rail's difficult train planning process – it seems likely that the remaining players in the sector will continue to strive hard to maintain their place in the highly competitive and crowded arena that is today's privatised railway.

BELOW Class 47/4 No 47832 heads the 'Cruise Saver Travel' train from Southampton Docks to Glasgow Central through Berkswell on 2 January 2009. *Bob Sweet*

Factfile G: **Rolling Stock**

Table G1: Investment in trains

	New Coaches		Refurbished	
	1984-94	**1996-2012**	**1984-94**	**1996-2012**
Anglia	0	42 Class 170	0	120 Mk3
CrossCountry	0	251 Class 220/1	0	50 HST
East Coast	282	0	0	438 Mk4/HST
Gatwick Express	0	64 Class 460	0	0
Great Western	0	25 Class 180	0	548 HST
Midland Mainline	0	142 Class 222	0	100 HST
West Coast	0	684 Class 390	150	0
TOTAL	**282**	**1,265**	**150**	**1,256**

Sources: **Intercity (1984-94); train companies (1994-2012)**

Table G2: Productivity of HST fleet, 1990-2012

	1990 timetable			2012 timetable		
Route	Sets	Seats/set	Seats/fleet	Sets	Seats/set	Seats/fleet
East Coast	38 x 8	478	18,164	14 x 9	558	7,812
Midland Mainline	10 x 8	478	4,780	10 x 8	468	4,680
Cross Country	12 x 7	448	5,376	5 x 7	475	2,375
Great Western	24 x 7	396	9,504	37 x 8	572	21,164
	6 x 8	472	2,832	16 x 8	488	7,808
Grand Central	-	-	-	3 x 5	269	807
TOTAL SEATS	**90 sets**	**-**	**40,656**	**85 sets**	**-**	**44,646**

Notes: 1990 fleet: 90 operational sets formed from 197 power cars and 705 Mk3 coaches (including 21 spare)

2012 fleet: 85 operational sets formed from 191 power cars and 713 Mk3 coaches (including 33 spare)

2012 fleet strengthened by conversion of 38 Mk3 locomotive-hauled coaches

Three power cars withdrawn following accidents and three used for Network Rail Measurement Train

Source: **Gordon Pettitt**

Table G3: train fleets, 1994-2012 (including spare coaches)

Train Fleet 1994			Train Fleet 2012		
	Sets/ locos	Coaches/ power cars		Sets/ locos	Coaches/ power cars
Anglia					
Class 86 locomotives	14	-	Class 90 locomotives	15	-
Mk2 coaches	9	124	Mk3 coaches + DVTs	11	120
CrossCountry					
Class 47 locomotives	30	-	Class 220 'Voyager' (4-car)	34	136
Class 86 locomotives	17	-	Class 221 'Super Voyager' (5-car)*	23	114
Mk2 rolling stock	34	264	HST sets (2+8 cars)	5	50
HST sets (2+7 cars)	23	161	Class 170 'Turbostar' (3-car)	16	48
Mk3 sleepers	2	26	Class 170 'Turbostar' (2-car)	13	26
Class 158 'Express' (2-car)	5	10			
East Coast					
Class 91 locomotives	31	-	Class 91 locomotives	31	-
Mk4 coaches	30	302	Mk4 coaches + DVTs	30	307
HST sets (2+8 cars)	10	104	HST sets (2+9 cars)	14	131
			Class 67 locomotives	4	-
Gatwick Express					
Class 73 locomotives	14	-	Class 460 'Juniper' (8-car)**	8	64
Mk2 coaches	10	84			
Great Western					
HST sets (2+7 cars)	39	319	HST sets: micro-buffet (2+8 cars)	26	269
			HST sets: buffet (2+8 cars)	27	279
Mk3 sleepers	2	20	Class 180 'Adelante' (5-car)	5	25
Class 47 locomotives	4	-	Mk3 sleepers	2	18
			Class 47 locomotives	4	-
Midland Mainline					
HST sets (2+8 cars)	14	140	HST sets (2+8 cars)	10	100
Class 47 locomotives	3	-	Class 222 'Meridian' (7-car)	6	42
Mk2 coaches	3	24	Class 222 'Meridian' (5-car)	17	85
			Class 222 'Meridian' (4-car)	4	16
West Coast					
Class 86/87/90 locomotives	76	-	Class 390 'Pendolino' (11-car)	31	341
Mk2 coaches	26	280	Class 390 'Pendolino' (9-car)	21	189
Mk3 coaches	26	270	Class 221 'Super Voyager' (5-car)	21	105
Mk3 sleepers	6	116	Class 57 locomotives	7	-
ScotRail					
	-	-	Mk3 sleepers (ScotRail)	12	121
			Class 90 locomotives (hired)	4	-
			Class 67 locomotives (hired)	2	-
Hull Trains					
		-	Class 180 'Adelante' (5-car)	4	20
Grand Central					
		-	Class 180 'Adelante' (5-car)	3	15
		-	HST sets (2+5 cars)	3	21
Total coaches	-	**2,244**		-	**2,652**

* one four-car set / ** replaced by Class 442 units in 2012 / Sources: **Colin J. Marsden, train companies**

ABOVE On a London Euston–Holyhead service, 'Thunderbird' No 57302 hauls a 'Pendolino' along the North Wales coast at Penmaenmawr. *Gavin Morrison*

BELOW Topped and tailed by HST power cars Nos 43062 *John Armitt* and 43014, Network Rail's Measurement Train passes through Newton Abbot on 27 July 2012. Fitted with in-cab signalling and a third headlight at each end, this unit can now operate on HS1. *Antony Christie*

Table G4: Projected IEP fleet, 2016-20

Route	Trains	Length	Mode	Vehicles
Phase 1 Great Western	21	9-car	Electric	189
	36	5-car	Bi-modal	180
Total Great Western	57			369
Phase 1 East Coast	12	5-car	Electric	60
	10	5-car	Bi-modal	50
	13	9-car	Bi-modal	117
Total East Coast	35			227
Phase 1 Options	30	9-car	Bi-modal	270
Total Phase 1	122			866

Source: **DfT announcement, July 2012**

Table G5: Extent of electrification

	2012	Post 2014-19 HLOS investment
% network electrified (single track km)	41%	53%
% electric train miles (passenger vehicle miles)	64%	76%

Source: **Network Rail**

Table G6: Comparative costs, diesel v electric

	Diesel	Electric
Maintenance cost per mile	60p	40p
Fuel cost per mile	47p	26p
Track costs per mile	9.8p	8.5p
Lease costs per vehicle (per annum)	£100k	£90k

Sources: **ATOC, Network Rail**

ABOVE A Class 222 is dwarfed by the overarching elegance of Ely Cathedral. *East Midlands Trains*

Table G7 Rail electrification by 2019

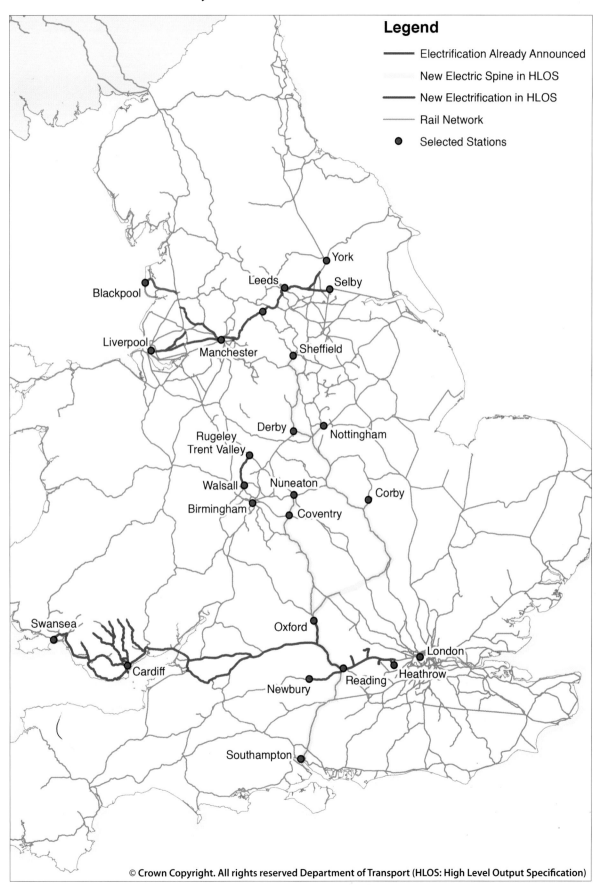

Legend

— Electrification Already Announced
— New Electric Spine in HLOS
— New Electrification in HLOS
— Rail Network
● Selected Stations

Factfile H: **Railway People**

Table H1: Government leadership, 1990-2012

Secretary of State	Period in office	Political party	Prime Minister
Cecil Parkinson	1989-1990	Conservative	Margaret Thatcher
Malcolm Rifkind	1990-1992	Conservative	John Major
John MacGregor	1992-1994	Conservative	
Brian Mawhinney	1994-1995	Conservative	
Sir George Young	1995-1997	Conservative	
John Prescott[1]	1997-2001	Labour	Tony Blair
Gavin Strang[2]	1997-1998	Labour	
John Reid2	1998-1999	Labour	
Helen Liddell[2]	1999-1999	Labour	
Lord Macdonald of Tradeston[2]	1999-2001	Labour	
Stephen Byers[2]	2001-2002	Labour	
Alastair Darling	2002-2006	Labour	
Douglas Alexander	2006-2007	Labour	
Ruth Kelly	2007-2008	Labour	Gordon Brown
Geoff Hoon	2008-2009	Labour	
Lord Adonis	2009-2010	Labour	
Phillip Hammond	2010-2011	Conservative	David Cameron
Justine Greening	2011-2012	Conservative	
Patrick McLoughlin	2012-	Conservative	

Sources: **Wikipedia, BBC,**

1. Secretary of State for Environment, Transport and the Regions
2. Minister of State with responsibility for Transport

ABOVE Driver Tommy Farr in 'Pendolino' No 390039 keeps a careful eye on the track ahead. *Paul Bigland*

Table H2: InterCity leadership – the Board, 1993

British Rail InterCity 1993	
Managing Director	Chris Green
Route Directors	Andy Cooper (Anglia & Gatwick)
	Brian Burdsall (East Coast)
	Brian Scott (Great Western)
	Richard Brown (Midland & CrossCountry)
	Ivor Warburton (West Coast)
HQ Directors	Geoff Ashton (Finance)
	Brian Clementson (Fleet)
	Barry Woledge (Human Resources)
	John Elliot (Infrastructure)
	John Cimelli (Marketing)
	Terry Coyle (On Board Services)

ABOVE Train maintainers at work at Craigentinny depot, near Edinburgh. *East Coast Main Line Co Ltd*

Table H3: OPRAF, ORR, ATOC and SRA

OPRAF: Office of Passenger Rail Franchising 1993-2001	
1993-1996	Roger Salmon
1996-1997	John O'Brien
1997-1999	Mike Grant

ORR: Office of Rail Regulator 1995-2004 (Office of Rail Regulation 2004-12)	
1995-1998	John Swift QC
1998-1999	Chris Bolt
1999-2004	Tom Winsor, Rail Regulator
2004-2009	Chris Bolt, Chair – Office of Rail Regulation, with statutory Board
2009-2010	Anna Walker, Chair – Office of Rail Regulation
2011-	Richard Price, Chief Executive, Office of Rail Regulation

Strategic Rail Authority 1999-2004	
1999-2001	Sir Alastair Morton (Chairman)
1999-2001	Mike Grant
2001-2004	Richard Bowker (Chairman & Chief Executive)

ATOC: Association of Train Operating Companies 1995-2012		
	Chairman	Director General
1995/1996	Chris Tibbits	-
1996/1997	Chris Tibbits	-
1997/1998	Ivor Warburton	Major General James Gordon
1998/1999	Ivor Warburton	Major General James Gordon
1999/2000	Giles Fearnley	Major General Gordon
2000/2001	Richard Brown	George Muir
2001/2002	Richard Brown	George Muir
2002/2003	Christopher Garnett	George Muir
2003/2004	Keith Ludeman	George Muir
2004/2005	Keith Ludeman	George Muir
2005/2006	Adrian Shooter	George Muir
2006/2007	Adrian Shooter	George Muir
2007/2008	Mike Alexander	George Muir
2008/2009	Mike Alexander	Michael Roberts (CEO)
2009/2010	Tom Smith	Michael Roberts (CEO)
2010/2011	Tom Smith	Michael Roberts (CEO)
2011/2012	Tom Smith	Michael Roberts (CEO)

Table H4: Senior management leadership, 2012

Greater Anglia (Abellio)	
Managing Director	Ruud Haket
Customer Services Director	Andrew Goodrum
Finance Director	Adam Golton
Projects Director	Thijs Jan Noomen
Engineering Director	John Ratcliffe
Operations Director	Nanouke van't Riet
Commercial Director	Andrew Camp
Asset Management Director	Simone Bailey

CrossCountry (Arriva Trains)	
Managing Director	Andy Cooper
Commercial Director	David Watkin
Finance Director	Jonathan Roberts
Customer Service Director	Jeremy Higgins
Production Director	Helen Waters
HR Director	Maria Zywica
Head of Safety	Des Lowe

East Coast (Directly Operated Railways)	
Managing Director	Karen Boswell
Business Planning Director	Phil Cameron
Operations Director	Danny Williams
Finance Director	Tim Kavanagh
Commercial & CS Director	Peter Williams
Engineering Director	Jack Commandeur
Stations/Property Director	Tim Hedley-Jones

East Midlands Trains (Stagecoach)	
Managing Director	David Horne
Safety & Operations Director	Ian Smith
Engineering Director	Tim Sayer
Finance Director	Tim Gledhill
Human Resources Director	Clare Burles
CS & Commercial Director	Neil Micklethwaite

First Great Western (FirstGroup)	
Managing Director	Mark Hopwood
Engineering Director	Andrew Mellors
Operations Director	Kevin Gale
Projects & Planning Director	Matthew Golton
Director of Communications	Sue Evans
Finance Director	Ben Caswell
Head of Sales & Marketing	Diane Burke
Head of Human Resources	Sharon Johnston
Head of Safety & Envir'ment	Sharon Vye-Parminter

Virgin West Coast	
Chief Executive	Tony Collins
Chief Operating Officer	Chris Gibb
Exec Director, Commercial	Graham Leech
Human Resources Director	Patrick McGrath
Finance Director	Phil Whittingham
Communications Director	Arthur Leathley

Grand Central (Arriva)	
Managing Director	Richard McLean
Marketing Manager	David Crocker
Fleet Engineer	Dave Hatfield
Operations Director	Sean English

First Hull Trains (FirstGroup)	
Managing Director	Cath Bellamy
Service Delivery Director	Keith Doughty
Finance Manager	Glenn McLeish-Longthorn
Head of Engineering	Richard Elwen
Performance Manager	Louise Mendham
On Board Standards Manager	Katie Beckett
HR Manager	Victoria Evans

Table H5: General Secretaries of railway trade unions

Period in office	General Secretary
ASLEF	
1990-1993	Derek Fullick
1993-1998	Lew Adams
1998-2003	Mick Rix
2003-2004	Shaun Brady
2004-2011	Keith Norman
2011-	Mick Whelan
RMT	
1990-2001	Jimmy Knapp
2001-	Bob Crow
TSSA	
1989-2004	Richard Rosser
2004-2011	Gerry Doherty
2011-	Manuel Cortes

(Excludes general unions serving the rail industry)

Table H6: Employee numbers, 2010/11

	2010/11	Change on 2009/10
East Anglia	2,869	+1.3
CrossCountry	1,610	- 0.4
East Coast	2,807	- 5.3
East Midlands Trains	2,042	+2.4
First Great Western	4,431	-6.0
Great Central	121	0.0
Hull Trains	105	0.0
Virgin West Coast	2,913	+0.2

Source: **McNulty Report (AECOM/University of Leeds/First Class Partnerships)**

Table H7: Employee costs (£000s), 2008/9

TOC	Staff costs	Other operating costs	Earnings	Pension	Other staff costs	Employee costs as a % of other operating costs
CrossCountry	75,016	561,654	63,447	6,277	5,292	13%
East Coast	106,718	565,885	87,709	9,323	9,686	19%
East Midlands Trains	76,768	240,931	65,872	5,525	5,371	32%
First Great Western	201,912	577,611	170,769	17,940	13,203	35%
East Anglia	122,127	388,869	97,903	9,787	14,437	31%
Virgin Trains	127,774	552,580	107,671	10,682	9,421	23%

Source: **McNulty Report (AECOM/University of Leeds/First Class Partnerships)**

Table H8: Average staff costs by company, 2008/09

TOC	1996/97	2008/09	Growth 1996/97-2008/09	Growth 1996/97-2008/09
CrossCountry	34,812	39,526	31%	14%
East Coast	28,234	44,447	31%	57%
West Coast	29,753	41,921	51%	41%
Midland Mainline	30,790	n/a	33%	n/a
First Great Western	28,509	41,165	51%	44%

Source: **McNulty Report (AECOM/University of Leeds/First Class Partnerships)**

Table H9: Average driver pay and hours, 2011/12

	Pay 2011/12 £	Working week Hours
Eurostar	48,661	35
CrossCountry	48,628	35
Virgin West Coast	46,812	35
East Coast	46,228	35
First Great Western	41,950	35
Hull Trains	40,978	35
DB Schenker (Charter Trains)	40,000	35
East Midlands Trains (ex MML)	39,003	35
East Midlands Trains (ex Central)	37,988	35
National Express East Anglia	37,357	35
East Midlands Trains (Maintrain)	31,732	37
Deutsche Bahn (DB)	30,534	36

Source: **ASLEF**

Table H10: Workforce productivity, 1996/97 v 2008/09 (train km per member of staff)

	96/97	08/09	Growth 96/97-99/00	Growth 99/00-08/09	Growth 96/97 - 08/09
Cross Country	18,197	18,587	12%	-8%	2%
East Coast	5,906	8,304	19%	18%	41%
West Coast	4,778	9,318	71%	14%	95%
Midland Mainline	6,004	n/a	n/a	n/a	n/a
First Great Western	5,516	8,588	14%	37%	56%

Source: **McNulty Report (AECOM/University of Leeds/First Class Partnerships)**

ABOVE Happy to help in the buffet – a friendly smile completes the purchase. Some 97% of long-distance trains offer the choice of trolley or buffet-car services. *Anglia Railways*

Factfile J: **Finances and fares**

Table J1: Long-distance passenger subsidy

1998 prices	Total subsidy		Subsidy per passenger mile (pence)			
	1998/99	1999/2000	1997/98	1998/99	Total subsidy (£m)	2000/01
CrossCountry	101.4	86.8	9.3	7.4	5.8	5.4
West Coast	70.3	59.1	3.7	3.4	2.8	2.7
Great Western	55.5	48.6	4.3	3.9	3.3	2.9
GNER	37.4	17.6	2.5	1.7	0.7	0.2
Anglia Railways*	26.9	23.6	10.1	6.8	5.2	3.8
Midland Mainline	2.5	0.9	1.6	0.4	0.1	0.1
Gatwick Express**	- 8.2	-10.3	-6.7	-6.7	-8.7	-10.0
Overall	285.8	26.3				

* Anglia subsidy includes East Anglia branches
** Gatwick and Thameslink only TOCs not in subsidy
Sources: **OPRAF Performance Bulletin 1999 and SRA Performance Trends 2000**

Table J2: CrossCountry finances

£000	31/12/2007	31/12/2008**	31/12/2009
Turnover	543,400	558,089	446,172
Operating costs	544,000	551,781	454,606
Operating profit	2,500	6,308	(8,434)*
Turnover/employee	324,000	335,793	276,267
Track-access charges	228,100	215,572	115,282
Rolling-stock lease	129,300	41,772	44,075
Revenue grant	221,900	n/a	111,942

* loss
** pro rata of a 60-week year
Source: **The Modern Railway Directory 2012**

Table J3: East Coast finances (operating as East Coast Main Line Co [DOR])

£000	31/12/2007	31/12/2008	31/12/2009
Turnover	20,647	648,958	231,595
Operating costs	36,135	621,644	230,292
Operating profit	(15,488)*	27,314	1,303
Turnover/employee	6,776	270,287	85,712
Track-access charges	8,330	145,718	16,087
Rolling-stock lease	4,396	73,998	31,407
Revenue grant	1,732	5,382	n/a

* loss
Source: **The Modern Railway Directory 2012**

Table J4: East Midlands Trains finances

£000	26/04/2008	02/05/2009	01/05/2010
Turnover	183,288	324,619	289,232
Operating costs	180,052	317,699	285,864
Operating profit	3,236	6,920	3,368
Turnover/employee	91,828	158,971	143,043
Track-access charges	59,790	58,080	65,378
Rolling-stock lease	14,061	31,210	30,984
Revenue grant	59,204	32,283	0

Source: **The Modern Railway Directory 2012**

Table J5: Great Western finances

£000	31/12/2007	31/12/2008	31/12/2009
Turnover	705,441	766,710	845,011
Operating costs	682,158	775,521	834,968
Operating profit	23,283	(8,811)*	10,043
Turnover/employee	153,892	6,312	174,589
Track-access charges	223,080	249,940	131,443
Rolling-stock lease	58,341	58,703	49,450
Revenue grant	49,371	56,690	133,097

* loss
Source: **The Modern Railway Directory 2012**

Table J6: Virgin West Coast finances

£000	01/03/2008	28/02/2009	06/03/2010
Turnover	787,662	779,456	848,921
Operating costs	714,913	680,767	780,639
Operating profit	72,749	98,689	68,282
Turnover/employee	280,706	255,727	283,446
Track-access charges	257,384	152,752	170,552
Rolling-stock lease	180,503	209,978	215,608
Revenue grant	119,595	24,118	68,120

Source: **The Modern Railway Directory 2012**

Table J7: Financial results 2009/10

Year end	CrossCountry 31/12/09	East Coast 31/03/10	Great Western* 31/03/10	MML* (inter-city) 01/05/10	West Coast 06/08/10	Total inter-city
Turnover	£446m	£567m	£845m	£289m	£849m	£2.996m
Profit (Loss)	(£8m)	(£48m)	£10m	£3m	£3m	£25m
Revenue grant	£112m	-	£133m	-	-	-

* includes local trains run by the company
Source: **TAS**

Table J8: Long-distance fares — increase (%) 1994-2012 (inflation = 60%)

	Anglia	Cross Country	East Coast	Great Western	Midland Mainline	West Coast
First Single	150	275	145	220	185	215
Standard Single	130	140	155	200	190	195
Super Off Peak	--	120	100	115	130	125
Off Peak Saver	70	70	195	100	140	75
Off Peak Day	-	-	-	-	-	-
First Season	65	-	100	155	80	65
Standard Season	55	-	75	100	50	60

Source: **Barry Doe**

Table J9: Long-distance fares — cost (£) of 100-mile journey in 2012

	Anglia	Cross Country	East Coast	Great Western	Midland Mainline	West Coast
First Return	150	205	180	245	185	225
Standard Return	95	100	130	155	140	140
Off Peak Return (Saver)	43	50	85	60	80	42
Super Off Peak Return	-	-	50	50	54	-
Off Peak Day Return	-	-	35	-	-	-

Source: **Barry Doe**

Factfile K: **High Speed 2**

HS2: InterCity reborn for the 21st century

Before delving into the detail of its two planned implementation phases, it is vitally important to understand the underlying concept of HS2 within the UK's broader rail future seeing HS2's boldness and imagination as truly taking the InterCity brand forward into the 21st century.

Weaving together all former InterCity main lines running north from London, HS2 will – for the first time – crucially provide an important cluster of major northern cities with high speed quality services and connections. It will do this from both London Euston and from Birmingham Curzon Street and it will do so in ways that the former InterCity business – through no fault of its own - was never able to do.

HS2 will redraw the rail map of Britain, strengthening Birmingham as an additional centre of gravity for train travel. Most importantly, through creating a new northern high speed rail network, HS2 will help reflect and rebalance the improving rail connectivity currently being experienced in

southern England with projects such as Crossrail 1 & 2, Thameslink and Great Western electrification.

At the same time, HS2 has the potential to transform journeys between the overworked airports at Manchester, Birmingham and Heathrow – the latter via a change at Old Oak Common – in times that slash those currently in operation. Finally, it will provide a long overdue direct link with continental Europe from destinations beyond London through HS1 and the Channel Tunnel.

With the enormous increase in intercity business over the last twenty years, the future development of traditional intercity routes depends on HS2 being built. With the £9 billion West Coast upgrade due to reach full capacity around 2025 both the DfT and Network Rail say that there are no credible alternatives to building the new line. Construction is planned to take place in two phases.

HS2 Phase 1: London–Birmingham 2026

On 17 January 2012 the Government announced its firm intention to build Phase 1 of HS2 from London to Birmingham at a cost of £17 billion. It also declared its intention of subsequently projecting it northwards to Manchester and Leeds in Phase 2 at a cost of a further £15 billion. However, even at this early stage of the project, there is already considerable business and political pressure to extend it onwards to Scotland.

Phase 1, between London and Birmingham is due to open by 2026 and, although at the time of writing the route of this core line is well-identified, further changes are likely to emerge as part of the project's ongoing consultation work.

Starting from an expanded London Euston, Phase 1 will head north reconnecting with the West Coast Main Line at a point near Lichfield. In the West Midlands a westwards-diverging line will head for Birmingham city centre, reaching Curzon Street, the site of the former London & Birmingham Railway's terminus and abandoned in 1854 as a regular passenger station.

At the southern end of the line there will be new stations at Old Oak Common in west London and this will provide connections with Crossrail, Heathrow Express and Great Western services. Heading north, HS2 would run close to the National Exhibition Centre (NEC) and serve a new Birmingham Interchange station with a people-mover connection to the airport, the latter then being just 40 minutes from London and able to provide extra runway capacity for the capital.

Phase 1 is planned to include a connection between HS2 at Old Oak Common and HS1 just outside St Pancras International thus allowing through services to run between HS2 and continental Europe. Indicative journey times could be three hours fifteen minutes from Birmingham to Paris with Birmingham-Brussels being just three hours.

HS2 Phase 2: East Midlands, Leeds and Manchester 2032

On 28 January 2013, the DfT issued its preferred route options for the second phase of the planned HS2 network. In this phase, one branch of the 'Y' shaped route will be built beyond Lichfield following the WCML to Crewe where it will then head towards Manchester Airport. Taking a new route to the north towards Warrington, it will re-join the West Coast Main

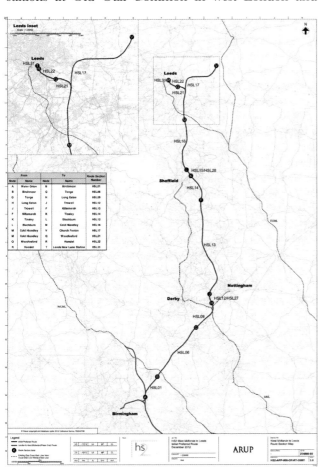

ABOVE Route Map 1: East Midlands & Leeds

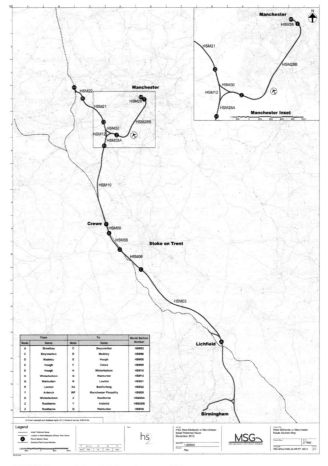

ABOVE Route Map 2: Manchester - HS2

ABOVE Visualisation of London's Euston station – exterior view. *HS2*

Line near Wigan having thrown off a second branch – via a triangular junction – into Manchester city centre.

The other side of the 'Y' will serve new interchanges in the East Midlands and South Yorkshire before rejoining the ECML at Church Fenton south of York. A spur to Leeds would essentially follow the existing Castleford-Leeds line.

Purpose-built intermediate stations are planned at Manchester Airport and at an East Midlands Hub, midway between Derby and Nottingham. The DfT has confirmed that this Hub would be served by connecting passenger trains from both Derby and Nottingham although the former city, as well as Stoke-on-Trent, have already made it widely known that they are keen to have their own HS2 stations. From the Hub the line would continue on to Meadowhall situated on the eastern edge of Sheffield.

The proposals envisage new terminal stations at Manchester Piccadilly adjacent to the existing station and at Leeds New Lane located to the south of today's station.

London Euston would be completely rebuilt as a 24-platform station with more and longer platforms and with a much better interchange to London Underground, including the Circle Line. The proposed Chelsea–Hackney tube line (Crossrail 2) – new plans for which are emerging as this book goes to press – would also pass under the new Euston to help distribute extra passengers generated by the new high-speed railway.

In a change of policy from previous documents, the work to develop a spur from the main HS2 route to London's Heathrow Airport has been 'deferred' pending the publication in the summer of 2015 of a government-commissioned report examining the UK's long-term aviation strategy. Passengers heading for Heathrow Airport will have to change onto Crossrail for transfer services to the airport's terminals.

A Hybrid Bill for Phase 2 – currently being prepared for submission to parliament – is also planned before the end of 2013.

ABOVE Visualisation of Euston station – interior view. *HS2*

Journey Times

The high journey speed will ultimately bring London–Newcastle journey times down to 2hr 18min and London–Glasgow/Edinburgh down to 3hr 38min, which should at last provide the competitive journey times that rail needs to capture the lucrative high-yield domestic air market, whilst providing alternative connections to Manchester, Birmingham and Heathrow airports (for indicative journey times see Tables K1 and K2)

Customer service

HS2 will be a great opportunity to display the very latest and very best in meeting the growing expectations and needs of customers. The trains will certainly have two classes of travel, and may even have the three classes that Eurostar offers. Most importantly, it will give the chance for Britain to showcase what other UK inter-city rail companies have so admirably done – provide excellent customer service.

Final thoughts

With countries such as China, France, Germany, Spain and Japan already well-established in the high-speed rail arena, some sources have suggested that further delay in building HS2 could ultimately contribute to the UK's future economic decline. In November 2011 the Commons' Transport Committee reported that HS2 has

ABOVE Visualisation of Birmingham Curzon Street – interior view. *HS2*

'a good case' and that it 'offered a new era of inter-urban travel in Britain'. Although Labour has some criticisms of the proposed route, remarkably all three of the major political parties have shown support for its construction.

Let us hope that those responsible for promoting and building today's HS2 can show the same strength and stamina of vision that Victorian rail builders demonstrated when constructing the wonders of today's under-valued and over-worked rail network.

Table K1: Indicative journey times from London on HS2 will be:

London to:	2012 Current Journey Times	HS2 Projected Journey Times	Intermediate Stations
Birmingham	1hr 22 (New St)	49mins (Curzon Street)	Old Oak Common & Birmingham Interchange
East Midlands Hub	n/a	51mins	Old Oak Common
Derby Midland (via East Midlands Hub)	1hr 31	1hr 11	Old Oak Common
Sheffield Midland (via Sheffield Meadowhall)	2hrs 5	1hr 19	Old Oak Common & Birmingham Interchange
Leeds	2hrs 12	1hr 22 (New Lane)	Old Oak Common & East Midlands Hub
Newcastle	2hrs 52	2hrs 18	Old Oak Common & York
Manchester Piccadilly	2hrs 8	1hr 8	Old Oak Common
Manchester Airport	2hrs 24	59mins	Old Oak Common
Preston	2hrs 8	1hr 24	Old Oak Common & Birmingham Interchange
Liverpool	2hrs 8	1hr 36	Old Oak Common, Crewe & Runcorn
Glasgow	4hrs 8	3hrs 38	Old Oak Common & Carstairs
Edinburgh	4hrs 23	3hrs 38	Old Oak Common & Carstairs

Source: HS2

Table K2: Indicative journey times from Birmingham Curzon Street on HS2 will be:

Birmingham Curzon Street to:	2012 Current Journey Times	HS2 Projected Journey Times	Intermediate Stations
Nottingham Midland (via East Midlands Hub)	1hr 13	36mins	East Midlands Hub
Sheffield Meadowhall	n/a	38mins	East Midlands Hub
Sheffield Midland (via Sheffield Meadowhall)	1hr 11	48mins	East Midlands Hub & Sheffield Meadowhall
Leeds New Lane	1hr 58	57mins	East Midlands Hub & Sheffield Meadowhall
York	2hrs 10	1hr 3	East Midlands Hub & Sheffield Meadowhall
Newcastle	3hrs 14	2hrs 7	East Midlands Hub, Sheffield Meadowhall, York, Darlington & Durham
Manchester Piccadilly	1hr 28	41mins	Manchester Airport
Manchester Airport	1hr 44	32mins	-
Preston	1hr 31	53mins	Wigan North Western
Edinburgh	4hrs 1	3hrs 14	Wigan North Western, Preston, Oxenholme, Carlisle & Lockerbie
Glasgow	3hrs 57	3hrs 22	Wigan North Western, Preston, Lancaster, Penrith, Carlisle & Lockerbie

Source: HS2

Bibliography

Chapter and Factfile references

All Change — *British Railway Privatisation*, edited by Roger Freeman and Jon Shaw (McGraw Hill, 2000)

Better Rail Stations — An Independent Review (Department for Transport, 2009)

British Rail 1974-1997 — From Integration to Privatisation by Terry Gourvish (OUP, 2004)

Broken Rails by Christian Wolmar (Aurum Press, 2001)

High Speed in Japan by Peter Semmens (Hubbard Printers, 2000)

HST Silver Jubilee by Colin J. Marsden (Ian Allan, 2001)

Realising the Potential of GB Rail — Report of the Rail Value for Money Study by Sir Roy McNulty (Department for Transport, May 2011)

The Comprehensive Guide to Britain's Railways (Rail, 2012)

The InterCity Story by Mike Vincent and Chris Green (Haynes Publishing [Oxford Publishing Co], 1994)

The Modern Railway Directory — The Definitive Guide to the UK's Railway Industry (Ian Allan, 2011 and 2012)

Sectional Maps of Britain's Railways (Ian Allan, 1985)

The Privatisation of British Rail by Nigel G. Harris and Ernest Godward (Railway Consultancy Press, 1997)

'Save Our Railways' — Trade Union Briefing (TUC, 2012)

Virgin Trains — A Decade of Progress by John Balmforth (Ian Allan, 2008)

Virgin Trains — From HST to Pendolino by John Balmforth (Ian Allan, 2012)

Specific article references

'Another Country' by Kate Silvester, *Rail Professional*, December 2011

'A year to remember', *Rail* 686 (29 December 2011 - 10 January 10 2012)

'Aggregate Level Analysis of Train operating Company Average Salary & Productivity Performance' by Dr Andrew Smith, Professor Chris Nash and Jeremy Drew (University of Leeds, 2010)

'At last: Government says "yes" to High-Speed 2' by Chris Milner and Nick Pigott, *The Railway* Magazine, March 2012

'Britain's Railways: A political plaything!', *Rail* 693 (4-17 April 2012)

'Discussing Devolution', *Rail* 694 (18 April - 1 May 2012)

'East Coast: Targeting a First Class Service' by Peter Williams, *Rail* 691 (7-20 March 2012)

'Foreign Foes?' by Nigel Wordsworth, *Railstaff*, April/May 2012

'High Speed Three Bid by Meridian', *Railstaff*, July 2012

Hotline Commemorative Special Edition for CrossCountry (Virgin CrossCountry, October/November 2007)

'HS2 resistance persists as protestors turn to courts'; Rail 694 (18 April - 1 May 2012)

'HS2 Special', Railnews, February 2012

'Intercity Passenger Rail Transport in the UK' by Caroline Finch (IBIS World Industry Report H49.100, February 2012)

'McNulty in Europe', *The Rail Engineer*, February 2012

'McNulty means business', *Rail* 671 (1-14 June 2011)

ORR Annual Report 2003-2004 — Regulator's Foreword, Department for Transport, 2004

'Plastic takes over ticketing', *Modern Railways*, March 2012

'Privatised Rail Operators' (parts 1, 2 and 3) by Dennis Lovett, Bachmann UK, 2007 and 2008

'Railtours: Track Record' (charter trains), *The Railway Magazine*, March 2012

'Smart Ticketing for the Railway' by Steve Howes, ATOC, 2012

'The Franchise Dilemma', *Rail* 686 (29 December 2011 - 10 January 2012)

General references

Informed Sources (Roger Ford)
Modern Railways
Passenger Transport
Rail
Rail Engineer
Rail Professional
Railnews
Railstaff
The Railway Magazine
Virgin Train News (various issues)

Websites

En.wikipedia.org/wiki
Epp.eurostat.ec.europa.eu
www.abellio.com
www.aslef.org.uk
www.bbc.co.uk
www.crosscountrytrains.co.uk
www.dft.gov.uk
www.eurostar.com
www.firstgreatwestern.co.uk
www.hs2.org.uk
www.independent.co.uk
www.networkrail.co.uk
www.networkrailmediacentre.co.uk
www.railwaybritain.co.uk (recommended)
www.railuk.co.uk
www.renaissancetrains.com
www.rail-reg.gov.uk
www.stagecoach.com
www.statistics.gov.uk
www.tas.uk.net
www.thisismoney.co.uk (East Coast information)
www.virgintrains.co.uk

Glossary

Glossary of terms pertaining to UK long-distance passenger trains

APT-E Advanced Passenger Train – Experimental (gas-turbine version)

APT-P Advanced Passenger Train – Prototype (electric version)

ASLEF Amalgamated Society of Locomotive Engineers & Firemen (trade union)

ATOC Association of Train Operating Companies – incorporated association that was set up under the 1993 Railways Act by the train operating companies. It is the collective voice of the train companies and also provides common services such as ticket revenue allocation, National Rail Enquiry Service (NRES), Railcard marketing etc

ATP Automatic Train Protection

AWS Automatic Warning System

BAA British Airports Authority – a UK airport operator

BR British Rail(ways) – the state operator of the majority of rail transport in Britain from nationalisation in 1948 to privatisation in 1997

BRBR British Rail Board (Residuary) – organisation responsible for managing the remaining functions of the British Railways Board e.g. land disposal

BTP British Transport Police

CEO Chief Executive Officer

CP4 (NR) Control Period 4 2009-14 (Network Rail)

CP5 (NR) Control Period 5 2014-19 (Network Rail)

CTRL Channel Tunnel Rail Link

DB Deutsche Bahn

DfT Department for Transport – the Government department responsible for transport within Britain

DMU Diesel multiple-unit

DOR Directly Operated Railways – a Government-owned holding company currently managing the East Coast Main Line Co Ltd (East Coast) until re-franchising takes place in December 2013

DRS Direct Rail Services

ECML East Coast main line

EFQM European Foundation for Quality Management

EIL Eurostar International Ltd

EMT East Midlands Trains

EMU Electric multiple-unit

ERTMS European Rail Traffic Management System

EWS English, Welsh & Scottish Railway – freight company now running under the title of DB Schenker

EUKL Eurostar (UK) Ltd

FGW First Great Western

FOC Freight (Train) Operating Company

GNER Great North Eastern Railway

GNWR Great North Western Railway

HLOS High Level Output Specification – the outputs the railway has agreed to deliver in Network Rail Control Period 4 (2009-14)

HS1 High Speed 1 – the high-speed railway linking London St Pancras International and the Channel Tunnel

HS2 High Speed 2 – the planned and promoted high speed line linking London, Birmingham and eventually (through Stage 2) to Leeds and Manchester

HSE Health & Safety Executive

ICE InterCity Express

IEP InterCity Express Programme – a new fleet of trains to replace the former InterCity 125 High Speed Trains (HSTs) on the East Coast and Great Western main lines

ICRRL InterCapital & Regional Rail Ltd

LCR London & Continental Railways

LGV Ligne à Grande Vitesse – French high-speed line

MAA Moving Annual Average

MBO Management Buy-Out

MD Managing Director

MML Midland main line

NR Network Rail – the railway's current infrastructure owner

NRES A public information provider offering advice on timetables and other rail enquiries

NSARE National Skills Academy for Railway Engineering

OBS On Board Services

Open Access Open-access passenger companies identify a service that is not currently provided and apply to the ORR for the required track-access rights to Network Rail for train paths

OPRAF Office of Passenger Rail Franchising (1994-2001)

ORR Office of Rail Regulation

PPM Public Performance Measure – the percentage of franchised passenger trains arriving at their destination, having made all booked calls, and within a specified lateness margin (9min 59sec for long-distance)

PTE Passenger Transport Executive – these are bodies based across Britain [in the former

Metropolitan counties] that are charged with helping to integrate the use of public transport services within their boundaries

PUG1 Passenger Upgrade 1 (WCRM)

PUG2 Passenger Upgrade 2 (WCRM)

RAIB Rail Accident Investigation Branch – Britain's independent railway-accident-investigation organisation

RDG Rail Delivery Group

RM3 Railway Management Maturity Model as used with the McNulty Report 2011

RMT National Union of Rail, Maritime & Transport Workers (trade union)

RoSCo Rolling Stock Company, of which there are three — Angel Train Contracts, Porterbrook Leasing and Eversholt Rail Group

RSSB Rail Safety & Standards Board – an independent, industry-wide body formed to create and own technical standards for railway assets and operations

RT Railtrack – infrastructure owner from 1994 to 2002

RUS Route Utilisation Strategy

SNCB Société Nationale des Chemins de fer Belges – Belgian national train operator

SNCF Société Nationale des Chemins de fer Français – French national train operator

SoFA Statement of Funds Available

SRA Strategic Rail Authority (2001-6)

SWT South West Trains

TGV Train à Grande Vitesse – France's high-speed train

TOC Train Operating Company – franchised passenger-train companies

TPWS Train Protection & Warning System

TRS Train Running System – a computer system that monitors the railway's operational performance and associated delays

TSSA Transport Salaried Staffs' Association (trade union)

Vertical Integration where two or more firms combine their previously-separate activities into one integrated unit such as combining the management of the track with the running of the trains within a single, long-term concession held by one company

VRG Virgin Rail Group – the legal name for the Virgin Group's rail operations

VSOE Venice Simplon Orient Express

VT Virgin Trains – the brand name for the Virgin Group's rail operations

VWC Virgin West Coast

WCML West Coast main line

WCRM West Coast Route Modernisation

Index

Acknowledgements

The authors would like to thank the many people who have given their time, enthusiasm and energy to help us prepare this new edition of 'The InterCity Story'. Their contributions have provided an enormously insightful inside track on the imagination, issues and images of the privatised railway.

The railway managers who made it happen

Stuart Baker	Paul Emberley	Brian Johnson	Tim Shoveller
Charles Belcher	Sue Evans	Brenda Klug	Anthony Smith
Michael Beswick	Roger Ford	Steve Knight	Theo Steele
Karen Boswell	David Franks	Arthur Leathley	Chris Stokes
Bob Breakwell	Christopher Garnett	Dennis Lovett	John Swift
Rob Brighouse	Richard George	Adrian Lyons	Chris Tibbits
Richard Brown	Richard Gibson	Rob Mason	Peter Trewin
John Cimelli	Chris Gibb	Mac McIntosh	Jackie Townsend
Tim Clarke	Robin Gisby	Alec McTavish	Ivor Warburton
Tony Collins	Andrew Haines	John Nelson	David Ward
Andy Cooper	Nigel Harris	Ian Osborne	Ian Yeowart
Terry Coyle	Nigel G. Harris	Beverley Parkinson	
Jonathan Denby	Michael Holden	Gordon Pettitt	
Barry Doe	Mark Hopwood	Len Porter	
Alistair Dormer	David Horne	Denize Quest	
Richard Eccles	Charles Horton	Brian Scott	

The photographers and press officers who recorded it happening

Julie Beck-Richards	Paul Emberley	Steve Knight	Gavin Morrison
Paul Bigland	Sue Evans	Dennis Lovett	Ian Osborne
Sarah Boundy	Eimar Fitzpatrick	Keith Lumley	Ellen Rossiter
Katherine Button	Richard Gibson	Hazel Maguire	Bernard Slatter
Leigh Calder	Antony Guppy	Colin J. Marsden	Andrew Smithers
Antony Christie	Tim Hedley-Jones	Peter Middleton	Bob Sweet
Chris Dixon	Ben Herbert	Brian Morrison	Matthew Wilson

Those who put together this and the original book for publication

David Allan	Chris Heaps	Ian Hurst	Kevin Robertson
Michael Beswick	Nick Grant	Brian Perren	Peter Waller
Neil Butters	John Gough	Alistair Plumb	Matthew Wharmby
Sarah Burley	Roger Ford	David Rollin	Allan Williams